P9-CQJ-693

HYBRID

CRITICAL AMERICA

Richard Delgado and Jean Stefancic
GENERAL EDITORS

• • • • • • • • • • • •

White by Law:
The Legal Constructions of Race
Ian Haney López

Cultivating Intelligence:
Power, Law, and the Politics of Teaching
A Conversation between
Louise Harmon and Deborah W. Post

Privilege Revealed:
How Law, Language, and the American Mind-set
Uphold the Status Quo
Stephanie M. Wildman with Margalynne Armstrong,
Adrienne D. Davis, and Trina Grillo

Does the Law Morally Bind the Poor?
or What Good's the Constitution When You Can't
Afford a Loaf of Bread
R. George Wright

Hybrid:
Bisexuals, Multiracials, and Other Misfits
under American Law
Ruth Colker

HYBRID

Bisexuals, Multiracials,
and Other Misfits
under American Law

RUTH COLKER

CARROLL COLLEGE LIBRARY
Waukesha, Wisconsin 53186

KF
4749
. C6x
1996

NEW YORK UNIVERSITY PRESS
New York and London

NEW YORK UNIVERSITY PRESS
New York and London

Copyright © 1996 by New York University

All rights reserved

Library of Congress Cataloging-in-Publication Data
Colker, Ruth.
  Hybrid : bisexuals, multiracials, and other misfits under American
law / Ruth Colker.
      p.   cm.—(Critical America)
  Includes index.
  Contents: Introduction : living the gap—A bi jurisprudence—
Sexual orientation—Gender—Race—Disability—Bipolar
injustice : the moral code—Invisible hybrids under the U.S.
census.
  ISBN 0-8147-1520-6 (cloth : alk. paper).—ISBN 0-8147-1538-9
(pbk : alk paper)
  1. Discrimination—Law and legislation—United States.
2. Minorities—Legal status, laws, etc.—United States.   3. United
States—Race relations.   4. Sexual orientation—United States.
5. Law—Social aspects—United States.   I. Title.   II. Series.
KF4749.C64   1996
346.7301'3—dc20   95-50157
[347.30613]   CIP

New York University Press books are printed on acid-free
paper, and their binding materials are chosen for strength
and durability.

Manufactured in the United States of America

10 9 8 7 6 5 4 3 2 1

to C. C.-E.

may she have extraordinary experiences
living across boundaries

Contents

. . . .

Acknowledgments

....

Many people have assisted with the writing of this book through their inspiration, thoughtful conversations, devoted research, or careful reading of various drafts. The first inspiration came from Professor Ruthann Robson, who encouraged me to develop a "bisexual jurisprudence"—a jurisprudence that eventually broadened to encompass far more than bisexuality. Richard Delgado and Jean Stefancic, editors of the Critical America series, also served as valuable inspiration by offering to publish this work at a very early stage of production. Later inspiration came from the courageous writings of Dean Gregory Howard Williams and Professor Judy Scales-Trent, who have described vividly how it feels to live across the color line. Professor Linda Alcoff not only shared her experiences of living between ethnic categories with others but was gracious enough to offer me encouragement when I spoke with her about my own project.

Faculty at the University of Pittsburgh School of Law, as well as the students in my classes on constitutional law, feminist theory, and disability discrimination, have engaged in many lively conversations with me regarding these ideas as they developed. In particular, I benefited enormously from two faculty work-in-progress sessions at the School of Law and a symposium held at Yale Law School. Individual faculty members at the University of Pittsburgh also talked extensively with me about many of these ideas, including Jody Armour, Lisa Brush, Martha Chamallas, and Jules Lobel.

My research assistants were tireless in helping me discover wide-ranging material from the social sciences and law. Namita Luthra, Sharon Noble, Debra Sherman, and Colleen Zak have helped with nearly every idea contained in each chapter. In addition, my colleague, Bernie Hibbitts assisted me in finding valuable historical material on the U.S. Census. The word-processing staff at the School of Law, under the supervision of LuAnn Driscoll, did a marvelous job of polishing the typing, as well as proofreading a lengthy manuscript. Finally, the School of Law generously funded this research through summer writing grants and extra provision of research assistants in a time of fiscal austerity. I am very grateful.

As for careful reading of numerous drafts, no one deserves higher praise than my editor at New York University Press, Niko Pfund. Niko's gracious edits, sensitivity to the ideas underlying my project, and positive feedback enriched this project enormously. I cannot imagine a smoother and more helpful editing process than the one offered to me by New York University Press.

And, of course, my family deserves enormous thanks for putting up with the time commitments of this project. To my four-year-old daughter, Cara Colker-Eybel, I thank you for your patience while mommy spent so much time writing "that book." And to Edward Eybel, my husband, I thank you for all the hours you kept Cara away from my computer so that I could write without too much distraction. I should have more time to devote to the family now, that is, until I undertake the next big project.

Preface

. . . .

Bisexuals are blamed for spreading AIDS to the heterosexual community,[1] transsexuals for destroying America's moral fabric, interracial couples for having children who will not fit into American society, and the somewhat disabled for diverting resources away from the "truly disabled."[2] These hybrids are castigated and despised yet, in the eyes of the law, do not really exist. The 1990 U.S. Census rendered them invisible with marital categories that recognized only heterosexual unions, sexual categories that included only males and females, racial categories that were monoracial, and a disability category that counted only those unable to work. This book brings hybrids to the forefront.

The term "hybrid" usually refers to the offspring of two plants or animals of different races, breeds, varieties, species, or genera.[3] We do not usually mention "human hybrids" because we consider the differences between humans to be less significant than the differences in the plant and animal kingdom. The term "hybrid," however, is an apt description of people who lie between bipolar legal categories—bisexuals, transsexuals, multiracials, and the somewhat disabled. Their lives often constitute a unique set of traits and experiences not found at either end of the bipolar spectrum. Sometimes, they are considered exotic; other times, they are considered abhorrent; and yet other times, they are virtually invisible.

Human hybrids, however, are not produced by artificial technology or genetic mixing, but by law and society. When the law creates such bipolar categories as homosexual and heterosexual, white and black, able-bodied and disabled, it leaves a gap between categories. These hybrids befuddle courts, because the existing categories do not fit them. The time has come to incorporate human hybrids into the *legal* world.

Hybrids are beginning to come to the forefront in popular culture. Marjorie Garber writes six hundred pages on bisexuals,[4] Gregory Howard Williams shares a compelling story about his life on the "color line,"[5] *Newsweek* displays bisexuals[6] and multiracials[7] on their covers, the *New Yorker* features female-to-male transsexuals,[8] and talk shows overflow with personal accounts of transsexuality, bisexuality, and multiracial existence. But even Garber's comprehensive treatment of bisexuals pays little or no attention to the role of law in perpetuating the castigation and invisibility of hybrids. This book fills in that gap.

Although this study is an academic investigation, it also reflects my personal experiences with questions of identity. As I write these words, I can still hear my mother's voice saying to me as a four-year-old: "Ruth, you *must* wear a shirt if you are going to play outside!" And, much later, I remember being asked by my friends when I was going to decide whether I was "straight or gay." These questions haunted me until I learned that I could live between the gaps—that I could be neither male nor female, gay nor straight. People who are multiracial or somewhat disabled also have often confronted these questions of identity. Multiracial organizations are insisting that the

United States Census add a category to reflect their existence. Some people with disabilities speak of the "temporarily able-bodied" to emphasize the transient nature of our disability status. The invisibility of hybrids reflects the false belief that we can visually identify who is female, gay or lesbian, African-American, or disabled. But the National Women's Music Festival, for example, has discovered how difficult it is to exclude men from its annual music festival through visual identification alone, because people seek admission who have had sex-change operations or have very androgynous physiques. The U.S. military has struggled for decades to figure out how to identify and exclude the "true homosexual." Judy Scales-Trent's self-description as a "white black woman"[9] reveals that visual clues about race can be misleading. And the large numbers of people with "hidden disabilities" make unidimensional definitions of disability impossible.

Categorization under the law, however, is inevitable. Despite Garber's postmodern critique of sexual orientation categories, we can be sure that categories will always be the basis of our legal system. We don't live in the world of high theory; we live in the world of practical problems, day-to-day conflicts, pragmatism, and logistical concerns. My legal perspective therefore causes me to make an additional inquiry that is foreign to the perspective of Garber and others who have examined hybrids. Recognizing that categories are indispensable, we should consider how categories can be *improved* so as not to play a role in the destruction of human identity.

I therefore embark upon this project with both excitement and trepidation. It is particularly exciting to write this book now, with a four-year-old girl by my keyboard, who rejoices in taking off *all* her clothes when she plays outside. I write with trepidation because of the enormous scope of this study. This book could easily have been eight volumes instead of eight chapters, but I hope its general survey will inspire others who like myself want to learn better how to live between categories, and tolerate others who choose to do so.

ONE

Introduction:
Living the Gap

....

What I am—and have been for as long as I can remember—is someone whose sexuality and gender have never seemed to mesh with the available cultural categories.
—Sandra Lipsitz Bem, *The Lenses of Gender*

What is there about a continuum that is unsatisfying? frightening? Why must life—and we—be seen in either "black" or "white," with no shades in between?   —Judy Scales-Trent, *Commonalities*

I. Living the Gap between Categories

Sandra Bem is biologically female and has been married to the same man for nearly three decades, yet disclaims the gender category of "female" and the sexual orientation category of "heterosexual." She avoids such categories because they presume that she has ordered her gender and choice of sexual partners along the principle of biological sex.[1]

Judy Scales-Trent describes herself as a "white black woman" to emphasize that she transgresses boundaries of race, while also identifying as "black."[2] She finds that it makes people, including herself, feel uncomfortable when she moves among the static racial categories of "black" and "white." Categories, she concludes, "make the world appear understandable and safe."[3] Challenging categories unsettles and frightens people.

Linda Alcoff describes herself as "negotiating" the "gap" between her various racial and ethnic identities and observes that she never fully occupied any one of these identities. She has parents from Caucasian, Latina, and African backgrounds.[4] She remarks, "In white society I feel my Latinness, and in Latin society I feel my whiteness, as that which is left out, an invisible presence, sometimes as intrusive as an elephant in the room and sometimes more as a pulled thread that alters the design of my fabricated self."[5] Alcoff has discovered that "peace has come for me by living that gap, and no longer seeking some permanent home onshore."[6]

I, too, have found gender and sexual orientation categories to be unsettling. Starting at an early age, I embarrassed my mother when store clerks identified me as a boy. As an adult, however, I feel comfortable wearing both a dress and hiking boots and can even laugh when store clerks politely suggest that I might want to buy a "padded bra." Unlike Bem, however, I would acknowledge that my gender resistance is only partial. When I decided to have a child, for example, I am sure that some men became more attractive to me due to their ability to facilitate my pregnancy. When my husband and I discussed how to divide childrearing responsibilities after the birth of our child, my ability to lactate obviously affected our division of labor. On a less biological level, living in a married relationship with a man has a tangible effect on my sexual orientation because I am often treated as a heterosexual woman. And, as I raise a daughter, I realize that I often pass on gender rules to her. Complete resistance to gender and sexual orientation socialization is impossible. Bem, as a woman who has been married to the same man for nearly three decades, has been constructed, at least in part, by dominant society's view of her sexuality and gender. Nonetheless, such a label as "heterosexual woman" is an incomplete description of some women who are married to men.

The experience of living as a legal hybrid varies across gender, sexual orientation, and disability categories. Scales-Trent describes people responding to her hybrid existence with "fear." As a bisexual, I have often found that the most common reaction is moral disdain rather than fear. My strabismus (crosseyedness) which causes me to live between the categories of disabled and able-bodied sometimes makes people feel physically uncomfortable, which they express by avoiding eye contact. (Children and adults frequently cross their eyes to look scary.)

For any given individual, the experience of living within a hybrid category can also change in context. For example, Alcoff observes that her racial and ethnic identity changes depending upon the racial and ethnic identity of her community. At a primarily lesbian event, I acutely feel my status of being married to a man and at a heterosexual event, such as a traditional wedding, I feel uncomfortable as a bisexual.

Two individuals who share the same hybrid status, such as being multiracial, may also experience quite different reactions to that status. For example, law professor Maria O'Brien Hylton, of African-American, Hispanic, and Australian-Irish parentage, was caught in a public controversy concerning whether

her appropriate racial category was black, Hispanic, or white when she sought a faculty position at Northwestern Law School in 1994. Hylton has checked off the "black" racial category on employment applications and belongs to black community organizations. Hylton is a political conservative who does not believe that her racial identity should be a consideration in the appointment process. She also identifies with the "law and economics" movement within jurisprudence.

The community at Northwestern Law School engaged in a vigorous debate about whether Hylton's race should be a "plus" in the appointment process. One African-American member of the faculty concluded that Hylton should not be treated as "black" because of her racial background and political ideology. A Hispanic member of the student body concluded that Hylton should not be treated as "Hispanic" because that was not Hylton's self-identity. Hylton refused to comment on her "proper" racial identity during this controversy, because she considered such inquiries to be "racist and impolite in the extreme." [7]

The discussions of Hylton's candidacy were racially polarized. She was either "black" or "Latina" and therefore deserving of affirmative action, or "white" and therefore undeserving. No one suggested that she might fit a middle category of "mixed race." Nor did anyone probe whether individuals who fit into mixed-race categories should be beneficiaries of affirmative action.

Hylton and Scales-Trent share similar physical features (light skin and kinky hair), yet the responses to their ambiguous racial identity have differed radically. Hylton's conservative politics combined with her refusal to comment on her racial identity evoked strong disapproval from some blacks and Hispanics. Scales-Trent, by contrast, is a law professor who writes books and articles discussing her categoryless racial identity and who strongly supports affirmative action. The difference in treatment accorded Scales-Trent and Hylton was not the result of a difference in multiracial heritage or appearance, but in *identity* and *politics.* Nonetheless, their racial ambiguity has clearly affected their treatment by society. Hylton's background opened her up to political attacks concerning whether she was authentically "black," whereas her darker-skinned husband (who also seems to share her conservative politics) was not exposed to such racial categorizing when he sought an appointment on the same faculty. His darker skin and family background immunized him from claims that he was not "black" enough to count as black for affirmative action purposes. Clearly, the implications of living between racial categories are complex, acute, and varied.

The experiences of Hylton and Scales-Trent also reveal that racial identity is not always apparent. Our legal system, however, has been built on the assumption that race, unlike sexual orientation, is visually identifiable. Consider the following statement made recently by a three-judge panel of the Sixth Circuit Court of Appeals to justify its failure to invalidate an anti-homosexual initiative: "Because homosexuals generally are not identifiable 'on sight' unless they elect to be so identifiable by conduct . . . , they cannot constitute a suspect class."[8] The three-judge panel (including one African-American female judge) seemed ignorant of the fact that the infamous test case *Plessy v. Ferguson*[9] involved a plaintiff whose skin was so light that he had to be identified as "black" to the railroad conductor so that the lawsuit against segregation could be initiated. Racial civil rights litigation has been premised on the visual identifiability of "blacks"; homosexual civil rights litigation has been undermined by its inability to fit into that illusory visual-identification case law. Exposing the pervasive ambiguity of all categorization schemes, including racial ones, will help destroy some of the distinctions drawn between "genuine" racial civil rights claims and "inappropriate" homosexual civil rights claims. We need to understand that categorization schemes have been developed to pursue political and social policies ranging from the perpetuation of Jim Crow laws to the institutionalization of people with disabilities. No categorization scheme should be accepted as natural and inevitable.

Yet categorization schemes need not be eliminated altogether. Many feminist theorists, such as Bem, suggest that we abandon them because they perpetuate gender polarization and androcentrism (the power dynamic whereby men have more power in society than women). Similarly, law professor Neil Gotanda[10] suggests that we abandon racial categories because they perpetuate subordination. Others, such as Scales-Trent, are more open to the use of categories. Although Scales-Trent is certainly aware that racial categories have been constructed to perpetuate subordination, she is also an "identity" theorist who struggles to redefine such existing categories as black (with which she identifies) or to create such new racial categories as "white black woman" (with which she also identifies), because these terms have important cultural and political meanings for her.

Unquestionably, the categories typically used to describe our sexual orientation, gender, race, and bodies have perpetuated subordination. Nonetheless, categories need not *inevitably* perpetuate subordination. Categories can, in fact, help us overcome subordination through the development of a positive self-identity as well as through ameliorative programs such as affirmative action. Therefore, this book has both a *critical* and *constructive* agenda. I will critique existing categorization schemes while also offering constructive schemes for the future.

Categories can serve at least two constructive purposes. First, categories have value as a form of self-identity. The gay, lesbian, and bisexual communities have developed a rich cultural community which is only possible through self-identity. Sandra Bem's pervasive critical posture disavows the need for the label "bisexual." This perspective is unsatisfying because it results only in a negative definition of sexual orientation. She has not selected her partners based on biological sex. One might therefore ask: What are her positive values? A label such as bisexual can allow oneself to be part of a positive cultural community. Living in a society which subordinates people based on their minority sexual orientation makes it imperative to have labels as a part of positive self-identity. Moreover, Bem's description of her sexual orientation in negative terms leads her to conflate gender and sexual orientation, because she fails to identify the rationale for her choice of sexual partner. Sexual orientation takes on its own independent cultural meaning apart from gender when one attempts to develop a positive self-identity.

Second, categories are crucial for political, instrumental purposes. It is not enough for society to become nondiscriminatory, because not all groups in society currently operate on a level playing field. We need to develop and refine ameliorative programs, such as affirmative action, to achieve greater equality in society. Because law and society have imposed subordination on people due to their membership in group-based categories, we need to make reference to categories in order to develop fair and effective ameliorative programs. Categories used in ameliorative programs need not perfectly parallel the existing bipolar categories. Nonetheless, fair and effective ameliorative programs must make some reference to group-based categories. Interestingly, critical theorists rarely discuss ameliorative programs and therefore provide us with little insight as to whether and how group-based categories might be appropriate in ameliorative contexts.

II. Dilemmas of Categorization

The classification problems associated with hybrids are numerous, timely, and deeply perplexing. The U.S. Census Bureau is considering whether to add the category of "multiracial" to its survey instrument, because the current rules require that an individual mark only one racial designation.[11] Multiracial organizations have criticized these rules, and as a result they are under revision. Although the old rules are clearly problematic, it is not easy, as we will see, to develop appropriate rules that will work well in the future. Racial classification issues are also flaring up in adoption, tort litigation, and cases involving birth certificates. When adoption agencies decide to grant race-based preferences in adoption, how should multiracial children be classified?

Categorization problems also abound when we talk about gender, sexual orientation, and disability. Should transsexuals be considered victims of "gender" discrimination when they are discharged from employment for dressing in clothing that is considered not consistent with their anatomical gender? In proposing affirmative action plans on the basis of sexual orientation, some institutions are debating whether to provide affirmative action for bisexuals as well as gay men and lesbians.[12] In addition, many institutions are considering what criteria to establish for "domestic partners" who may wish to register for certain family-related employment benefits. Finally, the courts and society must decide who is sufficiently "disabled" to fall within the coverage of the Americans with Disabilities Act,

Supplemental Social Security, or the Individuals with Disabilities Education Act.[13]

Each of these classification dilemmas challenges us to construct classification schemes that serve ameliorative rather than subordinating purposes. We must find ways to allow individuals to identify as multiracial, transgendered, bisexual, and bi-abled without the fear that moving off of one polar point on the traditional bipolar scheme will subject them to subordination and necessarily preclude them from taking advantage of ameliorative programs. Our current system of affirmative action often gives an incentive to mixed-race individuals to label themselves as a minority racial category.[14] On the other hand, we need to make sure that programs that are designed primarily to assist individuals overcome a history of subordination are not used by individuals who largely have been shielded from that subordination through their presence in a hybrid category. Our current system of affirmative action often allows any member of a defined group to qualify for preferential treatment irrespective of how well affirmative action for that individual serves the purposes of the ameliorative program. Our awareness and recognition of hybrids should force us to be more individualized in understanding the structure of effective and fair ameliorative programs, while not forcing us to abandon group-based approaches entirely.

III. A Roadmap

This book responds to these perplexing legal and social problems through the application of a bi perspective. In chapter 2, I develop a bi jurisprudence, providing a broad overview of the differing implications of hybrid existence in the areas of sexual orientation, gender, race, and disability.

Chapter 3 applies a bi perspective to an examination of how courts and legislatures have attempted to create entitlements and benefits which flow from the categorization of persons as "homosexual" or "heterosexual." In contrast to the theoretical approach in chapter 2, I concretely examine the definitions of "homosexual" that courts and legislature have created. These definitions often break down when applied to individuals who have experienced sexual relationships with persons of both sexes. How the law responds to such "bad fits" reveals a great deal about society's determination to force people into neat "boxes," especially the tidy category of heterosexuality. This coercive attempt to define people on the basis of sexual orientation reflects society's discomfort with individuals who are "gay and proud" as well as with individuals who attempt to cross appropriate gender boundaries. Our sexual orientation policies are therefore inextricably connected to our gender policies.

Chapter 3 also asks how we can use the phrases "gay," "lesbian," or "bisexual" as part of ameliorative programs to overcome subordination. As society begins to permit partner registration systems irrespective of the gender of one's partner, how should we use the labels of gay, lesbian and bisexual? Do these attempts to allow people to self-identify as part of a committed partnership employ appropriate definitional categories? Because gay and lesbian people, unlike racial minorities, do not grow up in distinctive economically deprived communities, I also probe whether arguments for affirmative action are appropriate in this context and, if so, who should be considered entitled to affirmative treatment.

Chapter 4 explores how courts and legislatures attempt to use the terms "male" and "female" to fit individuals into gendered categories. Although we linguistically refer to the "opposite sexes" and consider biological sex to be an immutable characteristic, neither assumption is valid. Cases in which people cross gender boundaries through cross-dressing or sex-change operations baffle the courts and society enormously. Courts respond to these cases by maintaining the myth of the innateness and immutability of both gender and biological sex.

Constructively, I ask how the courts and society should respond to the historical mistreatment of people who cross gender or sexual barriers. Should individuals who "cross-dress" be considered victims of "gender" discrimination? Should we use the option of free-standing, unisex bathrooms, which has been developed in the disability context, to meet the needs of transgendered persons who often are not accepted in bathrooms for either biological sex?

Race is another area where the courts and society have imposed a false set of distinctions, categorizing people as "white" or "colored." Chapter 5 focuses on why such distinctions are of such importance to society despite the scientific bankruptcy of "whiteness" as a racial construct and the reality that most people have mixed racial histories. How can we devise fair and appropriate affirmative action and transracial adoption policies? Should individuals such as Hylton or Scales-Trent, who self-identify as African-American despite their multiracial background or light skin color, be eligible for affirmative action? Because racial identity is socially constructed, do race-based affirmative action programs perpetuate or ameliorate race-based subordination? Similarly, do race-specific labels in the adoption context perpetuate the subordination of minority groups? Again, how should racial categories be defined in that context?

The newly developing area of "disability" law is a final area that helps reinforce society's obsession with false categorization. Chapter 6 explores how society accords benefits and privileges based on whether one is "disabled" or "nondisabled" as if these are clear, bipolar categories. Whether individuals are considered "disabled" depends on what social policies are popular at the moment rather than on their needs as individuals. Nonetheless, disability nondiscrimination law is a novel model for redressing discrimination, in general. I therefore ask whether any of its innovations work well and should be exported to other areas of the law.

The courts are struggling constructively to develop a definition of "disability" which will further the purposes of our anti-discrimination laws. Do we need to determine whether people fit a single definition of "disability" for anti-discrimination laws to operate properly? Would an approach that recognized the spectrum of disabilities that people experience better serve the purposes of our anti-discrimination laws?

Chapter 7 moves the discussion to a broader theoretical plane. I inquire how the legal system is generally built upon a foundation of bipolar injustice and how such a perspective hinders our understanding of discrimination and subordination under federal anti-discrimination law. I argue that the courts have developed a narrow "sexualized harassment" doctrine that, in effect, provides justice for a very small portion of the victims of gender and race discrimination in our society.

Finally, in chapter 8 I return to the U.S. Census to suggest how we can construct racial categories while being mindful of the existence of racial hybrids. Categories can be used constructively without insulting our human dignity.

The central question of this book is: Why is law based on a bipolar framework in ways that denigrate hybrids and render them invisible? Why can't we see the nondichotomous spectrum on which people experience gender, race, sexual orientation, and disability? Why does the law need to use the labels of "homosexual and heterosexual," "male and female," "black and white," and "disabled and nondisabled" at all? The answer to that final question varies from chapter to chapter. In some cases, labels may be useful—for example, to help identify groups that have faced a history of subordination in our society. That usefulness, however, should not justify our attempts to misdefine humanity in order to achieve certain social policies. When categories are needed, a bi perspective allows us to develop a more pragmatic and humane jurisprudence, and thus a more complete and accurate worldview.

T W O

....

A Bi Jurisprudence

....

"Bisexuality: Not Gay. Not Straight. A New Sexual Identity Emerges" proclaims *Newsweek* on its cover. Shunned by heterosexuals and many gays and lesbians alike, bisexuals recently have been "discovered" by the popular media as well as conventional researchers. Nonetheless, the category of bisexuality remains elusive for most adults. Only about 1 percent of the adult population identifies as bisexual. Yet nearly 4 percent acknowledge that they are attracted to people of both sexes.[1]

Bisexual invisibility pigeonholes individuals into gay and straight boxes. A bisexual perspective allows us to ask ourselves who we find attractive and why, rather than to presume that sexual partners are chosen on the basis of gender. This perspective broadens to a "bi" perspective[2] as we reject conventional bipolar categories in the areas of gender, race, and disability in understanding our own lives, as well as in responding to others.[3]

I. Harms that Flow from Categorization

A. Invisibility to Ourselves and Others

Martin S. Weinberg and his colleagues report that one-fourth of self-identified bisexuals are currently "confused" about their

15

bisexuality, with more than half of the women and three-quarters of the men reporting previous confusion.[4] People who do not self-identify as bisexuals, yet have sexual relations with people of both genders, report even more identity confusion: "Some people who behave bisexually are confused and think that they may be in the process of becoming homosexual. Others simply deny their same-sex feelings and behaviors in order to preserve their self-image as heterosexuals."[5]

The pressure to identify with a monosexual label of "gay" or "straight" leads to some odd results. Some women continue to identify with the label "heterosexual" despite the fact that they are intimately involved with a woman. Other women who have had prior intimate relationships with a woman continue to identify with the label "lesbian" even when intimately involved with a man. One of the best-known examples of this phenomenon was Holly Near, a very popular songwriter and singer among lesbians, who persisted in labeling herself as a lesbian despite her intimate relationship with a man.[6] Alternatively, some women simply have felt immobilized by this need to fit into a category and have therefore chosen the "choose not to label" category.[7]

A bisexual perspective facilitates picking the "choose not to label" category rather than the static and bipolar categories of homosexual and heterosexual. Ruth Gibian describes the problematic, bipolar structure of the dominant sexuality categories: "The definition of a static sexuality is based on binary opposition. . . . Indeed, our entire Western system of thought is based on binary opposition; we define by comparison, by what things are not."[8] Bipolar injustice is of epidemic proportions; it is not limited to the area of sexual orientation. Although it is unrealistic to think that we can dismantle an entire system that is built on binary opposition, we can take small steps in the area of life that touches us most personally—our self-identity. We should not allow our bisexuality to be invisible even to ourselves. When I ended an intimate relationship with a woman and began dating a man about fifteen years ago, I remember telling him, "It's important that you recognize that I am a lesbian." I insisted on the lesbian label because I did not want to acknowledge to myself the dynamic nature of my sexual orientation. I thought I had to choose between being gay and straight and was having trouble reconciling the gender of my current partner with those choices. Five years later, when I became involved with another man, again ending an intimate relationship with a woman, I told a friend that I was sure that I was now a "heterosexual." My obsession with categorization precluded me from seeing the complexity of my feelings and the multiplicity of my prior relationships, harming the fullness of my self-identity.

The invisibility of bisexuals has had some profound social consequences. For example, it has rendered invisible the bisexual practices of many African-American men, thereby stalling our attempts to deal with the AIDS crisis. Although the Kinsey study[9] is often cited for statistics about sexual behavior, it is rarely noted that the study included only white American men who had engaged in a homosexual act at least once.[10] The statistics that do exist on the sexual behavior of African-American men are inconclusive but preliminary statistics suggest that African-American men may be somewhat more likely than white men to engage in both opposite-sex and same-sex sexual behavior.[11] These men, however, rarely identify as bisexual, in part because of disapproval of that status in their own community and in mainstream society.[12] A polarized straight/gay dichotomy and disapproval of bisexuals have caused us to ignore the sexual practices of this group of men. This lack of recognition has had profound consequences: it has deterred attempts to provide AIDS counseling to many African-American men who engage in same-sex sexual behavior, as well as to their female sexual partners. By rigidly assuming that people who primarily identify as heterosexual are not engaging in same-sex sexual behavior, health care professionals until recently have not targeted heterosexual African-American men and their female partners for safe-sex education. A bisexual perspective would make more apparent the sexual behavior of many African-American men and thereby would be more racially inclusive irrespective of what label these men[13] apply to themselves.[14]

Similarly, feminist theorist Brenda Marie Blasingame suggests that some minority communities recognize that many people engage in both same-sex and opposite-sex behavior while not expressly labeling it as bisexual:

In talking with older people of color who are queer, I've found that they often say that in their community people had relationships with people. Some people chose to be involved with both sexes, whereas others chose to be exclusively involved with same-sex partners. They spoke of how some people were bisexual. That was not what it was called, but that was what was taking place. It was not a subject of conversation: people knew who was in a relationship with whom, that was how it was and life went on.[15]

Blasingame provides excellent insight into the bridges that must be crossed if people of color are to feel more welcome in the "gay" movement. When we can start talking about people who have sex with people of the same sex without making any assumptions about whether they also have sex with people of the opposite sex, then we may have a more racially inclusive politics. Our bipolar orientation about sexuality therefore contributes to a misunderstanding of how people experience sexuality and also makes people in various ethnic communities feel alienated from the gay rights movement. How can we make more visible individuals who lie between sexual categories? One way is to embrace individualized storytelling rather than categories such as "bisexual":

To compensate for the lack of an adequate label, which I know would have its limitations anyway, I find myself telling my story, or as much of it as the situation warrants. It gives people the chance to hear, not *defector* or *fence-sitter*, but process, struggle toward self-understanding, self-claiming. It gives them room to hear about feelings and to tell their own. It gives me—and all of us—room to be larger than a name.[16]

Categories suggest stasis whereas storytelling reflects our changing life experiences. The way for individuals' sexual identity to become fully visible is not to embrace the new category of "bisexuality" but to explain fully the content of their sexuality. Sandra Bem embraces this perspective when she says that she has been involved intimately with a particular man for three decades but would not describe herself as having chosen him as a partner because of his biological gender. Her life description does a more complete job of explaining her sexuality than the label "heterosexual" or "bisexual." This perspective does not force us to agonize over whether Bem properly could be considered a "bisexual" given the monogamous nature of her sexual relationship of the last three decades. Applying or not applying the label "bisexual" to Bem's situation would not add to our understanding of her sexuality. Individualized storytelling, however, makes it clear how her sexuality differs from another woman who has also been married to the same man for three decades but who openly acknowledges that she organizes her sexuality around the biological sex of her partner.

There are times when we need categories for constructive purposes. The fact that categories may have pragmatic advantages in certain situations, however, should not make us forget that categorical thinking can also seriously misstate human feelings and experience. Where individualized storytelling is possible in addition to or instead of categorization, we should seek to promote storytelling.

Individuals who lie between racial categories often face similar dilemmas. As I will discuss further in chapters 5 and 8, some [17] individuals feel that they have to make a false choice on job application forms, census forms, or even birth certificates about their racial identity. Parents complain that such false choices undermine the self-esteem of their children. Although we do not usually think of race as a thought process based on our feelings in the same way that we think of sexual orientation, these stories reveal the element of conscious choice of racial category for certain individuals. Our dominant view of race as a biological category (which, itself, is inaccurate according to scientists and anthropologists) is undermined when we see the ways in which some individuals can move between racial categories or make choices about the racial categories to which they belong.

Nonetheless, sexual orientation and race have basic dissimilarities. Most of us are told as young children, either implicitly or explicitly, that we are heterosexual. It is only through a conscious thought process that we can move beyond that bipolar category. Similarly, most of us are told our race at a young age and few of us ever question our racial identity. However, some individuals discover new information about their racial heritage later in life through comments from their parents or official public records such as birth certificates. Irrespective of whether an individual has been informed of her multiracial background from a young age or whether she discovers it somewhat later in life, she may make a choice as to whether to identify with a multiracial category or, instead, to maintain a monoracial identity. (Most individuals, however, who have multiracial backgrounds do not make a conscious choice about racial identification, because the "one drop of blood rule" has defined them as fitting a monoracial category.) Racial identity, like sexual orientation, can therefore have a cognitive component for some individuals. That component becomes particularly apparent when we focus on certain individuals with multiracial backgrounds.

B. *Bipolar Classification Reinforces Pejorative Values*

Both the gay and straight communities often use the bipolar classification scheme to disparage bisexuals: "Switch-hitter. Swings both ways. Fence-sitter. AC/DC."[18] The term "hasbian," developed by the gay and lesbian community, reflects this disparagement. Stacey Young offers this critique of the term:

I object to the expression because it defines a person *only* in terms of what she once was. To refer to a woman as a "hasbian" implies that all one need know about her is her relationship to that exalted state, lesbianism. The term "hasbian" also, of course, evokes the word "has-been" which *Webster*'s defines as "a person or thing which was formerly popular or effective, but is no longer so." What interests, then, does this term serve? Who has the power to define here, and at whose expense?[19]

These negative connotations detract from the desire of bisexuals to work politically within the gay and lesbian community, thereby depriving us of valuable political energy and leadership. For example, the poet Nina Silver felt torn whether to come "out" to her lesbian editor, Tori, who was to visit soon.[20] When she wrote to Tori and told her that she was living with a man, whom she had also married, Tori wrote back and said that she could no longer have a working relationship with Nina, nor could Nina read her lesbian love poetry at a woman's bookstore. (The poems no longer genuinely reflected love for women.)

In a more public example of bisexual exclusion, the gay and lesbian community in one city decided to drop the word "bisexual" from the title of its lesbian and gay pride day march. A bisexual, Micki Siegel, had strongly supported the inclusion of the word "bisexual" in the march's title. Two lesbians responded to Micki's arguments in a gay newspaper by calling her "Mrs. Siegel" and criticizing her for trying to attach to the lesbian community rather than create a community of her own.[21]

An anonymous male political activist, who now identifies as gay rather than bisexual, summarizes the anti-bisexual sentiment that he has observed in the gay male community. Gay men, he reports, often believe that identifying as bisexual is:

a phony period of being pressured into conforming to society's standards, and it's a giving in to this pressure, therefore it's a lie; it's immaturity.... Another belief is that straights run the world and oppress gays. Gays are finally making progress. Progress is fragile, so you bisexuals shut up and let us gays have our time now.... Also, there is the belief that homosexuality, not heterosexuality is what people are really discriminating against, so bisexuality is a nonissue.[22]

My own experiences parallel those described by others. I was hurt and baffled when two lesbian friends explained that they would no longer be able to vacation with me once I became involved with a man. They had never met my male partner so they were speaking entirely from an abstract position; they could not imagine any man with whom they would want to share social space in a vacation setting. Oddly enough, they had repeatedly vacationed with one of their sisters and her husband. My friendship, however, appeared to be contingent on my being a "pure lesbian."[23] Similarly, I was shocked and dismayed when a feminist activist referred to me as a "hasbian" after I married a man, thereby erasing my feelings toward and experiences with women.

Ironically, the lesbian and gay community often criticizes female bisexuals for sleeping with men and diverting energy away from the lesbian community,[24] but it is sometimes the actions of lesbians and gay men rather than our male partners that keep us from working politically in the lesbian community. For example, when I was asked to serve as an openly gay delegate to the Democratic National Convention, I replied that I did not think that would be appropriate since I was currently involved with a man. The person who had "nominated" me immediately responded by agreeing with my assessment of the situation. I learned that he later described the conversation to someone else and called me a "coward" for being a bisexual rather than a lesbian. It was not until I met a woman who identified herself as a bisexual and who explained to me that there was a bisexual community that I came to feel more comfortable with that label and orientation.

Today, I feel comfortable with the label of bisexual and cannot imagine being involved with a man (or woman) who did not share my feminist vision and commitment to equality for lesbian and gay people. By doing childcare, housework, food shopping, and so forth, my male partner facilitates my feminist and lesbian political work rather than hinders it. The assumption that the reverse would be true is obviously the result of stereotypical thinking about "all men" but, in addition, is deeply insulting about my taste and preferences. Why would

anyone think that I would pursue a relationship with anyone—
male or female—that prevented me from doing legal and political work?

Not all lesbians and gay men have such a spiteful view of
bisexuals. I have found, in fact, that some lesbians and gay men
have been more supportive of my fluid sexuality than I have
been myself. The gay and lesbian community also seems to have
progressed in recent years toward greater inclusion of bisexuals;
recent anthologies on bisexuality[25] reflect this trend. Bisexuality, however, challenges people's feelings and actions concerning inclusiveness. When women who have had sexual relations
with people of both sexes, and who do not disavow those
relationships as authentic expressions of love and commitment,
can exist within the community of women in their wholeness
rather than as stereotypes, then we will have created a more
genuine feminist and lesbian politics.

Individuals who cross racial lines have suffered similar problems. Maria O'Brien Hylton was rejected by some members
of the black community during the Northwestern Law School
appointment process because she did not have a strong enough
black identity. One member of the black community described
Hylton as not authentically "black" because unlike most African-Americans, she was not the descendant of "twelve generations of enslaved Africans."[26] Other members of the black and
Latino communities questioned whether Hylton would be a
mentor and identify with the needs of minority students.[27] Hylton's multiracial background, along with her conservative law
and economics views, made her an unacceptable candidate for
some members of the black community.

Hylton's story also reflects how these negative attitudes can
make an individual feel uncomfortable in continuing to do political work within the black community. Before the controversy

surrounding her candidacy, Hylton described herself as being involved with many black community organizations and identified as "black." This experience, however, caused her to say: "Woe unto the next black person they try to hire. . . . May he or she have really thick skin."[28] Certainly, Hylton will pause before she checks "black" on an employment application in the future, and possibly she will pause before joining a black organization, wondering if she will be considered "black enough" to be a proper member. If such categorizing causes Hylton to retreat from political work on behalf of the black community then the categorization battle will have had a profound negative effect on her and others.

Gregory Howard Williams similarly has been stymied by racial categorization. Williams is the child of a white mother and light-skinned black father who "passed" as white when Williams was a young child. Williams looks "white" but, subsequent to his parents' divorce, was placed in an impoverished household with dark-skinned black relatives and friends. He tells a story of applying for a sheriff's position with the Muncie Police Department. Due to political pressures, they needed to hire a black sheriff. Williams applied for the position so that he could support himself to finish his college degree. A local black minister opposed Williams's appointment, claiming that the sheriff's department was trying to hire him in order to preserve a "lily white" appearance. Responding to such political pressures, Williams considered withdrawing his name from consideration. A cousin gave him the following piece of advice which convinced him to remain in consideration: "Let the politicians worry about who's black and who isn't. Nobody in Muncie ever gave you any breaks just because you looked white. You've had to take just as much crap as anybody I know, black or white. . . . If you're in a position to arrest some brothers, you are gonna be fair—not like some of the hillbillies they got on the department."[29] The cousin's prediction proved true, as Williams reportedly worked hard within the department to ensure that blacks and whites received fair treatment. Had he listened to the local minister, the community would have been deprived of Greg Williams's fair policing and he might never have been able to afford to finish college, attend law school, and eventually become the Dean of the Ohio State University School of Law.

Categories also have debilitating effects on people with disabilities. Children's behavior can be criticized or praised depending on whether they have been categorized as "disabled." A story told to me by an activist in the community of people with disabilities illustrates this point. Two children are on a hike with their parents and need to urinate. The able-bodied boy goes discretely behind a tree to urinate, and people say, "Oh, isn't that cute—that boy needed to pee and went behind that tree." Another child, with mental retardation, also goes discretely behind a tree to urinate, and people say, "Oh, isn't that horrible—that retarded boy has no control and had to pee in public!" The same behavior receives a different response depending upon the perceived category of the child. If we could move beyond labeling, we could respond to the children based on their behavior rather than on our stereotypes about the categories in which they belong.

II. Categories Can Serve Constructive Purposes

A. Categories Can Broaden People's Understanding of Identity

Nonetheless, categories also have a positive utility. The label "bisexual" can threaten a society that orders itself on neat bipolar concepts. The common stereotype of a bisexual person is one who always has at least two sexual partners. That stereotype arises out of the assumption that gay men, lesbians, and bisexual people are purely sexual creatures—at all moments being involved with all eligible sexual partners. (Society has trouble imagining a celibate or monogamous gay, lesbian, or bisexual person.)[30]

Naming bisexuality can broaden people's understanding of human sexual experiences by acknowledging the existence of a fluid spectrum rather than rigid bipolar categories. "Rather than naming an invisible, undernoticed minority now finding its place in the sun, 'bisexual' turns out to be, like bisexuals themselves, everywhere and nowhere. . . . The erotic discovery of bisexuality is the fact that it reveals sexuality to be a process of growth, transformation and surprise, not a stable and knowable state of being."[31] Bisexuality is not simply another static category.

The terms "gay" and "straight," by contrast, assume a sexual exclusivity—that a person always only has sexual partners of the same or opposite sex:

These terms [gay and straight] are convenient simplifications for the idea that most people engage in sexual relations with only one sex. To get a clear perspective on the part homosexual behavior plays in the total range of American sexual experience, we should first take a look at *bisexuality* to evaluate its significance in the gay (and straight world). There are certainly far more individuals with bisexual experience than there are lifelong exclusive homosexuals.[32]

For women, in particular, bisexuality often seems to be an accurate description of their feelings. In a 1976 *Ms. Magazine* article, a large number of women reported "that when they fell in love it was with a person rather than a gender."[33]

Gay and lesbian people have been defined by society so that

they have little identity beyond their sexual identity within mainstream culture. As one of my students once said, if you are defined as a lesbian, you have a lesbian breakfast, lunch, and dinner. Or, alternatively, as a gay activist in Louisiana observed, "I often wonder what people think I do in the two minutes of my day when I am supposed to not be engaged in sex!" Bisexual people can also be defined in that way—as irresistibly sexual creatures for whom *everyone* is a prospective sex partner.

There are many ways to deal with this problem. One common method is to insist that the words lesbian, gay, or bisexual are modifiers rather than nouns. In the disability rights movement, that linguistic move is commonplace. The preferred term is "person with a disability" to emphasize that an individual is a "person" who *also* has a disability. Unfortunately, that construction is a bit awkward. One would have to say, for example, I am a person who is bisexual, able-bodied, Jewish, white, middle-aged, middle-class, androgynous, and so forth, in order to emphasize that no one aspect of our identity defines us. Such constructions, however, are often preferable to such shorthand phrases as "the disabled" which suggest that one's entire existence is defined by one's disability status.

Labels can also help overcome the practical limitations of storytelling. For example, when asked about my sexual orientation, I could say, "I am currently married to a man but find both men and women sexually attractive" rather than say "I am a bisexual." That kind of storytelling could emphasize the fluid way that I define my sexual orientation. Unfortunately, such storytelling is not always practical. Moreover, in cases such as mine, most people probably just attach the label "married woman" to me with its assumptions about exclusive heterosexuality without even inquiring about my sexual orientation. Use of a simple category such as "bisexual" can force people to move quickly beyond their assumptions about my sexual orientation even if that label is problematic. One can hope that once a person learns that I attach the label "bisexual" to myself despite my married status that that individual would approach me and ask what the term "bisexual" means to me. At that time, I could try to describe the phrase's fluid meaning to me.

If it is true that far more people have experienced a bisexual lifestyle than is commonly recognized, why is bisexuality so often ignored?[34] Ignoring bisexuality allows society to perpetuate the stereotype that sexuality is rigidly dichotomous. That stereotype is male and white in that it hides women's and African-American men's sexual feelings and experiences.[35] Theologian John J. McNeill describes the impoverishment of the bipolar imagery of homosexuality and heterosexuality which is prevalent in our society:

The tendency to identify oneself as a person with one's sexual-identity image can, and frequently does, lead to a one-sided stress on certain qualities and the elimination of others. The heterosexual tends to define himself in contrast to the homosexual; the homosexual, in turn, tends to define himself in contrast to the heterosexual. The result is a narrow, impoverished, and dehumanizing self-image for both parties.[36]

McNeill's argument helps emphasize the importance of defining bisexuality with regard to *feelings* as well as conduct. In the *Ms. Magazine* study, many women described their sexual orientation based on their feelings of attraction toward men and women rather than based on their experiences in sexual relationships. Similarly, Weinberg found a much higher incidence of bisexuality among women if he inquired about their sexual feelings rather than sexual behaviors.[37] A more humanistic understanding of sexuality therefore would go beyond our conduct and try to understand our feelings. Since only our conduct is readily visible, this observation challenges each of us to verbalize our feelings about our sexuality in order to help society move beyond a narrow, noncontextual, and rigid understanding of sexuality. Saying the word "bisexual" aloud can help us begin to verbalize those feelings.

Finally, embracing the category of bisexuality would help society recognize that one can find an organizing principle other than biological sex to define sexual attractiveness. The labels homosexual and heterosexual are premised on the concept that biological sex is an organizing principle in the selection of a sexual partner. Only bisexuality challenges the significance that biological sex should have in one of the most important activities in our lives—our choice of sexual partner. As Weinberg reports: "instead of organizing their sexuality in terms of the traditional gender schema, bisexuals do so in terms of an 'open gender schema,' a perspective that *disconnects gender and sexual preference,* making the direction of sexual desire (toward the same or opposite sex) *independent* of a person's own gender (whether a man or a woman)."[38] This is a powerful message so long as people do not indulge in the stereotype that bisexuals are attracted to *everyone*. Bisexuals have organizing principles for determining whom they find attractive; that organizing principle simply is not biological sex.

Similarly, multiracial status in the United States is largely rendered invisible through our use of racial bipolar categories. As we will see in chapters 5 and 8, our legal system pervasively has insisted that people classify themselves as white or black with no room to check off a multiracial box. Accordingly, multiracial groups in the United States have begun to organize politically to proclaim their right to be counted as multiracial. In contrast to sexual orientation, however, no clear consensus exists that multiracial categories are appropriate or desirable. Because nearly all African-Americans are, in fact, of multiracial heritage, some people argue that recognizing the multiracial category will dilute the number of people recognized as African-American. This disagreement reflects the inherently political nature of such categories; the categories do not have any intrinsic meaning. If we recognize that categories are artificial because human behavior and experience exist on a spectrum, then we can be mindful of the implications of categories as we create them. The fact that we use certain categories for census reporting does not mean that we have to use them in the context of affirmative action.

Ongoing controversies over racial identity re-emphasize the point made earlier that racial identity is not entirely a biological or anthropological construct. Although we tend to think of race as a given, some people clearly make choices concerning their racial identity. The very existence of a multiracial identity movement, therefore, represents a positive political development because it emphasizes the socially constructed aspects of racial identity. It draws people's attention to the fact that we make decisions about how to label people racially. There is no "natural" racial categorization system.

Disability categorization also creates controversy although the dimensions of the problems are different. As with racial minorities, there is no monolithic understanding within or outside of the community of people with disabilities as to whom should get covered by various statutes. For example, people often complain that the Americans with Disabilities Act should not cover physical problems such as obesity. These comments are often premised on inaccurate stereotypes of such people, rooted in a belief that they "choose" their disability or are responsible for their problems. Real life stories can help overcome those stereotypes. In one poignant exchange on the internet, someone with a disability complained about people who are obese being considered disabled because they could control their weight. An obese individual wrote back, explaining that a physiological condition precluded her from losing weight; she also documented the extensive discrimination she suffered because of her body size. The original writer immediately recanted his criticism, ironically noting that his own disabilities precluded him from *gaining* weight. Yet, it had never occurred to him that people who are obese also can have physiological problems affecting their body weight. By putting a story behind the labels, these individuals were able to overcome their stereotypes. Had there been no way to identify the subcategory of "obesity" within the label "disabled," this helpful exchange might not have occurred.

B. Categories Can Serve Ameliorative Purposes

Not only are categories needed to facilitate ordinary conversation, but they are needed for legislative purposes. We have to define who is "gay, lesbian, or bisexual" if we are to create nondiscrimination statutes, same-sex partner registration, or affirmative action.

Similarly, we need categories in the race context to develop affirmative action. Who should qualify for such programs? The Hylton controversy brings this question explicitly to the forefront. Why do we have affirmative action? Should Hylton have been rendered ineligible because of her economic background, unwillingness to promise to serve as a "black" role model, or because of her racial background, light skin, or conservative politics? We need to articulate more precisely *why* we have affirmative action in the education context to know how to resolve Hylton's candidacy.

Nonetheless, the implications of a bi perspective are not monolithic. A bi perspective on sexual orientation and gender may be very different from a bi perspective on race and disability. An individual who identifies as a bisexual may only be making a statement about her feelings. If she has not formed sexual relations with people of both biological sexes during her lifetime, she is not making a statement about actions. In other cases, it may reflect a statement about her actions. In virtually no case will a bisexual identity reflect a statement about her discernable physical appearance or family history.

Similarly, a bi perspective on gender usually reflects a statement about feelings or attitudes. Embracing a "bi" identity often means that one rejects or questions the traits that are considered "normal" for one's biological sex. A bi perspective on gender may also reflect a statement about actions. A person may cross-dress, pursue a nontraditional occupation, or even have surgery to align one's biological self with one's psychological self. These actions or traits may also make an individual visually discernable as transgendered, although many individuals who are transgendered "pass" as fitting one pole of the bipolar categorization scheme.

By contrast, a bi perspective on race may not correspond to any particular feelings, attitudes, or life experiences. In some cases, such as that of Scales-Trent, one may be light skinned and appear "white" but identify as black because both of one's parents are black. Society may view Scales-Trent as multiracial or even white because of her appearance, yet she self-identifies as black. Like some multiracial individuals, Scales-Trent may easily "pass" as belonging to one pole of the bipolar categorization scheme. Some of these individuals have a strong self-identity of being multiracial, and resent society trying to force them into the categories of black or white. Nonetheless, most individuals who have multiracial family histories prefer to be considered members of a monolithic racial category such as "black." Being multiracial can therefore be a statement about identity or can simply be a statement about one's ancestry. Often, it is physically indiscernible and may be unknown to the individual herself.

There is no parallel social movement for individuals who are between categories of disability. There is not even a label for this category. Thus, it is hard to argue that lying between categories can be a source of identity. In some cases, however, individuals who lie between disability categories have received public attention as "unworthy" of being considered disabled. For example, in one *Wall Street Journal* article, reporter Heather MacDonald questioned why mental impairments, drug addiction and alcoholism, and learning disabilities should be labeled as "disabilities" under the Social Security Act, because individuals with these disabilities purportedly "choose" or fabricate these impairments for financial gain. In a broadscale critique of "learning disorders," she reports that "stories abound of parents coaching their kids to misbehave in school or fail their tests . . . to ensure that they will fall back several grades and thus fail the 'age-appropriate' test"[39] so that their parents can receive a monetary windfall. Her claim that "stories abound" of parents coaching their kids to misbehave is seemingly based on one isolated story from Wynne, Arkansas. Nowhere does she mention that most children only receive money to pay for designated medical and educational needs to specified providers.[40] By disputing that these children have any genuine disabilities and by promoting the stereotype that their parents coerce their children into appearing disabled for money, Mac-Donald heightens the mistreatment of individuals who fit between the categories able-bodied and disabled. Her article highlights the need for us to recognize the category of people who are somewhat disabled yet do not fit the stereotype of the "truly disabled" in order to make sure that they are receiving assistance in the face of public criticism like that of MacDonald. One purpose of MacDonald's article was to criticize the Supreme Court decision, *Sullivan v. Zebley*,[41] in which the Court concluded that the Social Security Administration had too restrictive a definition of "disability" for the purpose of determining whether a child qualified for Supplemental Social Security. The Social Security Administration's definition failed to include such obviously disabling impairments as spina bifida, Down's syndrome, muscular dystrophy, autism, AIDS, infant drug dependency, and fetal alcohol syndrome.[42] Plaintiff Brian Zebley had been denied SSI despite the fact that he had congenital brain damage, mental retardation, development delay, eye problems, and musculoskeletal impairment, because his problems did not meet or equal any single disability category.[43] The Supreme Court required the Social Security Administration to move to a more functional approach so that children who fell between discrete categories, and combined categories of disabilities could be covered by SSI. MacDonald's broadside would leave such children unprotected by federal law.

The *New York Times* also published a critique of special education programs for children diagnosed as learning disabled but, unlike the *Wall Street Journal*, chose to attack a program at one of New York's elite private schools.[44] In that article, the schools and parents were not criticized for trying to get a free financial windfall from the government; instead, the parents were criticized for going along with researchers who told them that their children had learning disabilities. The parents of the children in the elite school often supplemented the free special education that was offered to their children with additional special education. In their case, the diagnosis of a learning disability was costly. The combination of the *Wall Street Journal* and *New York Times* stories suggest that parents of all classes want educational and medical assistance for their children with disabilities. The skepticism displayed by the *Wall Street Journal* and *New York Times* suggests that schools and parents are wise to devote whatever resources are available to solving these problems since mainstream society is unlikely to empathize with their children's problems. These children do not appear to be "truly disabled" yet need our assistance *because* they fit into an unnamed middle category.

A bi perspective therefore provides us with different insights on race, gender, sexual orientation, and disability. The implications of living between categories also varies enormously within categories. A bi perspective requires that we be very attentive to context. Nonetheless, openly transcending categories makes a difference, one worth exploring.

III. The Critical Aspects of a Bi Perspective

Critical theorists have offered arguments parallel to, yet different from, my bi perspective. Angela Harris and Kimberlé Crenshaw have questioned how feminists have historically used the word "woman" to mean "white woman" and how civil rights activists have used the word "black" to apply to all persons with any African-American heritage.[45] They have also questioned how judges have tried to force African-American plaintiffs in discrimination lawsuits to fit the category "woman" or "black" without considering the intersections of race and gender. This is sometimes called "intersectionality" theory. Other critical theorists, such as Scales-Trent, have questioned how lawmakers have created the labels "black" or "colored" to force multiracial individuals to conform to a single racial category. The Harris and Crenshaw critiques of racial categories are somewhat different from the critique offered by Scales-Trent. Harris and Crenshaw consider how an individual crosses several categories—race, religion, and gender. They accept the fact, however, that such markers as "black" have an intrinsic meaning. They are therefore interested in the special ways in which race, religion, and gender intersect to construct identity. Scales-Trent adds to the discussion by considering the ambiguity of the categorical markers themselves; in particular, she focuses on the ambiguity of racial markers. Scales-Trent's intersections lie within; they are really *intra*sections.

The Scales-Trent critique, as opposed to the Crenshaw or Harris views, parallels the bi perspective found in this book, insofar as a bi perspective is an intracategorical perspective rather than an intercategorical perspective. A bi perspective can provide us with special insights that we might attain through an intracategorical perspective that are overlooked in the work of Crenshaw or Harris. Questioning the meaningfulness of the labels that they employ can add to intersectionality theory.

In applying a bi perspective to race, I have asked myself why critical race theorists have not tended to ask the intrasection questions that are central to my perspective as a bisexual. The answer, I believe, depends upon the difference between the constructions of our sexual orientation and our race. One of the first components of our identity is race: are we African-American? Caucasian? Asian-American? We consider it to be a given, an immutable fact. The significance of that racial identity may differ but it is something we "know" like most of us "know" our gender. Our sexual orientation is something that we discover as we grow older. In particular, people who have come to identify with a minority sexual identity have had to grapple with the recognition that they have moved away from the expected category, heterosexuality, to another category such as homosexuality or bisexuality. Intracategorical movement is therefore a typical experience for people who are members of a minority sexual-orientation category but is not a typical experience for people who are members of a minority racial category.

Nonetheless, a bi perspective needs to investigate racial categories because they are, in fact, as socially constructed as sexual orientation categories. Anthropologists, for example, believe that there is insufficient difference between supposed human racial categories to constitute genuine racial categories. In addition, anthropologists agree that the vast majority of people who are labeled as "African-American" have a multiracial background. The fact that most of us do not investigate our race to question whether we belong in a monoracial category reflects the power of socialization rather than any biological reality. Thus, although multiracial existence may be quite different from bisexual or transgender existence, it is worth examining closely, as it reveals the social construction of bipolar racial categories. A bi perspective may therefore enhance our understanding of race by encouraging us to make an intracategorical investigation of racial categories. It is essential that a bi perspective investigate sexual orientation, gender, race, and disability to provide us with a comprehensive understanding of the construction of bipolar injustice in our society.

THREE

....

Sexual Orientation

....

In a 1981 decision, the South Dakota Supreme Court thought it reasonable to ask Sandra Jacobson to forego a sexual relationship with a person of the same sex. "Concerned parents," the Court wrote, "in many, many instances have made sacrifices of varying degrees for their children."[1] The law of sexual orientation routinely gives bisexuals the "choice" of avoiding the negative consequences of the legal system (i.e., loss of custody of children, discharge from the military, imprisonment for sexual conduct) if they will disavow their attraction to people of the same sex and flaunt their attraction to people of the opposite sex. But as one Ninth Circuit judge asked: "Would heterosexuals living in a city that passed an ordinance banning those who engaged in or desired to engage in sex with persons of the *opposite* sex find it easy not only to abstain from heterosexual activity but also to shift the object of their sexual desires to persons of the same sex?"[2] Because bisexuals find some people of both biological sexes attractive, society considers it especially appropriate to visit upon them coercion that would be unthinkable for heterosexuals.

The blatantly coercive history of sexual-orientation policies should make us wary of developing any sexual-orientation categories under the law. Yet, some categories are necessary to develop ameliorative policies. Should the definitions that are used for ameliorative purposes parallel the definitions that have been used for subordinating purposes? Is it possible for society to create privileges and benefits for the gay, lesbian and bisexual communities without perpetuating negative stereotypes about these communities? We need to consider carefully which policies we are trying to promote as we construct these new categories in order to avoid importing destructive values and policies into the gay, lesbian, and bisexual communities.

I. Homosexual Policies That Cause Harm

A. Cincinnati: "Homosexuals Are Not Identifiable"

Many grass-roots attempts to restrict the rights of gay and lesbian people through voter referenda have occurred in the last decade.[3] Oregon and Colorado received considerable national publicity overshadowing a lesser-known attempt in Cincinnati, Ohio, which has produced the most peculiar case law relating to the definition of "homosexual."

In November 1992, the city of Cincinnati passed a Human Rights Ordinance prohibiting discrimination based on race, gender, age, color, religion, disability status, *sexual orientation,* marital status, or ethnic, national, or Appalachian regional origin in employment, housing, and public accommodations.[4] The passage of this ordinance caused an immediate backlash. An organization called Equal Rights Not Special Rights (ERNSR) was formed to eliminate special legal protection that was accorded to individuals because they were gay men, lesbian, or bisexual.

ERNSR's strategy was to get the voters to pass a ballot initiative which would invalidate the Human Rights Ordinance as it applied to individuals who are "homosexual, lesbian, or bisexual." [5] (Presumably, it did not invalidate the Human Rights Ordinance insofar as it protected *heterosexuals* from sexual-orientation nondiscrimination.) The initiative passed by a popular vote of approximately 62 percent in favor and 38 percent opposed and became Amendment XII to the Cincinnati City Charter.

Six days later, a lawsuit was filed challenging the implementation of the initiative. Plaintiffs prevailed in the trial court and the case was appealed to the Court of Appeals. The lower court found that the initiative penalized gay, lesbian, and bisexual people based on their status as persons oriented toward a particular sexual attraction or lifestyle. In reaching this conclusion, the trial court noted that having the *status* of being gay, lesbian, or bisexual does not require an individual to engage in any particular *conduct*. (One can be, after all, a celibate homosexual.) Instead, homosexual status requires an individual to have an "innate and involuntary state of being and set of drives." [6] This conduct/status distinction was needed to distinguish the initiative from the sodomy statute unsuccessfully challenged in *Bowers v. Hardwick.*[7] In *Bowers,* the U.S. Supreme Court had ruled that states could constitutionally proscribe homosexual sexual *conduct*. In order to conclude that the Cincinnati initiative was unconstitutional, the trial court had to be able to conclude that the initiative regulated *status* rather than *conduct*.

The Court of Appeals rejected the trial court's analysis that the initiative regulated status rather than conduct. It concluded that the initiative could not be discriminating on the basis of status because we have no way to identify gay, lesbian, or bisexual people except by their conduct:

The reality remains that no law can successfully be drafted that is calculated to burden or penalize, or to benefit or protect, an unidentifiable group or class of individuals whose identity is defined by subjective and unapparent characteristics such as innate desires, drives, and thoughts. Those persons having a homosexual "orientation" simply do not, as such, comprise an identifiable class. Many homosexuals successfully conceal their orientation. Because homosexuals generally are not identifiable "on sight" unless they elect to be so identifiable by conduct (such as public displays of homosexual affection or self-proclamation of homosexual tendencies), they cannot constitute a suspect class. . . .

Those persons who fall within the orbit of legislation concerning sexual orientation are so affected not because of their orientation but rather by their conduct which identifies them as homosexual, bisexual, or heterosexual. . . . for purposes of these proceedings, it is virtually impossible to distinguish or separate individuals of a particular orientation which predisposes them toward a particular sexual conduct from those who actually engage in that particular type of sexual conduct.[8]

The Sixth Circuit's logic is difficult to comprehend. It suggests that all individuals who are affected by the Cincinnati initiative are currently engaging in sexual conduct with people of the same biological sex. Because *Bowers* allows a state to regulate such conduct, it concludes that the Cincinnati initiative must be constitutional.

The Cincinnati initiative, however, never mentions sexual conduct so the court makes a big leap from the initiative language to its conduct conclusion. It makes that leap by broadly defining the word "conduct" and then ignoring its own definition. In the paragraph quoted above, the court concludes that we cannot identify homosexuals except by their conduct. Conduct, however, is broadly defined to include both "public displays of homosexual affection" *and* "self-proclamation of homosexual tendencies." The latter aspect of conduct acknowledges the existence of a celibate homosexual who publicly proclaims his or her sexual feelings or desires. By the end of the quoted passage, however, the court has forgotten this part of the conduct definition because it concludes that one cannot distinguish between individuals who are predisposed toward homosexual conduct and those who engage in such conduct. But, if "conduct" included self-proclamations by individuals not currently engaged in relationships, then, of course, one could readily distinguish between the two categories. The *Bowers* conduct rule, which only related to homosexual activity, would then be inapposite to the Cincinnati initiative which regulated homosexuals irrespective of their current sexual activity.

Many problematic assumptions underlie the Court of Appeals' decision in the Cincinnati case. First, the court assumes that definitional problems are unique to the area of sexual orientation. Identification problems make gay, lesbian, and bisexual people ineligible for suspect class treatment but somehow do not cause problems for racial or religious minorities. But, racial identification can be equally difficult. As Judy Scales-Trent so vividly demonstrates in her book, *Notes of a White Black Woman,* one can be black but look white.[9] Yet, it is unthinkable that a court would deny suspect class treatment to blacks because we cannot correctly identify all blacks through visual observation. The court assumes that most gay, lesbian, and bisexual people choose to be invisible or closeted. It is only a small minority through public displays of affection (that could and *should* be curtailed) that become identifiable as gay or lesbian.

Second, the court assumes that bisexuals do not exist. Although the initiative specifically mentions "bisexuals" as does the Human Rights Ordinance, the court never considers the application of the initiative to bisexuals. Instead, it limits its discussion to "homosexuals" who are found to exist only through their conduct and not through their identity. Such reasoning causes monogamous bisexuals to be labeled as heterosexual or homosexual, depending on the sex of their current partner. Under the court's reasoning, it would not be possible for a woman, like myself, who is married to a man (thereby meeting the "public display of heterosexual affection" test) to hold myself out as a bisexual. The court assumes that public displays of affection and self-proclamations will be consistent along the bipolar categories of heterosexual and homosexual. Thus, although the court rejects the ease with which we can define people's sexual orientation, the court adopts a very bipolar notion — one is homosexual if one engages in public displays of affection with someone of the same sex and one is heterosexual if one engages in public displays of affection with someone of the opposite sex. Bisexuals do not exist.

Given the court's perverse logic, the political and legal implications of the Cincinnati decision are amusing to consider. Let us assume, for example, that an organization in Cincinnati decides to allow individuals to join if they will sign a piece of paper saying that they are predisposed to find people of the same sex sexually attractive. (One can join even if one also finds individuals of the opposite sex to be sexually attractive.) If you sign the paper, you became an official member of the "H" club. Could the city of Cincinnati then pass an ordinance protecting members of the "H" club from being discriminated against? If so, could the voters of Cincinnati pass a referendum prohibiting the city from granting special protection to members of "H" club? In such a case, the members of "H" club would be discrete and identifiable. They would be definable without reference to their conduct. Of course, members of the gay, lesbian, and bisexual communities are currently members of the "H" club but the Sixth Circuit Court of Appeals mistakenly believes that most gay, lesbian, and bisexual people are in the "closet" when they are not engaged in public displays of affection. And, unfortunately, such decisions as the Cincinnati case drive gay, lesbian, and bisexual people into the "closet" because such cases take away their newly granted nondiscrimination protections. As we will see below, courts and legislatures consistently encourage gay, lesbian, and bisexual people to remain closeted. Self-deprecating gay, lesbian, and bisexual people, who attempt to hide and criticize their own sexual orientation, are rarely targeted by anti-gay policy measures. The message from the Sixth Circuit is that gay, lesbian, and bisexual individuals do not need or deserve nondiscrimination protection because they have the choice of remaining closeted or, in the case of bisexuals, heterosexual.

B. The State of New Hampshire: Conduct-Based Definition of Homosexuality

The Sixth Circuit limited the definition of homosexuals to individuals who engage in same-sex conduct in order to facilitate an initiative aimed at hurting gay men, lesbians, and bisexuals. The New Hampshire Supreme Court, by contrast, narrowed the definition of homosexuals so as not to include all individuals who have engaged in same-sex conduct. An individual could thus move from Cincinnati to New Hampshire and be reclassified from a homosexual to a heterosexual. (Neither court, of course, would consider labeling an individual who had engaged in both same-sex and opposite-sex conduct as a bisexual.)

In 1987, the state of New Hampshire passed a bill barring "homosexuals" from adopting children, being foster parents, or working in day care centers. This was its definition of "homosexual":

a homosexual is defined as any person who performs or submits to any sexual act involving the sex organs of one person and the mouth or anus of another person of the same gender.[10]

This definition divided people into two stark categories: heterosexual or homosexual. Any act of same-sex sexual activity made a person homosexual. Presumably, most bisexuals would be labeled as homosexuals under this definition. Moreover, homosexuality was defined exclusively on the basis of sexual experience. Sexual orientation was equated with sexual experience rather than sexual desire or identity. Thus, a bisexual or homosexual who had not yet experienced sexual relations with individuals of the same sex would be labeled a heterosexual.

Because of the blatantly coercive aspects of this bill against individuals classified as homosexuals, the New Hampshire House of Representatives was concerned about its constitutionality. Pursuant to the New Hampshire Constitution's rules regarding advisory opinions, it sought an opinion from the New Hampshire Supreme Court concerning its constitutionality.

The New Hampshire Supreme Court (including now-U.S. Supreme Court Justice David Souter) advised the state legislature that this bill would be constitutional in the adoption and foster care setting but not in the day-care setting. In determining the constitutionality of the bill, the court, however, was troubled by the definition of homosexuality. It stated: "This very narrow definition of homosexual behavior contains no requirement that the acts or submission thereto be uncoerced, nor does there appear to be any temporal limitation regarding when the acts are to have occurred." [11] Because the court believed that the statute was too broad in defining homosexuality, it decided to assume that the homosexual acts had to be voluntary and knowing. Moreover, the court created this temporal rule:

we interpret the definition's present tense usage to mean that the acts bringing an individual within the definition's ambit must be or have been committed or submitted to on a current basis reasonably close in time to the filing of an adoption. This interpretation thus excludes from the definition of homosexual those persons who, for example, had one homosexual experience during adolescents, but who now engage in exclusively heterosexual behavior.[12]

This commentary by the state Supreme Court was an attempt to narrow the New Hampshire definition to include only individuals who were currently engaging in same-sex sexual activity. A person who engaged in same-sex sexual activity only at a young age could be excluded from the definition based on the combination of the coercion and timing exceptions. Because the event had occurred in the distant past, one did not have to consider this event to be indicative of the individual's current identification. The fact that the event had not recurred even might be evidence that the individual was repulsed by such activity. Moreover, if the individual could allege coercion then the label "homosexual" would not apply at all. This definition had the effect of excluding bisexuals from its definition if the bisexual was currently engaged in opposite-sex sexual activity.

After the state Supreme Court issued its advisory opinion, the state legislature enacted a statute prohibiting homosexuals to adopt or to be foster parents. (Based on the court's legal advice, it dropped the ban on homosexuals working as day-care workers.) It used the following definition of homosexuality: "any person who knowingly and voluntarily performs or submits to any sexual act involving the sex organs of one person and the mouth or anus of another person of the same gender."[13] The legislature explicitly imposed the requirement that the sexual behavior be knowing and voluntary but it did not explicitly impose a temporal requirement. It retained the present tense usage but left open the question of how recently one would have had to engage in a homosexual act to be deemed a homosexual. Would the act have had to occur in the previous day, the previous week, the previous year, or the previous decade? These interpretations are awkward because they require a past-tense interpretation of the statute. Certainly, the legislature did not mean to require that the person engage in a homosexual sexual act while being interviewed about his or her suitability as a parent! Nonetheless, it did construct a conduct-based definition of homosexuality.

Although the legislature was alerted to the ambiguity with respect to timing, it did nothing to solve the problem.[14] It continued to believe that it could neatly divide the world into the homosexual and heterosexual to achieve its purpose. Although the legislature was subtly alerted to the fact that bisexuals exist, it chose to continue to ignore their existence. Therefore, it is hard to know whether it intended to exclude bisexuals, who were currently sexually involved with individuals of the opposite sex, from its definition.

In sum, the state of New Hampshire initially created a legal disability for homosexuals without considering how hard it might be to define the "homosexual." When confronted with definitional difficulties by a state Supreme Court that seemed to recognize the ambiguity that was created for some bisexuals, the legislature did not budge much. It maintained bisexual invisibility in the face of criticism by the state Supreme Court.

In the state of New Hampshire, therefore, the "homosexual" who was excluded from being an adoptive parent was the individual who had engaged in same-sex sexual activity and would not express regret concerning those experiences by claiming that they were coercive. The state of New Hampshire did not intend to exclude all individuals who had same-sex sexual experiences from being adoptive or foster parents. It only intended to exclude those individuals *who felt positively* about their same-sex sexual experiences. A closeted, self-deprecating homosexual or a bisexual who was currently engaging in opposite-sex sexual activity and was willing to disavow same-sex sexual experiences was considered to be a more appropriate parent than an open, proud homosexual or bisexual who was engaging in same-sex sexual activity.

Oddly, however, the state does not even appear to have considered another category of homosexual or bisexual—an individual who is open about his or her identity but is not currently engaged in same-sex sexual conduct. For example, both an open bisexual who is married to a person of the opposite sex and an open homosexual who is currently not in a sexual relationship would seem to qualify as adoptive parents under the state's definition. One would not expect that the state of New Hampshire wants open homosexuals or bisexuals to adopt children since they might inculcate gay-positive values to their children. The failure to mention such individuals reflects the state's stereotypes and ignorance. Like the Sixth Circuit, it does not believe such people exist because they have the "option" of being closeted. The federal government, however, has become well aware of such individuals as it has tried to write policies to govern the military.

C. Federal Government: Keeping Homosexuals out of the Military and in the Closet

Like the State of New Hampshire, the federal government has distinguished between conduct and status so as not to sweep too broadly in limiting the rights of gay, lesbian, and bisexual people in the military.[15] While the state of New Hampshire's definitional story is relatively straightforward, the military's is far from simple. The military has had a long-standing problem trying to define "homosexual" and has adjusted its definition many times in order to better achieve its intended social policies as well as to avoid constitutional difficulties. Its definition-making has been so unsuccessful and problematic that it has recently developed a definition that is radically more encompassing, and less bipolar, than prior definitions. The military currently excludes nearly all gay men, lesbians, and bisexuals from military service based on both conduct or status. It finally has realized that it cannot fully perpetuate the subordination of all nonheterosexuals unless it opens up its rigidly bipolar definition of sexual orientation.

First Definition: A Sweeping Rule

The first definition used by the military to exclude homosexuals provided for the mandatory discharge of individuals who engaged in "homosexual acts." "Homosexuality" was defined as including "the expressed desire, tendency, or proclivity toward [homosexual] acts whether or not such acts are committed." Unlike the definition used by the Sixth Circuit in the Cincinnati case, this definition recognized that there could be a "celibate homosexual"—that conduct and orientation can be distinct. The definition, however, was silent on whether it covered bisexuals.

The definition soon led to problems because it resulted in broader exclusion than desired by the military, as exemplified by *Beller v. Midendorf.*[16] This case challenged the discharge of three individuals because they allegedly engaged in activity prohibited by Navy regulations. These three individuals presented three different categories of individuals who might be covered by the military's exclusion policy: (1) an avowed homosexual, (2) an avowed bisexual who admittedly engaged in same-sex activity, and (3) an avowed heterosexual who admittedly had engaged in same-sex sexual activity.

1. *The Avowed Homosexual.* Mary Saal, a Navy air traffic controller, signed a statement in 1973 admitting that she had homosexual relations with another member of the Navy. At her disciplinary hearing, she admitted to having had homosexual relations since she signed that statement and indicated that she intended to continue her homosexual relationship.[17] She easily fit the Navy's definition of homosexual since she acknowledged engaging in homosexual conduct.

2. *The Avowed Bisexual.* Dennis Beller, an enlisted member of the Navy, admitted during an investigation that he had current contacts with homosexual groups. Subsequently, Beller acknowledged that he had sexual activities with men for the first time after enlisting in the Navy, and that he considered himself to be bisexual.[18] The initial evidence suggested that Beller fit the Navy's definition somewhat less perfectly than Saal, because it only included information about his associational activities. He did not appear to engage in public acknowledgment of his homosexuality. Moreover, he was not known to have engaged in homosexual activities. His subsequent disclosure, however, soon brought him under the Navy's "expressed desires" definition. Nonetheless, Beller insisted on labeling himself a "bisexual," by which he presumably meant that he had opposite-sex as well as same-sex sexual desires. That expression, however, did not remove him from the category of "homosexual." Bisexuals were an unacknowledged, but apparently covered, category.

3. The Avowed Heterosexual. James Miller, a Yeoman Second Class, admitted during an investigation that he had participated recently in homosexual acts with two civilian men. A medical officer who examined Miller concluded that "he did not appear to be 'a homosexual,' and that he found no evidence of psychosis or neurosis."[19] According to the court, Miller "at various times denied being homosexual and expressed regret or repugnance at his acts."[20] Miller fit the Navy's definition of a homosexual because he was found to have engaged in homosexual activity. His expressed repugnance at his homosexual conduct did not exempt him from discharge.

The homosexual acts clause therefore allowed the Navy to discharge Saal and Miller, and the "expressed desire" clause allowed them to discharge Beller. Although the military claimed it had the discretion to retain a "known homosexual" during this discharge process, it did not exercise that option.[21]

Second Definition: "It Only Happened Once, and I Regret It"

Miller's case apparently troubled the Navy because of the rules' inflexibility. Although the Navy made no effort to retain Miller, and denied his request to reenlist, it did modify its regulations after he was discharged. Under the new regulations, the Navy could decide to retain a "known homosexual" if the following conditions were met:

A member who has solicited, attempted, or engaged in a homosexual act on a single occasion and who does not profess or demonstrate proclivity to repeat such an act may be considered for retention in the light of all relevant circumstances.[22]

This was a modest modification of the regulations because the modification required the existence of two separate conditions: the homosexual act occurred only once and the person expressed disdain for such activity. Although Miller might have been able to meet the second requirement, he could not meet the first requirement since he acknowledged having engaged in more than one homosexual act.

Nonetheless, the modification shows that the Navy was troubled by a perceived conflict between its understanding of who are "true homosexuals" and who it was discharging. Moreover, the modification demonstrates the Navy's attempt to get military employees to conform their statements and actions to the categories of "true homosexual" and "normal heterosexual." Subsequent to the modification, the Navy gave individuals who were found to have engaged in homosexual activity the opportunity to stay in the military if they said that the event was their sole homosexual experience and that they did not intend to commit such acts again in the future. The Navy could then operate under the confirmed illusion that people typically experiment *exactly once* in homosexual activity, discover they do not enjoy the experience, and therefore fit the category of normal heterosexual. The illusion could persist so long as people tailored their statements about their sexual activity to fit within the modified regulation.

Not everyone who engaged in exactly one incident of same-sex sexual behavior, however, could meet the Navy's new exception. An unsuccessful attempt to tailor one's statements to the new regulations occurred in *Dronenburg v. Zech*.[23] James Dronenburg had been a petty officer with the Navy for nine years. In August 1980, a seaman recruit gave sworn statements to the Navy alleging that he had engaged in repeated homosexual acts with Dronenburg. Dronenburg's first response was to deny those allegations.[24] Later, he acknowledged their accuracy.

Since the only evidence of Dronenburg's conduct were his

actions with one sexual partner, he could have tried to come under the "one act" exception. Dronenburg's problem, how-ever, was that he fit the court's and society's stereotype of a "true homosexual." According to the Court of Appeals:

This very case illustrates dangers of the sort the Navy is entitled to consider: a 27-year-old petty officer [Dronenburg] had repeated sexual relations with a 19-year-old seaman recruit. The latter then chose to break off the relationship.[25]

The court (in an opinion written by Judge Robert Bork and joined by Judge Antonin Scalia) criticized Dronenburg's actions at great length, because they demonstrated the "powers of mili-tary superiors over their inferiors, to enhance the possibility of homosexual seduction."[26] In other words, like the state of New Hampshire, the D.C. Circuit was particularly horrified because of what it perceived to be a coercive homosexual sexual act between an older man and a young man. Those are the acts of a stereotypical "true homosexual" even if they could technically fall within the "one act" exception. The military and the court therefore made no attempt to allow Dronenburg to fit into the "one act" exception for those who have only had one sexual partner.

By putting Dronenburg in the stereotypical "true homosex-ual" category, the court and the military could also make the seaman recruit blameless. The younger recruit could argue that the sexual activity was limited and not reflective of his sexual orientation—that he was repulsed by the actions and therefore sought to end the relationship. In the language of the New Hampshire statute, he could argue that he did not *knowingly* and *willingly* engage in homosexual acts, but that he was sub-ject to coercion by an older officer. This version of the story allows the court to believe that homosexual conduct is deviant, only performed when one person is acting in a coercive way. Like the version accepted by the New Hampshire legislature, this version does not require the military to recognize homosexual acts as frequent consensual activities. It also allows the military to ignore bisexuality by allowing people to be labeled heterosexual if they predominantly engage in opposite-sex sexual activity.

The "one time" exception clause, however, was not the only problem facing the military in enforcing its regulations. It was also having difficulty with its broad definition of homosexuality which included "the expressed desire, tendency, or proclivity toward [homosexual] acts whether or not such acts are committed." That definition was written to encompass the "true homosexual" whose homosexuality was known on the basis of identity rather than action. The problem with this regulation, however, was that it allowed the military to penalize someone solely on the basis of speech, seemingly in violation of the First Amendment.

That problem soon emerged in the first round of *benShalom v. Secretary of Army.*[27] Miriam benShalom, a member of the U.S. Army Reserves, had publicly acknowledged her homosexuality during conversations with fellow reservists, in an interview with a reporter for her division newspaper, and in class, while teaching drill sergeant candidates.[28] She was then informed by letter that she was being considered for discharge from the Reserves.[29]

The district court concluded that the regulation which dictated her discharge violated the First Amendment because it "directly infringes on any soldier's right at any time to meet with homosexuals and discuss current problems or advocate changes in the *status quo,* even though no unlawful conduct would be involved."[30] Moreover, the court concluded that the regulation infringed on a soldier's right to receive information and ideas about homosexuality.[31] In other words, the regulation went further then allowing the Army to discharge the "true homosexual." It also permitted the Army to discharge people who simply associated with homosexuals or received information about homosexuals. (Such people, of course, are dangerous because they undermine the view that homosexuals are immoral and deviant.) Because of such constitutional problems, the military was forced to abandon its attempt to reach individuals purely on the basis of status. It needed to link that status to *conduct*. Hence, the next round of definitions.

Third Definition: A Broader Disavowal Exception

In response to *benShalom* and *Dronenburg,* the military issued new regulations which stated that:

a member of the armed forces shall be separated from the armed forces under regulations prescribed by the Secretary of Defense if one or more of the following findings is made and approved in accordance with procedures set forth in such regulations:

(1) That the member has engaged in, attempted to engage in, or solicited another to engage in a homosexual act or acts unless there are further findings, made and approved in accordance with procedures set forth in such regulations, that the member has demonstrated that—

(A) such conduct is a departure from the member's usual and customary behavior;

(B) such conduct, under all the circumstances, is unlikely to recur;

(C) such conduct was not accomplished by use of force, coercion, or intimidation;

(D) under the particular circumstances of the case, the member's continued presence in the armed forces is consistent with the interests of the armed forces in proper discipline, good order, and morale; and

(E) the member does not have a propensity or intent to engage in homosexual acts.[32]

These regulations constituted a much more complicated attempt to distinguish between the "true homosexual" and the "true heterosexual." Unlike the previous exception for individuals who engage in one homosexual act, these regulations allowed exceptions for individuals who have engaged in many homosexual acts as long as they expressed disapproval of such acts. Miller, as well as the seaman recruit in the *Dronenburg* case, could probably have fit under this broader exception. In addition, Beller, the "avowed bisexual" discharged under the first definition of homosexual could probably have fit under the exception.

These regulations no longer permitted the military to discharge an individual entirely on the basis of his or her association with homosexuals, or his or her receipt of information about homosexuals. There would have to be a positive statement of identity through public acknowledgment of homosexuality or marrying someone of the same sex. These public statements would put the individual into the category of a "true homosexual."

These regulations, however, did not end the military's legal troubles, because they continued to treat someone adversely based on status rather than conduct. The attempt to criminalize the status of an individual's sexual orientation poses grave constitutional problems.[33] The government, however, did not want to limit itself to cases in which there was known homosexual conduct because it was threatened by individuals, such as ben-Shalom, who were willing to publicly state their status as homosexuals. Those individuals were apparently more threatening to the military than individuals who engaged in homosexual conduct but expressed disdain at such conduct. Thus, the military created fewer status exceptions than conduct exceptions.

The new regulations continued to give the military First

Amendment problems in the "status" cases where there was evidence of identification but no evidence of homosexual conduct. Three cases raised that problem. In *Woodward v. United States,*[34] *Watkins v. United States Army,*[35] and the second round of *benShalom v. Marsh,*[36] individuals were discharged from the military because of their sexual status rather than sexual conduct. In each of these cases, there was no proof that the individual had engaged in homosexual acts. The only proof was that he or she identified as a homosexual. James Woodward acknowledged that he was sexually attracted to members of his own sex and sought the company of gay officers, but there was no finding that he had engaged in homosexual conduct.[37] Miriam benShalom publicly acknowledged she was a lesbian but there was no finding that she had engaged in homosexual acts.[38] Finally, Perry Watkins had always acknowledged that he was a homosexual but there was no finding that he had engaged in homosexual conduct.[39] The military wanted to discharge these individuals because they belonged to the ranks of the "true homosexual" but there was no evidence of homosexual conduct.

In Woodward's case, the military achieved its desired end by discharging him for reasons other than his homosexuality. Disciplinary proceedings were brought against Woodward because he visited an officer's club in the company of an enlisted man who was awaiting discharge from the Navy because of homosexuality.[40] Woodward never acknowledged engaging in homosexual acts but did acknowledge that he identified as a homosexual.[41]

On the basis of those statements, Woodward was recommended for discharge. The discharge, however, was not processed and, instead, Woodward was made available for reassignment or release from active duty. His file was then reviewed by a personnel officer. As a result of this review (which would not have taken place but for the allegation of homosexuality), the Navy determined that Woodward's record placed him below the cutoff point for retaining a reservist.[42] These "nonhomosexual" reasons were used to release him from reserve status. The Navy therefore did not have to defend its right to discharge him solely on the basis of his homosexual status by finding another explanation for his discharge.

In the case of Sergeant Perry Watkins, the military did not resolve the status problem as successfully. It had known of Sergeant Watkin's homosexuality for more than a decade, had no current evidence of homosexual conduct, and had no reason to discharge him other than his homosexuality. Nonetheless, his public acknowledgment of his homosexuality made him a "true homosexual" whom the military wanted to discharge.

This case was very difficult for the courts because Watkins fit the category of a "true homosexual" yet the military had tolerated his homosexuality. Moreover, the only indication that Watkins had engaged in homosexual activity was quite old. In 1968, Watkins admitted engaging in homosexual acts with two other soldiers, actions that occurred fourteen years before the Army tried to discharge him.[43] Thus, he would seem to have met the New Hampshire Supreme Court's "temporal exception" but for his refusal to repudiate his homosexuality. His unwillingness to repudiate his homosexuality, coupled with the military's lack of knowledge of recent homosexual acts, made his case one that squarely challenged the military's power to create penalties solely on the basis of status.

When the Ninth Circuit heard this case for the first time, it viewed the case as one requiring it to determine whether the military could constitutionally penalize someone entirely on the basis of his status.[44] Proceeding from that assumption, the

Ninth Circuit concluded that such action violated the constitutional ideal of equal protection of the laws:

> we conclude that allowing the government to penalize the failure to change such a central aspect of individual and group identity would be abhorrent to the values animating the constitutional ideal of equal protection of the laws.[45]

The court disallowed the military to discharge an individual such as Watkins whose homosexuality was known solely on the basis of statements rather than conduct.

The Ninth Circuit's original decision, however, was not as pathbreaking as it might first appear, because it proceeded on the dominant assumption that homosexuality is immutable and bipolar. In other words, we are either fixed as homosexual or heterosexual:

> Scientific proof aside [about the immutability of sexual orientation], it seems appropriate to ask whether heterosexuals feel capable of changing *their* sexual orientation. Would heterosexuals living in a city that passed an ordinance banning those who engaged in or desired to engage in sex with persons of the *opposite* sex find it easy not only to abstain from heterosexual activity but also to shift the object of their sexual desires to persons of the same sex? It may be that some heterosexuals and homosexuals can change their sexual orientation through extensive therapy, neurosurgery or shock treatment. . . . But the possibility of such a difficult and traumatic change does not make sexual orientation "mutable" for equal protection purposes.[46]

This passage was strikingly bipolar because the court assumed that individuals have either exclusive heterosexual or exclusive homosexual innate sexual feelings. In the court's words, shock treatment is the only way to get people to move outside these bipolar categories. Bisexuals, therefore, do not exist. If the court were to recognize the existence of bisexuals, its reasoning might falter because it then would have to ask whether it is reasonable or constitutional for the government to try to affect the conduct of people who do not have an exclusive preference. The court's argument relied on the presumption of immutability and bipolarity. Thus, it had its own understanding of the "true homosexual" which rendered bisexuals invisible. Its understanding of the true homosexual simply differed from that of the military.

The Ninth Circuit's modest attempt to redefine the "true homosexual" was ultimately unsuccessful, as its reasoning was overturned by the entire panel of the Ninth Circuit when it sat to reconsider the case. The Ninth Circuit decided the case on estoppel grounds (i.e., not applying a rule on grounds of equity) rather than on equality grounds. It refused to permit the Army to discharge Watkins in the 1980s on an estoppel theory because the military had "affirmatively misrepresented in its official records throughout Watkins' fourteen-year military career that he was qualified for reenlistment." [47] Because of this affirmative misrepresentation, the Army was estopped from refusing to reenlist Watkins on the basis of his homosexuality. [48]

The *Watkins* decision sent out a clear message to the military: discharge a soldier as soon as he or she acknowledges his homosexuality. Do not tolerate the "true homosexual" at all if you want to maintain the integrity of your own regulations. Rather than creating more protection for individuals who may identify as homosexuals or engage in homosexual conduct, the Ninth Circuit's decision served as a reprimand to the Army for failing to comply with its own regulations to weed out "true homosexuals." Watkins was a homosexual whom the military and the court found had a "nonwaivable disqualification for reenlistment." [49] By treating that disqualification as discretionary rather than mandatory, the military took the risk of undermining its ability to weed out the "true homosexual." Watkins was therefore the exceptional "true homosexual" who was allowed to stay in the military only because of repeated attempts by the Army not to strictly enforce its own rules. The military's definition of the "true homosexual" was left unchanged.

Because of the Army's fourteen-year history of failing to enforce its own regulations against Watkins, the Ninth Circuit did not have to resolve the issue of whether the military could seek to discharge someone solely on the basis of status. That issue ultimately arose in the second round of *benShalom v. Marsh*.[50] As discussed above, a district court had ruled in 1980 that benShalom's discharge under the second set of regulations violated the First Amendment. The Army did not appeal that order and eventually reinstated benShalom for the eleven-month balance of her original enlistment.[51] Meanwhile, the Army modified its regulation. While serving the final period of her initial enlistment, benShalom sought to reenlist for another full six-year term under the old rules. The army notified benShalom that she was barred from reenlistment because of her acknowledgment that she was a lesbian.[52] In 1988, a new district court judge ruled that the Army was continuing to discriminate unconstitutionally against benShalom in violation of the First Amendment, because it was her statements about her sexual orientation that were precluding her from being reenlisted in the Army. The court granted benShalom's request for a preliminary injunction.[53]

That decision was overturned on appeal. The Seventh Circuit Court of Appeals concluded that the military had eliminated the problematic passage when it deleted the "desires or interest" language from the prior regulation.[54] The court saw no difficulty with the remaining language because it concluded that benShalom's admission that she was a homosexual implied, "at the very least, a 'desire' to commit homosexual acts."[55] Using that interpretation of the regulation, the court was able to avoid the status/conduct issue that had been raised by the first Ninth Circuit panel to hear the *Watkins* case.[56] It was able to resolve the constitutional dilemma that had plagued the Ninth Circuit by allowing the military to discharge or refuse to reenlist the "true homosexual" who was defined solely on the basis of status, not conduct. This finding that conduct and desire are synonymous (so that there is no such thing as a celibate homosexual) was similar to the Sixth Circuit's conclusion in the Cincinnati case that one cannot identify a homosexual other than on the basis of conduct. The court conflated status and conduct to uphold the military's regulation.

Fourth Definition: Don't Ask, Don't Tell, and Disavow

The third definition, which conflates status and conduct, however, did not end the military's attempts to define the "true homosexual" it wanted to exclude from military service. In a highly publicized dispute with President Clinton, who wanted to end discrimination against gay men, lesbians, and bisexuals in the military, Congress decided to codify its own version of who should be excluded from military service based on homosexuality.

Under the new rules, which for the first time were codified by *statute,* a member of the armed forces shall be separated if:

(1) the member has engaged in, attempted to engage in, or solicited another to engage in a homosexual act or acts unless there are further findings, made and approved in accordance with procedures set forth in such regulations, that the member has demonstrated that (A) such conduct is a departure from the member's usual and customary behavior; (B) such conduct, under all the circumstances, is unlikely to recur; (C) such conduct was not accomplished by use of force, coercion, or

intimidation; (D) under the particular circumstances of the case, the member's continued presence in the armed forces is consistent with the interests of the armed forces in proper discipline, good order, and morale; and (E) the member does not have a propensity or intent to engage in homosexual acts.

(2) the member has stated that he or she is a homosexual or bisexual, or words to that effect, unless there is a further finding, made and approved in accordance with procedures set forth in regulations, that the member has demonstrated that he or she is not a person who engages in, attempts to engage in, has a propensity to engage in, or intends to engage in homosexual acts.

(3) the member has married or attempted to marry a person known to be of the same biological sex.[57]

Although this rule received publicity as an attempt to moderate the military's treatment of gay, lesbian, and bisexual people, it actually empowers the military to discharge homosexuals more easily. The first part of the rule allows individuals to be excluded based on conduct alone. As with previous rules, it permits exceptions where the conduct is allegedly inconsistent with an individual's orientation. As such, it retains the exception for the individual who is willing to disavow his or her same-sex sexual feelings or actions.

The second part of the rule is broader than past rules, because it allows for the exclusion of individuals based on speech, irrespective of a finding of any sexual activity. Under the old rules, the military had to presume a connection between speech and action (as in the *benShalom* case). Under the new rules, no such presumption is required. The mere statement that one is homosexual or bisexual apparently conflicts with military morale and is a ground for discharge. In addition, the second part of the rule provides explicitly for the exclusion of bisexuals. One does not have to label bisexuals as "homosexuals" in order to exclude them.

The third part of the definition also expands the scope of the military's exclusion policy by clarifying that off-base activity can cause one to be excluded from military service. An individual who marries someone of the same sex in an off-base ceremony but who intends to be celibate while serving on-duty, can be excluded. The military no longer confines itself to conduct or statements. Coupled with the second part of the definition, it is clear that newspaper interviews as well as private marriage ceremonies can form the basis for exclusion.

This new rule is described as "don't ask, don't tell," but it could be more properly described as "don't act, don't tell, and disavow your homosexual or bisexual conduct." As with earlier rules, it gives individuals an incentive to disavow their prior same-sex sexual activity. Unlike prior rules, it also makes it clear that being open about one's sexual orientation, if it is homosexual or bisexual, can be very dangerous to one's military career. No longer can such individuals as Perry Watkins be open about their homosexuality, while refraining from being "caught" in homosexual acts, and expect to be retained in the military.

The broad reach of the existing rules has caused a district court to declare them invalid. In *Able v. United States of America,*[58] the federal district court entered a preliminary injunction, and ultimately a permanent injunction,[59] to prevent the military from enforcing these rules to discharge six individuals from the military. In concluding that the free speech provision of the First Amendment had been violated, the court observed that: "The Act and Regulations restrict their speech not only while they are in uniform and on duty, or on base, but in every conceivable aspect of their lives, including the prosecution of this lawsuit. . . . This court holds that there is a serious question as to whether a regulation goes beyond what is reasonably necessary to protect any possible government interest when it inhibits six service members from continuing to speak in court to make a constitutional challenge." [60]

The sweeping nature of these regulations reflects that the government is moving in a new direction in its attempt to define the "true homosexual" who should be excluded from military service. Unlike the state of New Hampshire, which apparently wanted to limit the scope of its anti-gay rules to individuals who engage in certain kinds of same-sex sexual conduct, the federal government wants to reach as broadly as possible to exclude any individual who has a homosexual identity or who has engaged in same-sex sexual conduct. The fact that many good soldiers will be discharged, who had been able to be retained under the old versions of the rules and represent an enormous financial investment for the military, seems not to be of concern. At this time, the private sensibilities of heterosexuals in the military, who do not want to shower or bunk with individuals who find *some* members of the same sex attractive, seem to be paramount through the exclusion of all open homosexuals and bisexuals. Good discipline and morale supposedly cannot be retained through the presence of any "out" homosexuals or bisexuals. A bipolar model has been retained of "good" soldiers and "bad" soldiers; for the first time, bisexuals clearly have been placed in the "bad" soldier category along with celibate homosexuals. The bipolar model now seems to have shifted to "heterosexuals" and "others," with "others" including a much broader category for exclusion than in the past.

In sum, the military has had a tortured history of trying to decide whom exactly to exclude from service based on homosexuality. It started with a pure identity definition, moved to a pure conduct definition, and now has a broad definition that includes both conduct and identity. To the military's credit, one might say that its current definition best achieves its apparent purpose of excluding as many gay, lesbian, and bisexual people from military service as possible. In terms of human rights, however, the current definition is extremely troubling because of the ways it forces gay, lesbian, and bisexual people to curtail same-sex sexual conduct as well as open same-sex sexual identity in order to serve in the military.

D. State Sodomy Law: An Attempt to Target Bisexuals

One final example shows that social policies do not always target the "pure homosexual" for mistreatment; sometimes, bisexuals can be the central target. Ironically, in their search for a "middle ground" in the gay rights debate, Professors Arthur Murphy and John Ellington have proposed blatant discrimination against bisexuals.[61] They suggest that existing sodomy laws be modified to make it illegal to engage in sexual intercourse by mouth or anus with another person of the same sex unless the accused can prove by a preponderance of the evidence that the individual with whom they had sex was "reasonably believed by the accused to be a true homosexual."[62] A "true homosexual" is defined as an individual whose "sexual orientation is predominantly towards persons of the same sex as himself or herself."[63] They justify this rule by arguing that it is permissible to direct the bisexual to "make a choice":

The only people whom the statute inevitably frustrates are those (rare?) bisexuals who are powerfully, equally attracted to both men and women—the truly "double gaited" in Damon Runyon's phrase.

But as the majority of the justices recognized in *Bowers,* a state may define and proscribe deviant behavior in its pursuit of secular morality. A state may frustrate a bisexual's desire for homosexual intercourse just as it may frustrate any adult's libidinal hankering for a fifteen year old Lolita, a close adult relative, a prostitute or a willing animal.[64]

Murphy and Ellington's proposal openly condemns bisexuals (and tolerates the "true homosexual") thereby turning the New Hampshire perspective on its head. While the legislature in New Hampshire was determined to find the "true homosexual" for legal sanction, Murphy and Ellington are determined to provide limited protection to the "true homosexual" while proscribing the same-sex conduct of the "true bisexual." Clearly, to some people, bisexuals are the most threatening category whereas, to other people, "true homosexuals" are the most threatening. In either case, social policy is created to conform human behavior to a set of arbitrary norms.

In sum, social policies act coercively to construct individuals' sexuality. These classifications substantially affect people's lives. Children are languishing in foster care who could be adopted by loving and committed homosexual parents in New Hampshire and elsewhere. The quality of our military is eroded through open acceptance of homophobia. Gay and lesbian people are routinely denied family rights and other benefits because of their "illegal lifestyle." These definitions are not simply irrational attempts to classify human behavior and identity but are powerful mechanisms to perpetuate the subordination of gay, lesbian, and bisexual people in society. Unfortunately, instead of consistently arguing for the elimination of these debilitating categories, some argue for the creation of new, more debilitating categories.[65]

II. Positive Categorization

In the prior examples, courts, legislatures, and academics have proposed categorization schemes for the purpose of harming the gay, lesbian, and bisexual communities. Is categorization for *constructive* purposes also possible?

A. Marriage versus Domestic Partnership

The gay and lesbian community has pursued two separate, but related, strategies with respect to the law of marriage. First, it has sought to extend the right to marry to same-sex partners. Because the marriage strategy has been generally unsuccessful,[66] it has also sought to create a new legal category—domestic partnership—which can be used to provide same-sex partners with the option of obtaining some benefits that are normally limited to married couples. The attempt to obtain domestic partnership registration has been extremely successful with many cities and corporations providing same-sex couples the opportunity to register and obtain benefits otherwise only accorded to married couples.[67]

Both strategies, however, have their problems. The marriage approach is arguably flawed because it strengthens the patriarchal institution of marriage by extending it to a new group. We should be seeking to weaken or destroy the institution of marriage rather than extend it to a new category of people. The domestic partnership approach is arguably flawed because it gives same-sex couples an unacceptable second-class status. We should be seeking formal equality rather than separate and unequal benefits. But are these flaws fatal?

My bisexual perspective gives me a special insight into the

marriage and domestic partnership movement because I have been in a long-term (but legally unrecognized) relationship with a woman and in a long-term (but legally recognized) relationship with a man. On an emotional and symbolic level, I understand how much easier it is to sustain a married relationship with someone of the opposite sex than an unmarried relationship with someone of the same sex. Familial and societal support can strengthen opposite-sex married relationships. On an instrumental level, I also appreciate the material benefits that become available through the institution of marriage. My husband was able to immigrate easily to the United States because I was able to sponsor him through the "first-preference" that is accorded spouses under immigration law; I have also been able to obtain inexpensive health insurance for him through my employer. Without the legal and emotional benefits of marriage, we would probably not even be living in the same country at this time. The law of marriage as well as the emotional support of marriage therefore have profound influences in people's lives.*

For that reason, I fully endorse attempts to extend the benefits of marriage to same-sex couples although I question why these benefits must be marriage-dependent. For example, as a university employee, why can I only offer my tuition benefits to my spouse and child? Why can't I offer them to a poor child in my city? It seems peculiar that the spouses of highly compensated employees get tuition waivers. The community would probably benefit more from a poor child receiving a tuition waiver to attend my university than my husband receiv-

---

*My friends who have entered into interracial or interreligious marriages have suggested to me that their relationships, while receiving formal legal recognition, did not receive the familial support usually accorded to marriages. It is therefore hard to predict whether same-sex couples would attain familial support if they were allowed to legally marry. Nonetheless, they would receive numerous legal benefits.

ing a tuition waiver, since my husband could otherwise afford to go to the university.

Marriage-related benefits are unlikely ever to disappear, but we could and should take conscious steps in that direction. In Canada, for example, health insurance is provided universally irrespective of marital or employment status. Similarly, all tax returns are filed in Canada by individuals rather than jointly by couples. Even in the United States, argues Martha Fineman, we often define family without respect to the public law of marriage by encouraging, for example, antenuptial agreements and separation agreements.[68]

The elimination of some marital-based rules, however, does not necessarily foreshadow equality for same-sex couples. For example, the Canadian system offers numerous benefits on the basis of marital status such as immigration privileges, social assistance, family emergencies, tax benefits, pensions, custody, property division, spousal support upon divorce, and intestacy benefits.[69] Canada has a Human Rights Code in six Canadian jurisdictions that protects against sexual orientation discrimination,[70] and constitutional law that recognizes that gay men and lesbians constitute a "suspect class,"[71] yet a recent Canadian Supreme Court decision, *Egan v. Canada,* suggests that many marital-based privileges will remain unavailable to same-sex couples.[72] The Court justified the unavailability of federal pension benefits to same-sex partners based on the stereotype that "It is the [heterosexual] social unit that uniquely has the *capacity* to procreate children and generally cares for their upbringing."[73] Oddly, the Court overlooked that poor same-sex couples like the petitioners who had lived together for nearly fifty years especially needed federal assistance because they did *not* have children to help support them in their advanced years. The Court, of course, also overlooked the lesbian babyboom, made possible by the oldest of reproductive technologies—artificial insemination. It seemed to accept a commonplace stereotype— that lesbians are inherently infertile.*

Unfortunately, the lesson from Canada is that mere recitation that same-sex couples should constitute a suspect class does not mean that the Court has overcome stereotypes about homosexuals in our society. Not all gay men are wealthy and thereby undeserving of pension benefits; not all lesbians are infertile.

Although marriage could provide important benefits to samesex partners, domestic partnership constitutes an unacceptable second-class citizenship that has so little value that it is not worth the price of extending a bipolar model of relationships. The purpose of domestic partnership registration is to allow the gay and lesbian community to obtain benefits that are currently only available to married couples. This movement has two problems. First, the gay and lesbian community has accepted very problematic definitions of domestic partnership in order to qualify for benefits. Second, and more importantly, the gay and lesbian community has helped perpetuate a bipolar model of family relationships through its endorsement of domestic partnership registration in exchange for very few benefits.

Problematic Definitions of Domestic Partnership

The definitions of domestic partnership are consistently more rigorous than the definitions of marriage. Nearly all entities require evidence of shared finances and a waiting period of at least six months since the last domestic partnership. At the University of Pittsburgh, for example, couples need to specify

---

*When I was contemplating having a child, a colleague reportedly said to a friend of mine, "But Ruth can't have a child, she's a lesbian!" That same individual expressed no surprise or shock when I bore a child as part of a heterosexual partnership. My perceived reproductive ability fluctuated depending upon the gender of my partner.

that they are responsible for their "common welfare" and that at least two years have passed since a statement of termination of a prior domestic partnership agreement. The City of San Francisco requires that individuals "live together," "agree to be responsible for each other's basic living expenses," and have not had a different domestic partner in the last six months.[74] Similarly, the City of Berkeley requires that individuals "reside together and share the common necessities of life," and have filed a statement of termination of a prior domestic partnership at least six months before. Finally, the City of Boston requires individuals to specify that they "share basic living expenses," and "assume responsibility for each other's welfare and for the welfare of any dependents."

These definitions are far more rigorous than existing definitions of marriage. Many people, of course, remarry within days of finalizing a divorce. In addition, many married individuals live in separate cities or choose not to commingle assets or finances. In fact, feminists often encourage women *not* to commingle financial assets so that they will have independent credit and finances in the event of divorce. Domestic partnership rules reflect a heightened patriarchal definition of marriage—financial and emotional dependence coupled with a prior period of apparent chastity. "A checklist of features used to determine who is 'in' and who is 'out' of family normalizes the dominant conceptions of family, and reinforces the notion that difference is deviance. Resort to such a test preserves the exclusionary function of family, albeit with slightly adjusted boundaries."[75]

On close examination, these definitions are filled with more burdens than benefits. Individuals who register under a domestic partnership system are not guaranteed any meaningful benefits such as health insurance for their partner. At the University of Pittsburgh, for example, individuals who register under this system get library privileges and modest tuition reduction but no health insurance benefits for their partner. In return for these quite limited privileges, the individuals in the domestic partnership agree to be responsible for each other's financial welfare. Since catastrophic illness is one of the most common ways that an individual can incur substantial financial debt, one wonders whether it makes sense to sign up for a domestic partnership without any guarantee of health insurance benefits for one's partner. Registration is particularly problematic due to the open discrimination that same-sex couples experience in our society. Holding themselves out as a couple by sharing a residence or using a joint bank account may allow a couple to register but it also may expose them to victimization because of their sexual orientation and family status.[76] In making same-sex couples conform their behavior to the domestic partner registration checklist, we may be heightening their exposure to discrimination while according them few benefits.

One cynical way to understand domestic partnership is that mainstream society has capitalized on gay and lesbian people's desires for symbolic manifestations of their relationships by offering them a domestic partnership registration system. In registering, however, domestic partners largely agree to accept social welfare responsibilities that would otherwise be borne by the state. They achieve few gains except at the symbolic level, and even that symbolism is tainted by the second class status of domestic partnership as compared to marriage.

The response to these arguments is that domestic partnership registration is a step toward official legal recognition of same-sex marriage. As society becomes more comfortable extending *some* benefits and recognition to same-sex partners, it becomes more comfortable with extending the privilege of marriage. This is a plausible argument but only if domestic partnership registration is sufficiently analogous to marriage that such long-term steps might occur. Highly restrictive definitions of domestic partnership and limited allocations of benefits do not help us attain that long-term strategy. In fact, the effect of these programs may be exactly the opposite of their intended affect, giving society the false sense that same-sex couples who can register as domestic partners do not need marriage because they already have domestic partnership.

When I give public speeches about same-sex marriage, I am usually confronted with a member of the audience who is positive that same-sex couples can marry in California. It is true that hundreds of same-sex couples have registered as domestic partners in San Francisco and Berkeley while receiving few benefits and many potential liabilities for such registration. But same-sex marriage bills have repeatedly stalled in the California assembly and have virtually no chance for passage in the immediate future. If domestic partnership were not so commonplace, members of the public would not be so misinformed about the status of marriage in the gay and lesbian community.

My university has a highly restrictive registration system for domestic partners with limited benefits that do not include the highly important benefit of health insurance. A strong backlash has arisen over even these limited privileges, forcing, in part, the resignation of the university president. It is thus clear that no extension of these benefits will happen in the short-term or even near long-term. Yet, there is also broad misinformation about the existing available scope of benefits. I routinely hear from well-informed individuals that same-sex couples do have access to family-based health insurance benefits although that information is entirely wrong. The larger community therefore falsely believes that same-sex couples have been extended extensive benefits while the reality is that same-sex couples have an onerous registration system with few benefits. Politically, it might be more useful for the larger community to believe that same-sex couples have no benefits whatsoever than to be deluded into believing that same-sex couples have extensive benefits. The existence of minimal benefits has stalled political work without creating meaningful reform.

The solution to these problems is not to oppose all moves toward domestic partnership, but we should be aware of the problematic nature of domestic partnership and seek to eliminate its problems. We should push for definitions of domestic partnership that parallel state marriage law. If state marriage law has no waiting period, then we should insist that domestic partnership also has no waiting period. Moreover, we should be vigilant in trying to make domestic partnership a registration for benefits rather than a registration for obligations. Admittedly, gay, lesbian and bisexual people also should take on their share of social obligations but those obligations must be borne proportionately. At the current time, same-sex couples help finance many of the benefits available to married couples by paying higher insurance premiums, higher income taxes, and higher inheritance taxes, and by receiving fewer tax deductions. If domestic partnership simply becomes a method of *increasing* the liabilities of same-sex couples, then we should be loud in our criticism of that result. The gay, lesbian, and bisexual community should not be asked to bear a disproportionate set of obligations in our society in the name of domestic partnership.

Unfortunately, moving domestic partnership in this more progressive direction has proven quite difficult. In Ontario, Canada, for example, the New Democratic Party (when it controlled the provincial legislature) introduced Bill 167 to provide for the equal treatment of same-sex partners who are in spousal relationships.[77] Although the bill had the support of the governing party, and passed first reading by a close margin, it never became law. Unlike the domestic partnership ordinances that have been passed in the United States, this bill would have provided equality on the provincial level between common law opposite-sex and same-sex couples.[78] (Marriage is codified in Canada at the federal law, so the Ontario government could not modify the definition of marriage.) Equality, however, proved to be politically unacceptable. The bill faltered at its second reading and was defeated. The failed Ontario attempt, however, reveals that the public only accepts domestic partnership registration if it is truly a second-class citizenship. When it becomes the functional equivalent of common law marriage, it becomes unacceptable.

Bipolar Model of Family Relationships

More fundamentally, however, these definitions are flawed because they perpetuate a bipolar model of family relationships. In *The Neutered Mother, the Sexual Family*,[79] Martha Fineman argues that we should abolish marriage as a legal category and with it any privilege based on sexual affiliation:

Instead of seeking to eliminate [the stigma of nonmarital relationships] by analogizing more and more relationships to marriage, why not just abolish the category as a legal status and, in that way, render all sexual relationships equal with each other and all relationships equal with the sexual?[80]

The problems that Fineman identifies can be seen in the domestic partnership examples cited above. Individuals signing up for domestic partnership registration must state that they have only *one* domestic partner. A family unit can only consist of *two* unrelated adults. The assumption of two adults derives from the heterosexual model of one male and one female parent in a family unit.

Some of these definitions, such as the San Francisco program, also requires individuals to indicate that they have an "intimate, committed relationship of mutual caring." The defeated Ontario domestic partnership bill required the individuals to be in a "conjugal relationship." But why must families be built on intimate relationships? Why cannot groups of people choose to live together as a domestic partnership even if they do not share a sexual relationship? As Fineman argues, there is no reason to privilege sexual affiliations above other kinds of affiliations.

The bipolar model reflected in the law of domestic partnership is reflective of the bipolar model generally found in family law. Based on our heterosexual model of parenthood, the law generally only acknowledges two parents of the opposite sex. Most recently, the law has moved toward recognizing two parents of the same sex, but only when the original opposite-sex parent relinquished his rights to parenthood. Because the law has been formulated under the heterosexual model, people rarely question the two-person limitation which, as I showed above, is replicated in the domestic partner registration system.

Many contemporary family law situations cry out for recognition of more than two parents. For example, in *Thomas S. v. Robin Y.,*[81] the court was faced with the difficult question of who should be the legally recognized parents when two women, Robin and Sandra, raised a child together jointly. The child was biologically related to Robin as well as a male friend, Thomas. Thomas became somewhat involved in the child's life at the age of five when the child began to be interested in her biological origins. After five years of periodic interaction with the child, Thomas sought to be legally recognized as a parent due to a dispute with the child's female parents over visitation. Due to the limitations of family law, only one of the women was legally recognized as a parent. The legal issue in the case was whether Thomas should also be recognized as a parent. The court found for Thomas so that the legally recognized parents became the biological mother, Robin, and Thomas. Sandra was a legal nonentity. If Robin were to die, Thomas not Sandra would become the child's sole parent.

The court's resolution of the case is not surprising under existing bipolar family law, because the legal system searches for one male and one female parent. If rights to children, however, were defined with regard to *relationships* rather than heterosexualized biology, Sandra would be a legally recognized parent. Moreover, if our model were not rigidly bipolar based on our heterosexual premises, this child would have *three* parents. Our system of bipolar injustice, however, gives preferential rights to married couples often ignoring same-sex couples and always ignoring threesomes, foursomes, and so forth. Rather than seeing a child as potentially blessed because she has three individuals who desire to be her parents (with parenthood's many responsibilities), our legal system tries to find the biologically appropriate opposite-sex partners to parent *irrespective* of their emotional relationship to the child. (In this case, Sandra had a much stronger connection to the child than Thomas yet she was legally unrecognized.)

Unraveling the bipolar assumptions that form the basis of family law is a formidable task. Some modest movement in this direction, however, has occurred. For example, the law increasingly recognizes the rights of stepparents to visitation.[82] Stepparents' rights are a dramatic departure from the two-parent model because they reflect rights to nonbiological emotional parents *in addition* to the rights of legally recognized parents. At a minimum, stepparent statutes should be extended to accord rights to same-sex partners who help raise children but who are not related to their partner through marriage. Thus, women like Sandra could be ensured of maintaining a relationship with a child in the event of the dissolution of her relationship with Robin. Current law does not properly weigh the best interest of the child when it perpetuates the two-parent, heterosexual model.

B. Affirmative Action

Generally, the gay rights movement is silent about affirmative action out of fear that the Christian Right will use such talk as an excuse to undermine efforts to achieve more basic nondiscrimination.[83] Nonetheless, some authors have begun to tentatively speak about affirmative action for the gay and lesbian community, and some institutions have even begun to implement affirmative action programs on the basis of sexual orientation.[84]

Because of the complications and controversies involved in implementing affirmative action on the basis of sexual orientation, it is very important that we have a sound argument for how and why to implement such a program. A good place to begin is to determine why we consider an affirmative action policy to be appropriate. I would like to consider two rationales which I will explore more fully in later chapters. First, affirmative action might benefit people who have suffered prior economic or social disadvantage because of their group-based status. Second, it might provide "role models," particularly in settings where high status employment is involved.

Jeffrey Byrne and Bruce Deming justify affirmative action under the first rationale—societal disadvantage. Nonetheless, as they acknowledge, there is no monolithic treatment on the basis of sexual orientation:

For gay and lesbian people qua gays and lesbians, nondiscrimination may more effectively deliver the promise of substantive equality. We are raised as presumptively heterosexual members of families belonging to every race, religion, and socioeconomic class, and as Representative Barney Frank explains, "have not on the whole in this country suffered the kind of systematic discrimination in the allocation of educational resources that have affected other groups." Neither are our economic opportunities and social mobility as a group as systematically circumscribed as are those of African Americans and other groups.[85]

It may be the case that some gay, lesbian, or bisexual people have been largely shielded from the effects of prejudice. On the other hand, it may be the case that an individual gay, lesbian, or bisexual individual has faced dramatic discrimination that has disadvantaged her in an educational institution or workplace. Individualized storytelling of disadvantage may therefore be an appropriate requirement before affirmative action is implemented on an individual basis.

Storytelling may reveal many different life experiences that could be relevant to affirmative action in employment or higher education. For example, many gay, lesbian, and bisexual people are cut off from their families when they "come out." These events can be emotionally and financially traumatic. Others are subjected to beatings or blatant harassment because of their perceived homosexuality. Yet others are suspended, or even expelled from school for violating rules against homosexuality. By contrast, some people, like myself, were "out" to very supportive families and faced few experiences that interfered with academic performance. Individualized storytelling may be especially appropriate in the context of sexual orientation, because gay, lesbian, and bisexual people rarely live in communities defined by sexual orientation and economic disadvantage at a young age. Nonetheless, because of blatant discrimination often visited upon gay, lesbian, and bisexual people as teenagers or adults, the disadvantage rationale is often but not always appropriate in this context.

The second justification—the role model theory—would arrive at different conclusions based on group-based status and necessitates less individualized storytelling.[86] Under a role model theory, I would have been entitled to affirmative action as a law school applicant as an "out" lesbian because I hoped to serve as a role model for other lesbians and generally serve that community. Under that justification, it would not matter whether I had suffered disadvantage due to my lesbian status. What would matter would be my commitment to the community. Others who have faced disadvantage, but have little or no interest in serving as a role model, might not be deserving under that rationale.

To further complicate the problem of categorization, we have to consider the situation of bisexuals. Should bisexuals be included under the social disadvantage or role model theories? Little attention has been given to how to define the beneficiary group in the sexual orientation context. One law firm has defined it as "self-identified gay men and lesbians" whereas another institution has defined it as "declared gay men, lesbians, and bisexuals."[87] Jeffrey Byrne, the only author who discusses how we should define the beneficiary group, argues that we should include bisexuals along with lesbians and gay men:

Bisexual persons have suffered oppression and invisibility such that the justifications articulated for affirmative action for lesbians and gay men warrant inclusion of bisexual persons in the beneficiary group. In particular, bisexual women and men face the same widespread societal and employment discrimination faced by lesbians and gay men.[88]

Byrne makes his argument for the purpose of extending protection of gay men and lesbians to bisexuals under the disadvantage justification but I believe his argument actually helps demonstrate the flaws with his basic categorization scheme. Bisexual individuals vary widely in terms of what that category means to them.[89] Individual F, who has had exclusive relationships with someone of the same sex, may consider herself to be bisexual along with individual G, who is married to someone of the opposite sex and has never been sexually involved with someone of the same sex. Individual H may have recently had relationships with individuals of both sexes. For those three categories of people, the meaning of their sexual orientation might be entirely different in their lives. Individual F may have suffered extensive discrimination by individuals who considered her to be a "lesbian" rather than bisexual. Individual G may have suffered virtually no discrimination because few people recognize that he considers himself to be bisexual. Individual H may be being treated as an outcast by both members of the heterosexual and homosexual communities because she does not seem to "fit in."

A particular bisexual individual may be any one of those three characters during his or her lifetime. (In fact, I have taken these stories from my own life experiences as a bisexual individual.) We therefore need to recognize the fluidity of our sexual orientation in creating rules about the meaning of our sexual orientation in our lives. Before deciding that these bisexual individuals are deserving of affirmative action, I would want to hear their histories. How has their sexual orientation disadvantaged them such that affirmative action makes sense?

The role model theory might be a more appropriate justification for bisexuals although it also has some problems. Although I am currently an "out" bisexual in that I openly acknowledge my sexual feelings and history, my sexual orientation is also largely hidden through my wearing of a traditional wedding ring. I may be a positive "bisexual" role model but only to those individuals who are sufficiently perceptive to recognize my bisexuality. By contrast, when I was involved with a woman (but still considered myself to be a bisexual), I was generally perceived as a lesbian because I did not have the false signifier of a well-known marriage to a man. In fact, when I broke up with a woman and got involved with a man, I was told that it was too bad that I was dating a man because I had been such a good lesbian role model! It never occurred to the speaker that I had just become an excellent bisexual role model by openly changing the gender of my partner. It can be difficult to serve as a bisexual role model, although I have found it to be true that students who identify as bisexual (or who are considering such identification) often seek me out for conversation. I may therefore serve as a role model for some students seeking to come to terms with their bisexual identity.

The problem of applying the role model theory to bisexuals reflects the problem previously noted by the Sixth Circuit—gay, lesbian, and bisexual people are not always readily identifiable. Racial minorities, however, also are not always visually identifiable. The role model theory only works as a justification for people who choose to be identifiable. An institution should therefore only apply the role model theory to individuals who it reasonably believes will make themselves identifiable and available as role models. Closeted gay men, lesbians, or bisexuals do not serve as positive role models; neither do identifiable racial minorities who prefer to have little contact with minority students or colleagues. Unlike the Sixth Circuit, however, I would suggest that gay men, lesbians, and bisexuals are often quite identifiable by their words, deeds, or conduct. In an educational institution, especially, I find that my reputation quickly becomes the source of considerable gossip although I have certainly never engaged in sexual activity on campus. The Sixth Circuit lives in a highly sheltered environment if it does not recognize the visibility that is often accorded to gay men, lesbians, and bisexuals in the community. Therefore, unlike the Sixth Circuit, I would not presume homosexual invisibility anymore than I would presume racial minority invisibility.

Because few institutions have adopted affirmative action plans on the basis of sexual orientation, we have an opportunity to develop those rules with a fresh start. Rather than mimic the rules that we have used in the race and gender areas, it makes sense to ask broad questions about the nature of these rules. We need to have a mechanism to determine who is deserving of affirmative treatment as well as a rationale for our affirmative action policy. If, instead of probing into "status," we probed into an individual's experience of disadvantage and willingness to serve as a role model, then I believe we would have a fair method of determining who is entitled to affirmative action with little or no fraud problem.[90] We do not need to repeat the "status" categorization problem that has been historically used against gay, lesbian, and bisexual people in order to structure appropriate affirmative action.

Because affirmative action for gay, lesbian, and bisexual people is likely to be firmly resisted, it is especially important that we develop strategies that will be effective. Deming and Byrne, in writing the first articles on this subject, already recognize the wide variation in treatment about gay, lesbian, and bisexual people. As a first step, let us build on that recognition rather than repeat the shortcomings of our racial experience. Let us use affirmative action programs as an opportunity to share experiences of disadvantage and stories of positive role modeling to target appropriate beneficiaries as well as to educate us about the scope of mistreatment suffered by gay, lesbian, and bisexual people.

It is fashionable in postmodern circles to say that society constructs sexuality. Usually, however, these comments are made at a broad, theoretical level, asking us to consider the social policies that create "compulsory heterosexuality."[91] In this chapter, we have seen that this construction also occurs at the definitional level. Legislatures and courts have consciously created awkward definitions of "homosexuality" to achieve social policies. These definitions are not universal; instead, they vary depending upon the context in which they are applied. Thus, an individual may not be a homosexual under military regulations but might be a homosexual under state adoption law. There is no one definition of a "true homosexual." Instead, there are definitions which conveniently exclude certain people from privileges and opportunities based on their sexual practices or identity. It takes a lot of double-speak for society to attack the "true homosexual" while leaving safe the normal heterosexual who happens to engage in sexual activity with someone of the same sex but who repudiates that conduct. The bisexual must remain invisible for this legal system to survive.

Nonetheless, we should not simply get rid of all uses of the word homosexual, heterosexual, or bisexual because we may sometimes need to use those terms to develop ameliorative categories to overcome a history of subordinating treatment. Categories can be useful, but only when their ends are ameliorative. As we create new categories, we should be very mindful of whether these new categories are ameliorative or, instead, are themselves perpetuating bipolar injustice.

FOUR

Gender

. . . .

Sharon Bottoms lost custody of her two-year-old son, Tyler, in part because she had taught him to call her female partner "da da."[1] Michael Hardwick was arrested for having oral sex with a man rather than a woman.[2] Jane Doe, who was born anatomically male, was fired from Boeing for wearing "excessively feminine attire"—a pearl necklace.[3] In each case, these actions were unsuccessfully challenged in court. The law coerces lesbians, gay men, bisexuals, transsexuals, transvestites, and other gender hybrids to stay within the narrow gender roles assigned to their anatomical sex. The price for their hybrid status can be loss of custody, discharge from employment, and even imprisonment. Nonetheless, gender hybrids persist in challenging the relationship between genes and gender.

I. The Gender Hybrid Categories

The categorization system of homosexual, transsexual, and transvestite is as important to the affected class (as a means of self-identity) as to the society at large (as a means of oppression). But, as the following story illuminates, categorization can be elusive. Marty Phillip, an inmate who was a pre-operative transsexual, was denied estrogen and other treatment by prison authorities.[4] She unsuccessfully challenged her lack of medical treatment while in prison. Before incarceration, she had adopted a female name (despite retaining male genitalia) and was in a relationship with a man which she characterized as heterosexual. Because she was not receiving estrogen therapy, many of the female characteristics previously attained through treatment had been reversed.[5] She considered herself to be a heterosexual, pre-operative transsexual—not a homosexual, not a male, and not a transvestite. One could, however, have described her as a homosexual, male transvestite who was also a pre-operative male-to-female transsexual.

Transsexuals usually do not want to be considered to be homosexuals; transvestites frequently do not want to be considered to be transsexuals; and homosexuals often do not want to be considered transsexuals or transvestites.[6] Many male-to-female cross-dressers (be they transsexuals or transvestites) are sexually attracted to men. If the individual is a transvestite, then he is usually classified as a homosexual (or more commonly a "drag queen"). By contrast, if the individual is a pre-operative transsexual then the individual may identify as a heterosexual who is attracted to men but is trapped in a man's body.

Commentators typically try to distinguish neatly between transvestites and transsexuals by saying that both individuals may "cross-dress" but that the transvestite does not desire to become anatomically the opposite sex.[7] In fact, the distinction between the transvestite and the transsexual is not clear. After a period of cross-dressing, a transvestite may decide that he or she is actually a transsexual and seek surgery. But then, the question arises whether the individual who identified as a transvestite was really a transsexual all along.[8] Annie Woodhouse defines the distinction between the transvestite and the transsexual as follows (using the male-to-female cross-dresser as her example):

Perhaps a more easily recognizable point of departure would be to consider the transvestite as a person who identifies himself as a man-who-dresses-as-a-woman. In contrast, the transsexual will identify himself as a woman who has the misfortune of a male body; the solution being, in his terms, hormone therapy and sex reassignment surgery. In referring to the importance of changing genital sex, April Ashley, a post-operative transsexual, comments that as a biological male, "my genitals were quite alien to me." Typically, the transvestite will display the opposite attitude, enjoying the best of both worlds.[9]

Another way that transvestites and transsexuals are often distinguished is that a transvestite usually cross-dresses occasionally whereas a transsexual is a full-time cross-dresser. But this distinction becomes blurred in the case of the full-time cross-dresser who has not undergone sex reassignment surgery (and might not desire such surgery).[10] Woodhouse explains the distinction, in such cases, as follows: "In many respects the differences between the transvestite and the so-called transsexual lie with their own perceptions and definitions of self: whether they consider themselves 'real women' or whether they see cross-dressing as an end in itself which allows partial entry into the world of femininity."[11]

The classification system becomes even more complicated when we include hermaphrodites. By operating at birth on the hermaphrodite, we assign that person to one pole of the bipolar spectrum rather than allowing the person to live as a transgendered person. Instead of allowing a third, fourth, and even fifth sex to develop (given the three types of hermaphrodites),[12] we engage in surgery before the age of consent to eliminate each of these alternative genders to fix an individual purely in the male or female category. Thus, hermaphrodites become an invisible aspect of the male and female poles. Some civil rights activists are worried about a similar kind of erasure of identity through the adoption of biracial children (e.g., children born to a white mother and black father) by white parents. They worry that these children will be transformed into purely "white" children by the erasure of their black heritage.[13] The erasure of bi categories and identities can therefore happen through biology (i.e., surgery for hermaphrodites) or culture (i.e., adoption and child-rearing patterns).

Post-operative transsexuals also have an awkward place on the gender spectrum. Whether they fit on a pole depends on whether they "pass." The post-operative transsexual who does not pass is left in the indeterminate middle category (for example, with respect to sex-segregated bathrooms)[14] with neither men nor women wanting to claim him or her as their own.

The term "androgyne" does not inherently present a new category but, instead, a less negative way to describe some of the other categories. The word androgyne derives from the Greek *andro,* "male," and *gyne,* "female." It historically described individuals who were in possession of both sets of sexual organs—a hermaphrodite.[15] Today, however, androgyne is usually understood to be a cultural blending of gender, not a physical combination of sexual organs, and is even considered to be "chic."[16] Thus, we simultaneously use words with negative connotations—transsexual, transvestite, and hermaphrodite—to describe individuals who cross gender lines, while we also recognize (at least in some quarters) a new gender ideal in appearance, androgyne, for popular musicians such as Michael Jackson. (Although feminists who challenge gender roles are often maligned as "male hating dykes," suggesting that our tolerance for gender-crossing may extend to fashion but not politics.) The existence of the "androgyne" category reflects a modest attempt to move beyond sharp gendered divisions in appearance (at least where biological modifications have not occurred) while we also retain punitive treatment for the other transgendered categories.

Finally, the "bisexual transsexual" reveals the bipolar assumptions underlying many of these categories. A person who is born anatomically male can support his request for a sex change operation by stating that he has an exclusive interest in men as sexual partners. "This interest in the 'correct sex' is what the medical profession has usually required (among other things) as proof of transsexual status and a prerequisite for genital surgery."[17] The "true" transsexual moves to exclusive heterosexuality as a sexual orientation. The transsexual bisexual, however, shows the false assumptions underlying this framework. Gender and sexual orientation have no inherent interconnection.[18]

Exploring the "bi" within gender therefore shows an enormous range of hybrid categories which are virtually impossible to define but which are usually rejected and scorned by society. Because we believe that biology is destiny, we are shocked and dismayed at attempts to play with "mother nature" or, more modestly, to question the gender roles assigned to each biological sex. Society does its best to repress the proliferation of these hybrids. They abound nonetheless.

II. Gay Men, Lesbians, and Bisexuals

A. Family Law

In the last chapter, we saw that gay men, lesbians, and bisexuals are often denied custody of children because of their attraction to people of the same sex. They also are denied custody when they challenge the gender roles assigned to their biological sex.

Inappropriate Role Models: Who's the Mommy and Who's the Daddy?

In the early 1990s, I appeared on a TV show to discuss gay and lesbian issues with a conservative, fundamentalist minister. Our discussion soon turned to whether a lesbian should be able to adopt the biological child of her partner, so that the child would have two legally recognized parents of the same biological sex. I made what I thought was the rather obvious observation that it was better for a child to have two loving parents of the same sex than only one parent. Nonetheless, the minister disagreed with me, saying the child would be harmed in that situation because there would not be a proper male and female role model for the child. His statement was the clearest expression of the relationship between homophobia and heterosexism that I have heard. His belief that gender roles should flow directly from biological sex shaped his belief system about homosexuals.

Courts have, unfortunately, also adopted his reasoning. In 1995, the Virginia Supreme Court ruled that Sharon Bottoms was not a fit mother for her two-year-old son Tyler because of her "active lesbianism." [19] The state Supreme Court affirmed the trial court decision and overturned the opinion of the court of appeals. Custody of Tyler was transferred to Sharon's mother. The Virginia Supreme Court's opinion reflected "gender policing." Sharon Bottoms was not a fit mother, in part, because she had the poor taste to teach her son to call her female partner, April Wade, "da da." [20] This name purportedly confused him about the difference between women and men. [21]

If April were "Adam," April would most likely have been a positive factor in Sharon's custody battle. For example, in *Ferris v. Underwood*,[22] a Virginia Court of Appeals found that a positive factor in favor of a biological mother who sought custody in a battle with the child's grandmother was that the mother had remarried a man who "was willing to provide financial and physical support within his limitations."[23] His "limitations" were that he was blind and earned a modest income. Sharon and April were not legally married but only because marriage between same-sex couples is not possible in the state of Virginia. They had gotten matching tattoos with three sets of initials intertwined: Sharon, April, and Tyler, before the child custody dispute began. In the *Ferris* case, the mother was allowed to regain custody of her child, partly on the basis of her marriage to a man, despite the fact that the grandmother had had primary custody of the child for a lengthy time period and a sister who was a prostitute frequently visited the mother's home. The court of appeals affirmed the trial court decision to re-establish custody with the biological mother noting that this result has the "effect of re-establishing for [the child] the proper roles of her mother and her grandmother."[24] Sharon could not fit the proper role of mother because she lived with a woman rather than a man.

Another reason that Sharon lost her case was that she was too assertive, thereby not conforming to appropriate gender stereotypes for women. As we will see in the military cases, the label "lesbian" is often attached to independent and assertive women. Sharon's mother only contested custody when Sharon decided to rely less on her mother for child care.[25] Sharon had gone into therapy about the child abuse that she had suffered from her mother's long-term boyfriend and had finally developed the strength to begin to turn away from her mother. In response to Sharon's new assertiveness, the mother sued for custody. The lesbian label became the means through which the mother could retaliate against Sharon's increasing self-esteem and assertiveness.

Role model discussions often come to the forefront in cases involving gender hybrids. In a 1992 New York decision, the state court ruled that a father was not entitled to overnight visitation with his biological child because of the father's history of "cross-dressing." [26] The father's cross-dressing precluded him from being an appropriate "role model" for an "impressionable" five-year-old son. [27] Cross-dressing, of course, is not illegal and causes no harm to others. Yet, it was a sufficiently dramatic deviation from expected gender norms to preclude significant visitation with a child. Usually, men who seek custody of male children are given a presumption of fitness because they are thought to be especially good role models for a male child. [28] Men who cross-dress do not get to take advantage of that presumption when seeking custody or visitation of their male children because of the stereotype that they are perverted pedophiles. No father is better than a father who wears dresses or necklaces.

Presumption of Bad Mothering

Another gender theme that emerges from the cases involving lesbians and child custody is that lesbians, in contrast to heterosexual women, are not considered to be presumptively good mothers. Heterosexual women historically have been granted the benefit of custody in cases involving young children under the "tender years" presumption; [29] lesbians, by contrast, have sometimes had a reverse tender years presumption applied to them. [30] A Pennsylvania case explicitly states the rule that many courts implicitly follow: "We submit the law is and should be that, where there is a custody dispute between members of a

traditional family environment and one of homosexual composition, the presumption of regularity applies to the traditional
relationship and the burden of proving no adverse effect of the
homosexual relationship falls on the person advocating it." [31]
In other words, lesbians and gay men who are biological parents
do not get the presumption of fitness that is accorded to heterosexuals who are biological parents.

The *Bottoms v. Bottoms* case reflects this problem.[32] In a
case such as *Bottoms,* involving a custody dispute between a
parent and a nonparent, the law presumes that the child's best
interests would be served when in the custody of the biological
parent. (The father had voluntarily relinquished custody to the
mother. A grandmother who seeks custody of a grandchild has
the same status as any other nonparent under Virginia law.)
Thus, in order for the court to award custody to the grandmother, it had to conclude that Sharon Bottoms was unfit.

Sharon Bottoms, however, was never granted the standard
presumption of fitness. Under Virginia law, to rebut the parental presumption of fitness, a third party must prove by *clear and
convincing evidence* that the child will be *seriously harmed* if he
or she remains in the parent's custody. (It is not enough for the
evidence to demonstrate that the "best interests" of the child
would be served by living with the grandmother.) Such evidence
may not be merely "surmise and conjecture." [33] Moreover, as
recently as 1982, Virginia law had expressed a preference for
custody being given to the mother when the child was of
"tender years." [34] (Tyler was two at the time this dispute
erupted.)

The evidence of future harm in the *Bottoms* case was based
entirely on surmise and conjecture, and could hardly be described as serious. The *Bottoms* case contained no evidence that
could come close to meeting the high standards set by the

courts—there was no evidence of physical abuse or emotional abandonment which is the standard evidence considered in such circumstances. The only evidence about future harm emphasized by the trial court related to her "active lesbianism":

We have previously said that living daily under conditions stemming from active lesbianism practiced in the home may impose a burden upon a child by reason of the "social condemnation" attached to such an arrangement, which will inevitably afflict the child's relationships with its "peers and with the community at large." [35]

That finding, however, was very speculative and did not relate to immediate future harm. There was no evidence of any harm having actually occurred to the child by his exposure to his mother's "active lesbianism." The lesbian co-partner, in fact, appears to have been a very positive household factor because she supported the family financially and helped raise the child. The only negative evidence against April was that she had slapped the boy once. (She also reportedly cried for an hour afterward and regretted the action.) [36]

In cases involving heterosexuals, Virginia courts have granted custody to men despite evidence that they inflicted physical injury upon their spouse.[37] For example, a Virginia court concluded that a child's grandparents were not entitled to custody "merely" because the child's stepfather, who resided with the child's mother, had killed the child's natural father. The court refused to presume that the child would be harmed by living with his father's murderer.[38]

In most disputes between grandmothers and mothers, the biological mother has voluntarily relinquished childrearing to the grandmother for a considerable length of time. After the mother rehabilitates herself, she seeks return of her child over the grandmother's objections. In such cases, the mother typically prevails due to the strong presumption of maternal fitness despite the fact that the child's primary relationship is with the grandmother.[39] Although Kay Bottoms apparently did spend a lot of time with Tyler in his first two years, Sharon never relinquished childrearing to her mother. Heterosexual women who have engaged in inappropriate behavior toward their children are granted a presumption of fitness in the context of rehabilitation; Sharon had engaged in no inappropriate behavior, had no need to rehabilitate herself at all, yet could not obtain any presumption of fitness.

Even if the maternal presumption could be rebutted in the *Bottoms* case, custody should not transfer automatically to the third party-grandmother. The court is supposed to make a further, separate determination as to whether the best interests of the child require a transfer of custody to the third party. No such finding occurred in this case. In fact, a strong case could be made against Kay Bottoms's fitness as a parent if you accept the case against Sharon, herself. Kay, of course, raised Sharon. Moreover, Sharon testified that she had been the victim of child abuse at the hands of Kay's long-term boyfriend. Kay had a record of raising one person who the court concluded was an unfit parent. Why should we believe that she would do a better job raising Sharon's son? Sharon, on the other hand, had no childrearing record, except that of her son. If one were to judge either's suitability as a parent, it would seem that there is more evidence of the grandmother's unfitness than the mother's.

Finally, one should realize that the *Bottoms* case is not purely a "lesbian" custody case. Sharon's sexual behavior better fit that of a bisexual than a lesbian. Sharon had been married to a man and reportedly had several boyfriends before meeting April. Her brother Kenneth criticized Sharon by saying, "She isn't even a lesbian."[40] In Kenneth's mind, one apparently is not a "true lesbian" if one has recently been divorced and is raising a son. It is doubtful that Kenneth thought she was a "bisexual" so, presumably, he thought she was a heterosexual masquerading as a lesbian for publicity. Why, then, one must wonder, did he agree with his mother that Sharon was not fit to raise her son? Crossing bipolar categories seemed to bother Kenneth; the judges were too discrete to explain whether the boundary-crossing bothered them. Like the judges in family law cases involving bisexuals that we examined in the last chapter, they may be blaming Sharon for not "choosing" to express her heterosexual side.

In sum, the *Bottoms* case brings together many themes relating to bipolar injustice. Sharon was not considered to be a "real woman and mother" for the purposes of applying standard presumptions in favor of custody for biological mothers. Her "active lesbianism" took her outside the norm of womanhood. She was not considered to be sufficiently maternal because she attempted to challenge her own mother's assertion of authority over her child. Finally, Sharon's partner was not considered to be a positive factor like opposite-sex partners who provide financial and emotional support to a child. Instead, she was criticized for not providing the child with appropriate gender role models. Rules against "lesbianism" (applied against a woman whose experiences would seem to categorize her as a bisexual rather than as a lesbian) were used to help perpetuate gender norms. In the court's view, it was better for the child to be raised by an unmarried grandmother than by a same-sex couple that could provide him with both a mother and a "da da." "Da das" are only a positive factor when they are male. No father is better than a lesbian father.

B. The Military

After Mary Beth Harrison rebuffed a male crew member's sexual advances, he publicly shouted profanities and accusations that she was a lesbian.[41] When she filed a complaint against this harassment, she was discharged for being a lesbian although she maintained that she was not and had never engaged in lesbian activity. Rather than receive a fair hearing, she was tried and presumed guilty. Despite her record of outstanding job performance and the lack of evidence of lesbian sexual activity, she was discharged for being a lesbian. Other women have been discharged for the "crime" of putting their arm around the shoulders of a weeping female colleague.

Women are discharged from the military at a rate seven to ten times that of men for supposedly being a homosexual despite the fact that virtually no women are ever "caught" in the act.[42] These lesbian purges reflect attempts to keep women in their proper gender role—out of the military. These purges also reflect lesbian baiting as a form of sexual harassment.

The 1980s were characterized by a wave of investigations of women in the military for alleged lesbianism.[43] As the recession caused more men to enlist in the military, the military responded by placing a cap on the number of new female recruits and by seeking to discharge the women who had already enlisted. Some women in the military were threatened with jail sentences or the loss of custody of their children if they did not admit to being lesbian.

The ban on gays in the military did not require the military to have any evidence that an individual has engaged in same-sex sexual activity or even propositioned someone for such activity. All the military needed to show was that the individual who was discharged under the regulation was believed to be a "homosexual." Reputation evidence was sufficient.

The ban on homosexuals in the military therefore serves the gendered purpose both of keeping women out of the military who engage in same-sex sexual activity and of barring those who refuse to acquiesce to men's sexual advances. These women are, in a gendered sense, not "proper women."

C. Sodomy Laws

Georgia's anti-sodomy law states: "A person commits the offense of sodomy when he performs or submits to any sexual act involving the sex organs of one person and the mouth or anus of another."[44] This language does not refer to the sexual orientation or gender of the parties involved. Nonetheless, Georgia, like most states with such rules, uses this statute primarily to arrest men who are engaging in anal or oral sex with another man.[45] Michael Hardwick, for example, was arrested for having oral sex with another man in the privacy of his own bedroom. In *Bowers v. Hardwick*,[46] the Supreme Court upheld the application of Georgia's sodomy statute only to "homosexuals" despite the neutral language of the state statute. Had Michael Hardwick's partner been a woman, he could have been engaging in similar sexual activity but not been subject to prosecution.

The question that such cases raise is, why is the gender of one's sexual partner so important to society? Similarly, why do we define sexual orientation on the basis of the gender of one's partner? Why is gender-specific enforcement of sexual activity statutes permitted, and even encouraged, when we have constitutional rules against gender-based policy making? Kate

Bornstein provocatively engages these issues: "Sexual preference *could* be based on genital preference. . . . Preference could
also be based on the kind of sex *acts* one prefers, and, in fact,
elaborate systems exist to distinguish just that, and to announce
it to the world at large."[47] In the *Bowers* case, the state of
Georgia did define illegal activity on the basis of sexual acts,
not gender-specific genital preference, yet the prosecutors and
courts interpreted the statute to be gender-specific. In other
words, courts and society go out of their way to disapprove of
homosexuality irrespective of what language has been codified
by the legislature.

The courts have consistently refused to view sexual orienta-
tion-related discrimination as gender-based even when the answer to the hypothetical question: "Would a person of the
opposite sex have been treated differently?" is clearly yes.[48] In
fact, the state of Georgia's defense relied upon the fact that a
person of the opposite sex would have been treated differently.
Georgia understood that it could not constitutionally proscribe
sodomy practiced by married heterosexuals in the privacy of
their bedroom. Thus, they successfully had a heterosexual couple, the "Does," dismissed from the lawsuit by arguing that the
Does, as a heterosexual married couple, had no cognizable fear
of prosecution. The Does did not have "standing" to challenge
the Georgia statute because, despite the statute's gender-neutral
language, the state admitted that it only prosecuted people who
were engaging in sexual activity with people of the same sex.
Georgia managed to turn constitutional equality doctrine on its
head by defending a statute by reading into it an implicit gender-based rule. They succeeded in this effort because the courts
conveniently rule that discrimination is not sex-based when it
relates to sexual-orientation. Although this rule is linguistically

incoherent, it is widely accepted.[49] Sexual orientation cases such as *Bowers* therefore cleverly hide the gendered aspects of sexual orientation rules.

The Hawaii Supreme Court has understood the connection between rules challenged in such cases as *Bowers* and gender differentiation. In *Baehr v. Lewin*,[50] the plaintiffs challenged the Hawaii Marriage Law which precluded people of the same sex from marrying. The state tried to defend the rule by arguing that it appropriately precluded homosexuals from being married. The Court, however, refused to accept this analysis of the statute's effect. Noting that opposite-sex individuals who seek to marry do not have to proclaim themselves as "heterosexual" in order to get a marriage license, the court also pointed out that same-sex individuals who seek to marry need not consider themselves to be "homosexual." When two people of the same sex seek to marry, we only know that they are of the same gender. We do not know their sexual orientation. In the Court's words: " 'Homosexual' and 'same-sex' marriages are not synonymous; by the same token, a 'heterosexual' same-sex marriage is, in theory, not oxymoronic. A 'homosexual' person is defined as '[o]ne sexually attracted to another of the same sex. . . .' Parties to 'a union between a man and a woman' may or may not be homosexuals. Parties to a same-sex marriage could theoretically be either homosexuals or heterosexuals." [51]

Because the plaintiffs, who wanted to marry someone of the same sex, did not allege their sexual orientation in the pleadings, the court found that it was the defendants, not the plaintiffs, who sought to place the question of homosexuality in issue.[52] In other words, unlike the United States Supreme Court, the Hawaii Supreme Court understood that purported homosexual classifications are actually gender-based classifications, a powerful and unprecedented acknowledgment of how attempts to constrain homosexuals are also attempts to restrict people based on gender. If Michael Hardwick were a woman, he would not have been subject to prosecution.

In sum, discrimination on the basis of sexual orientation reflects, in part, the desire of law and society to force all people to conform to appropriate gender norms. When gay men or lesbians seek to raise children, norms about gendered role models break down and rules about the need for "traditional families" are imposed. Military women are accused of being lesbians in order to exclude them from military life. And when two men or two women have oral sex, the activity becomes "unlawful sodomy" although people of the opposite sex routinely engage in such behavior. Activity becomes tainted when gender barriers are not respected.

The group that most starkly challenges gender barriers, however, are transsexuals. To them, society imposes some of its most strongly voiced hatred and mistreatment. Their story is next.

III. Transsexuals

Although transsexuals are often misunderstood as people who crave one gender category, and thereby mutilate their bodies to acquire it, many transsexuals, in fact, have a discomfort with all gender labels. Kate Bornstein, a "woman" who was born biologically male, recounts:

I'm supposed to be writing about how to be a girl. I don't know how to be a girl. And I sure don't know how to be a boy. And after thirty-seven years of trying to be male and over eight years of trying to be female, I've come to the conclusion that neither is really worth all the trouble. . . . I'm sitting here tapping this out on my computer, and I'm thinking about who might be reading this; and I know that some of you really believe you are women. I want to get down on my knees in front of you, I want to get down on my knees, and I want to look up into your eyes and I want to say tell me! Tell me what it's like![53]

Bornstein explains that: "It was the absence of a feeling, rather than its presence, that convinced me to change my gender."[54] Changing her gender required her to change much more than her physical attributes. She had to learn new rules of etiquette, change her first name, learn new styles of communication, and change her sexual orientation since changing her gender did not change whom she found attractive. For example, as part of learning to pass as a woman, she had to learn to avoid eye contact when talking down the street, because looking someone in the eye is a male cue.[55] Because most of us have only lived our lives as one gender—male or female—we have not had to dissect all the ways we adapt our behavior to conform to our biological sex. The experiences of transsexuals can give us insight into the subtle aspects of our gender construction that we take for granted. Sandra Bem, for example, may attempt to structure her life without resort to gender but having lived her entire life labeled a "woman," she has not had to consider in detail the ways in which gender has subtly constructed her existence. Transsexuals, who have inhabited both gender worlds, can provide us with that insight.

Society, however, does its best to make it difficult for transsexuals to offer us those lessons. As we saw in the previous discussion, a man who cross-dresses (but probably would not be considered a transsexual) is precluded from spending much time with his son for fear that he would be a bad "role model." We hide "gender outlaws" for fear that they might influence others to question their socially constructed gender identity.

A. Employment

Jane Doe was discharged by the Boeing Company for wearing "excessively" feminine attire in violation of company directives—a strand of pink pearls.[56] This attire was unacceptable because Doe was an anatomical male who was awaiting genital sex reassignment surgery. She had already begun hormone treatments and electrolysis treatments, and legally changed her name from a masculine to a feminine name. In order to qualify for sex reassignment surgery, her physician had informed her that she would have to live full time, for one year, in the social role of a female. That social role included female attire. Doe's employer had agreed to accommodate this requirement so long as she did not wear "obviously feminine clothing such as dresses, skirts, or frilly blouses"[57] and did not use the women's restroom. The pants outfit that Doe wore on November 4, 1985, was deemed acceptable; similar attire the next day with the addition of a strand of pink pearls was not.[58] Doe challenged her discharge under Washington state disability discrimination law, and lost. Even assuming her gender dysphoria (i.e., transsexualism) was a handicap, the court found that Boeing had no duty to reasonably accommodate her desire to dress more femininely. "Boeing has a legitimate business purpose in defining what is acceptable attire and in balancing the needs of its work force as a whole with those of Doe."[59] Boeing could not and need not tolerate a person who was anatomically male wearing a strand of pearls while working as an engineer.

Similar cases have been brought under Title VII of the Civil Right Act of 1964 (which proscribes gender discrimination in employment) with the same results. Karen Frances Ulane was a licensed pilot for Eastern Airlines.[60] Unlike Doe, Ulane took a leave of absence while she underwent sex reassignment surgery. Eastern was not aware of her transsexuality, hormone treatments or psychiatric counseling until she attempted to return to work after her surgery. Ulane was not permitted to return to work, and was discharged. The trial court found in favor of Ulane but the Sixth Circuit Court of Appeals reversed, finding that Eastern discriminated against Ulane because she was a transsexual, not because she was a female.

Audra Sommers was dismissed from her job as a clerical worker for Budget Marketing, three days after being hired, because "she misrepresented herself as an anatomical female when she applied for the job." [61] After being told she could not use the restrooms, she was fired.[62] She filed suit under Title VII in federal court and lost in both the trial court and Eighth Circuit. She also filed suit under state anti-discrimination law on the grounds of gender and disability discrimination. She lost on both grounds.[63]

Reagan Kelly Kirkpatrick informed her supervisors at the beauty salon where she was employed that she was preparing to undergo a sex reassignment process from male to female.[64] Like Doe, she needed to live as a social female before undergoing surgery. When she began to wear female attire to work, she was fired. Kirkpatrick alleged gender discrimination in federal court and lost in both the trial court and Fifth Circuit.

Ramona Holloway was Head Multilith Operator at Arthur Andersen.[65] She informed her supervisor, at the time of her promotion, that she was undergoing treatment in preparation for sex reassignment surgery. She was terminated after a company official suggested she would be happier working at a new job where her transsexualism would be unknown. She brought suit under Title VII in federal court and lost in both the trial court and Ninth Circuit.

In each of these cases, the courts failed to take seriously the simple argument that the employer had imposed conditions on their employment because of their "sex" in violation of Title VII. (Title VII states "It shall be an unlawful employment practice for an employer . . . to discriminate against any individual with respect to his . . . conditions . . . of employment, because of such individual's . . . sex.") Jane Doe, an anatomical male, was not allowed to wear pearls; women, of course, were allowed to wear pearls. In each of the other cases, the employer insisted that the individual maintain an outward appearance in conformance with the employer's perception of his or her sex. Because the employer perceived these employees to be male, they were to wear male and not female clothing. By recasting the act of discrimination as "transsexual discrimination" rather than "sex discrimination," the courts created a circular argument. Under the courts' logic, plaintiffs were not discriminated against because of animus toward their biological sex but only because the employer did not want them to *change* their biological sex. Neither men nor women would have been allowed to change their biological sex, therefore the employer was even-handed in its practices.

But, as we will see in chapter 7, Title VII does not require an employer to discriminate against every woman in order for the woman targeted by sex discrimination to have a cause of action. Title VII also contains no requirement that an individual be discriminated against solely because of sex. Sex need only be a motivating factor for the challenged action. In the cases involving transsexuals, the employer targeted the employee for discharge because the employee, at the time of discharge, considered herself to be a woman. The employer did not have animus generally against women, but did have animus against women who were born as anatomical males. Although the employer's animus against this group of women can also be described as animus against transsexuals, the two categories are not separable. The word, trans*sex*ual, itself refers to one's sex. To say that one is discriminated against on the basis of transsexuality is therefore to admit that one has been discriminated against on the basis of sex. They are interrelated concepts.

Comparison with other kinds of cases can make the illogic of these courts' reasoning apparent. Some employers have, for example, discriminated against women who had young children. They defended their actions by saying that they did not have animus against women generally; they simply did not want to hire women who had young children and therefore might be absent from work. The Supreme Court has characterized these as "sex plus" cases — the employer used sex as a criterion along with another criterion.[66] Emphasizing that Title VII does not have a requirement that the discrimination be "solely on the basis of" an illegal criterion, the Court found for the female plaintiffs. Similarly, in sexual harassment cases, employers rarely target every woman for sexual advances or derogatory comments. It is no defense for an employer to say that it only targeted women that it found attractive or unattractive.[67] Yet that is exactly what is happening in the transsexual cases. The employer is only targeting women or men who, *for sex-based reasons,* it finds unattractive. That is sex discrimination plain and simple. The courts have to manipulate the language of Title VII to avoid reaching this category of hybrids.

Most significantly, the U.S. Supreme Court has rejected that illogic in the race context. In *Loving v. Virginia*,[68] it rejected Virginia's argument that an anti-miscegenation statute did not constitute race discrimination because it equally applied to whites and blacks. Noting that the purpose of the statute was to promote white supremacy, the Court found for the petitioner. A broad examination of rules against cross-dressing demonstrates that they help maintain male supremacy. The dress code cases do not involve only transsexuals. They also involve men and women who do not wish to dress in conformance with social expectations for their sex but have no interest in changing their biological sex. Courts have steadfastly refused to permit Title VII to protect individuals who face discrimination for failing to dress in accordance with gender norms. Often, the courts characterize this issue as too trivial for statutory protection.[69] Sandra Bem's story about her "cross-dressing" son, however, reveals the pervasive and pernicious nature of our appearance rules for gender policing:

[My son, Jeremy,] naively decided to wear barrettes to nursery school. Several times that day, another little boy insisted that Jeremy must be a girl because "only girls wear barrettes." After repeatedly insisting that "wearing barrettes doesn't matter; being a boy means having a penis and testicles," Jeremy finally pulled down his pants to make his point more convincingly. The other boy was not impressed. He simply said, "Everybody has a penis; only girls wear barrettes."[70]

The story may be "cute" when recounted in a day-care center but could have profound implications when replicated at the workplace if, say, a manager fired a "male" worker for wearing pearls at the workplace.[71] As Katharine Bartlett has argued, "Prejudgments about what is trivial and what is important without regard to the specific relationship between a rule and its cultural context take for granted the very habits Title VII should be used to scrutinize, and thereby undermine the Act."[72]

Title VII should recognize discrimination on the basis of appearance and clothing as covered by the statute. A rule that requires women to wear skirts and men to wear pants forces individuals to conform to rigid gendered standards. As uncomfortable as we may be with "cross-dressing," we need to recog-

nize that rules against cross-dressing are basic to gender policing. Our discomfort reflects the need for legal protection.
Appearance rules reinforce gender norms in at least two
ways. First, they promote bipolar understandings of appropriate attire for men and women. Men must wear a suit with
pants and a tie. Women must wear a suit with a skirt and
pantyhose. Men must not wear makeup, should shave their face
but not their legs; women must wear makeup and shave their
legs. These bipolar styles of dressing exaggerate the natural sex
differences between men and women. Men's and women's legs,
for example, are physically quite similar yet pantyhose and
shaving rules construct them to look artificially different. The
importance of reinforcing gender norms is profound in our
society yet rarely receives legal protection. For example, New
York City rules used to preclude a man and a woman from
getting married unless the woman wore a skirt or dress, and the
man wore a jacket and tie or turtleneck.[73] A court refused to
enjoin the rule concluding that it was not of sufficient importance for federal intervention. "The symbolism of abandoning
the traditional skirt or dress at one's wedding ceremony was
deemed trivial by the court."[74] In this context, gender rules help
construct the institution of heterosexual marriage, reflecting the
interrelation between gender and sexual orientation.

Second, appearance rules help perpetuate the objectification
and sexual harassment of women at the workplace. In many
cases involving appearance regulations, the rules do far more
than exaggerate gender difference. They also require women
to display themselves in ways that men might find sexually
objectifying. The best example of that phenomenon is the case,
EEOC v. Sage Realty Co.[75] Plaintiff Margaret Hasselman was
required to wear extremely revealing outfits as a lobby atten-

dant. Her mandated attire was so sexually provocative that she was subjected to sexual propositions, and lewd comments and gestures. Hasselman ultimately prevailed on a sexual harassment theory, making the court understand the connection between mandated appearances rules and sexual discrimination.

Unfortunately, the *Sage Realty* theory has not been extended to appearance cases in general. Men have lost cases in which they challenged a requirement to wear a tie[76] or keep their hair short.[77] The mere fact that an employer imposes different rules for men's and women's appearance is not enough to constitute liability under Title VII. One must also show that the rules for women are demeaning[78] or, as in *Sage Realty,* constitute sexual harassment. In other words, *demeaning* or *sexualized* appearance rules are unlawful gender discrimination even in such a case as Hasselman's where there is no evidence in the record concerning male attire. (There were no male lobby attendants.) *Nonsexualized,* but gender-differentiated, appearance rules do not constitute unlawful gender discrimination where one cannot prove they are demeaning. (This thesis will be further developed in chapter 7.) Unfortunately, courts often do not use Title VII of the Civil Rights Act to rid the workplace of gender or race differentiation. They only are comfortable using Title VII for the benefit of a particular type of plaintiff, such as Hasselman, who does not more broadly challenge rules with respect to gender or race differentiation. Such protection does not reach transsexuals.

Title VII prohibits "discrimination on the basis of sex in terms and conditions of employment." Explicit differentiation is purportedly illegal. But gender hybrids rarely can take advantage of that explicit prohibition.

B. Bathrooms

One awkward barrier for transsexuals that is reflected in many of these cases is the lack of acceptable restrooms, because public bathrooms are sex-segregated. In several of these cases, the employer discharged the employee because of complaints from other employees about plaintiff using their restroom. Patricia Williams tells a story about "S" who was a post-operative transsexual at an unidentified California law school, but who could not get either the male or female students to allow her to use their bathroom.[79] The Dean also refused to allow the student to use his private bathroom out of fear that he would be accused of preferential treatment. As Williams says, "Into the middle of that struggle, S. was coming to me because others had defined her as 'nobody.' " [80]

Sex-segregated bathrooms do not pose problems only for transsexuals. They create gender differentiation for all men and women. At my own institution, for example, we have a similar male and female bathroom for faculty and staff (with several private toilet areas), except that the male bathroom also has a shower room. When I joined the faculty and expressed a desire to have access to that shower area, the university was kind enough to make a "woman in shower" sign for me that I could put over the door to the man's bathroom to convert it temporarily into a "woman's space." That solution satisfied my needs without breaking down the rigid gender barriers. No one, of course, suggested that we simply designate each bathroom as sex-neutral with individuals who want privacy in the shower having the option of putting up a "person in shower" sign when they wanted to temporarily close off one of the two bathrooms to the public.

Gender-segregated bathrooms are a bedrock principle under

the law. In the seminal law review article on the proposed federal Equal Rights Amendment, the authors state that we must permit separate "toilet facilities in public buildings where separation carries no implication of inferiority for either sex." [81] Unfortunately, they do not define "inferiority." Does the impact on transsexuals who are rejected from both bathrooms constitute sufficient inferiority? What about the impact on women who typically have to wait in longer lines at public events than men because of an inadequate supply of women's bathrooms? (Plumbing codes as recently as the mid-1980s required more men's restrooms than women's in public buildings because of the assumption that more men attended sporting events and conventions than women; a woman was recently arrested for using the men's bathroom at a public event.) [82] Gender differentiation in bathrooms promotes transsexual discrimination as well as long lines for women at public places. Those are sufficient reasons to question the common acceptance of sex-segregated bathrooms. Segregation always carries a meaning; that meaning has largely gone unexamined in the context of sex-segregated bathrooms.

When I was in college, each year we had a "bathroom vote" whereby we voted whether to make the community bathrooms on each of the dorm floors single-sex or co-ed. Each floor got to vote separately so that there would not have to be uniformity on all floors. All of the toilets had stalls, and each of the showers had a privacy area for changing. Majority ruled each year, and, typically, all but a couple of bathrooms were voted to be "co-ed." This vote allowed each of us to use the bathroom closest to our dorm rooms rather than to travel to the closest one for the designated sex.

This regime of bathroom allocation quickly came to seem "normal." The only problem that I can remember with this arrangement was when an older male acquaintance was once visiting me before we were to go out for dinner. He said he needed to use the bathroom before we went to dinner and wanted to know where was the "men's room." I explained that there weren't any "men's rooms" but that a unisex bathroom was down the hall. He blushed and said he would wait until we got to the restaurant.

This story is amusing because men are socialized to be comfortable with using urinals that offer no privacy between men. Had this man used the community bathroom, he would have had the benefit of an enclosed cubicle. He apparently preferred a urinal in a "men's room" to a private cubicle in a co-ed bathroom. Our socialization with regard to our sense of privacy reinforces gender differentiation while actually providing little privacy.

In a perfect world, we should move to the model of community bathrooms with enclosed cubicles and private showering areas. That would eliminate the long lines in front of women's restrooms as compared with the relatively short lines in front of men's restrooms. It would eliminate such incidents as the one Williams described at a California law school, caused initially by the fact that bathrooms are sex designated. If bathrooms were not sex designated, then transsexuals would not have difficulty finding an appropriate bathroom.

Realistically, however, I understand that many people's sense of privacy would be offended by that restructuring. A more modest solution is free-standing unisex cubicles. In airports, it is common for there to be single-standing stalls that are designated for people who use wheelchairs or who need to change a baby's diaper. These single stalls have helped solve the problem of people who use wheelchairs having opposite-sex attendants or men needing to change the diaper of a young child. It is time to make such a model more universally available so that transsexuals, among others, have the option of a single stall for their and other people's privacy. I am not suggesting that institutions should *only* rely on single stalls. Clearly, that would be expensive and architecturally infeasible in many situations. But one single stall on each floor or area of an institution would be feasible and could assist with problems of people who use wheelchairs, parents of young children, and transsexuals. If we dispose of our bipolar lenses and consider how different groups of people are similarly situated, we could see how single toileting areas could solve many problems at once.

IV. Ameliorative Treatment

Ameliorative treatment for transsexuals, transvestites, and hermaphrodites is rare. The most positive steps that have been taken include a failure to continue to coerce individuals to maintain a gender identity that they have abandoned. Thus, for example, courts often allow transsexuals to change their names from an obviously male name to an obviously female name,[83] although courts also sometimes refuse to allow transsexuals to have their birth certificates changed to match their sexual identity.[84] One of the most positive legal recognitions of a transsexual occurred in a divorce case where the ex-husband tried to avoid support and maintenance payments by arguing that his wife, a male to female transsexual, was really a man, so that the marriage was void.[85] Ruling in favor of the transsexual wife, the court said that the "transsexual is not committing a fraud upon the public. In actuality she is doing her utmost to remove any false facade."[86] Of course, however, the case was predicated on the bipolar assumption, which the court described as "almost universal," that "a lawful marriage requires the performance of a ceremonial marriage of two persons of the opposite sex, a male and a female." [87] The court therefore had to place the wife in a rigidly bipolar framework in order to conduct the appropriate legal analysis; in no way does the court's decision undermine the polarized conception of sex that underlies our marriage laws. Nonetheless, other courts have been less liberal in tolerating the desired gender status of a post-operative transsexual who sought to take advantage of the institution of marriage. [88]

Although "affirmative action" for transsexuals, transvestites, and hermaphrodites may seem implausible, one might argue that our tolerance for "corrective surgery" for transsexuals and hermaphrodites is an expression of ameliorative treatment. Transsexualism or "gender dysphoria," for example, is considered to be such a serious problem that surgery is covered under Medicaid. [89] Some argue that such treatment is clearly ameliorative because, without surgery, many individuals would commit suicide. [90]

But transsexuals only obtain favorable legal treatment in response to horrific fact patterns. For example, transsexuals in prison argue that it would be "cruel and unusual punishment" or "deliberate indifference" for them to be denied estrogen therapy or surgery. [91] Lawyers have to describe their situation in extraordinary terms to meet this exceedingly high standard. The American Psychiatric Association has recently concluded that not all transsexuals need be classified as having a personality disorder. [92] Yet, transsexuals have been taught that they virtually have to commit suicide in order to receive public assistance. [93] Judges must be convinced that the choice is between suicide or estrogen therapy. Little else would meet the stringently high standard. Our legal standards therefore reinforce a stark, bipolar model, because the courts are only presented with suicidal transsexuals.

Given the dramatic stories of suicidal behavior that are required to obtain public assistance for transsexuals, it is hard to describe the granting of public assistance as ameliorative treatment. Saving an individual from suicide does little to place him or her on the road to a happy and successful life. We have much further to go in our treatment of transsexuals before we could describe our treatment of them as truly benign. A postoperative transsexual still faces enormous hardships and barriers in a society that cannot accept his or her transgendered status.

As for hermaphrodites, it is very difficult to consider the surgery that is routinely provided at birth as ameliorative.[94] This coerced treatment has caused Anne Fausto-Sterling to ask:

Why should we care if there are people whose biological equipment enables them to have sex "naturally" with both men and women? The answers seem to lie in a need to maintain clear distinctions between the sexes. Society mandates the control of intersexual bodies because they blur and bridge the great divide; they challenge traditional beliefs about sexual difference. Hermaphrodites have unruly bodies. They do not fall into a binary classification; only a surgical shoehorn can put them there.[95]

Hermaphrodites are usually required to have surgery when they are infants, long before the age of consent. The decision to have surgery is virtually automatic rather than reflecting whether there was any medical[96] or even psychological reason for surgery. If we, as a society, were not so horrified at the existence of hermaphrodites, we would allow surgery decisions to be made by an informed adult rather than by a parent.

Hermaphrodites and transsexuals reflect two different kinds

of hybrid categories which we "cure" with surgery to the sex organs. Hermaphrodites reflect a mixing of biological sexual traits which we are not able to tolerate. Transsexuals reflect a mixing of gendered traits which we "cure" by changing the biological sex to match the gender. In both cases, we "solve" the problem by engaging in surgery on the biological sex organs. In neither case do we try to "solve" the problem by changing conventional understandings of sex and gender. It makes one wonder who is "sick"—hermaphrodites, transsexuals, or "able-bodied" society?

Because of the failure of Title VII to reach discrimination claims brought by transsexuals or people who dress outside gender norms for appearance, some cities have passed ordinances prohibiting such discrimination. These ordinances, however, usually have little teeth. At most, they usually can impose a modest fine and often have cumbersome and time-consuming enforcement mechanisms. These ordinances should also be unnecessary because Title VII already prohibits sex discrimination. It is time to remove the moral code from Title VII and let it reach out fully to protect gender hybrids who face explicit sex discrimination.

Rules promoting gender differentiation are everywhere. The way I cross my knees as I type these words has been constructed by the gender police. The best "informers" on the scope of gender policing in our society are transsexuals who have lived in both gendered worlds. Not surprisingly, law and society impose harsh treatment on transsexuals to preclude us from moving beyond our stereotypical conceptions of gender. In order for the gender police to be less effective, we must be more attentive to gender differentiation in our lives. We must also insist that the courts take seriously the statement by Congress that sex discrimination or differentiation is illegal at the workplace. The fact that such enforcement also would benefit some transsexuals should not be an excuse to ignore the clear statutory mandate of Title VII.

Race

....

The year 1967 was a watershed in the history of interracial relationships in the United States. In the landmark *Loving v. Virginia* decision, the U.S. Supreme Court struck down a Virginia statute that made it a felony for "any white person [to] intermarry with a colored person, or any colored person [to] intermarry with a white person."[1]

An interracial babyboom followed the Supreme Court's decision. Children born to parents of different races[2] accounted for more than 3 percent of births in 1990, up from 1 percent in 1968.[3] Since 1980, the number of interracial married couples has increased from 651,000 to 1.2 million.[4] The number of black and white interracial married couples has increased seventy-eight percent since 1980.[5] The rate of interracial marriage is even higher for other racial groups—38 percent of American Japanese females, 18 percent of American Japanese males, and 70 percent of American Indians enter into interracial marriages.[6] Our racial classification system, however, has not kept up with this demographic trend.[7]

Our predominant classification system remains white/black with little recognition of other racial groups, or racial mixing of white and black.[8] The Virginia statute itself reflected this classification system—the state was concerned with whites intermingling with "coloreds" but did not object to various "colored" subgroups intermingling with each other. The purity of the "white" race was the state's only concern. Despite this historical concern, the terms multiracial and biracial are not part of contemporary legal discourse.

Nonetheless, color and mixed-race heritage (which are not synonymous) can define an individual's experiences. Maria O'Brien Hylton, a multiracial candidate for an appointment at Northwestern University, became a source of public controversy in the affirmative action debate because she was not a "pure" black in appearance or heritage.[9] Gregory Howard Williams lived "on the color line" because, in his early years, his light-skinned African-American father and Caucasian mother tried to "pass" the immediate family as white.[10] After living with black friends and family, and attending segregated black schools for more than a decade, he was not readily accepted as authentically "black" for affirmative action purposes. Shirlee Taylor Haizlip's family tree was divided depending upon whether her relatives could "pass" as white.[11] Her "darker-skinned" mother was separated from her "lighter-skinned" sister at a young age because her mother's presence would prevent the family from "passing." When Haizlip finally reunited her mother and aunt, then both in their seventies, she found that they could not discuss the reason for their separation although they clearly knew that color had been a major factor.

The racial classification system also renders invisible individuals who do not fit the two or three categories recognized by the legal system. Chinese-Americans, for example, were labeled as "Indian" in nineteenth-century California because the only available categories were white, Negro, and Indian.[12] The current U.S. census form contains numerous classifications yet still lumps together quite dissimilar groupings of people. The global category of "Asian or Pacific Islander" includes Native Hawaiians along with eight other distinctive national groups[13] that have about as much in common with each other as Chinese-Americans had with Indians in nineteenth-century California.

Although Americans generally prefer to ignore issues of mixed-race and color, legal issues involving such individuals have been part of our history since 1896, when a light-skinned "black," Homer Plessy, attempted to sit in the "white" section of a segregated Louisiana railroad car. One hundred years later, the U.S. Census Bureau is contemplating changing its forms to allow individuals to indicate their multiracial heritage. At the same time, we are struggling to develop rules governing affirmative action which will determine whether the Hyltons and Williamses will be eligible for affirmative action. What then is race, and when should it matter?

I. Mulattoes, Quadroons, and Octoroons

Louisiana has been a hotbed for legal challenges to the system of racial classification because so many people of mixed-race historically have resided there. The local language reflects this racial and color landscape with such terms as mulatto, quadroon, and octoroon. The courts have been confronted continually with the existence of people of mixed-race, yet have resisted overturning a bipolar classification system of "negro" and "white."

The first major case challenging Louisiana's classification system was the infamous *Plessy v. Ferguson*,[14] decided by the U.S. Supreme Court in 1896. Lawyer Albion Tourgée wanted to challenge the arbitrariness of the racial classification system underlying the Louisiana statute, although the case is usually only remembered as a challenge to Louisiana's practice of segregating railway cars. Tourgée urged his associates to select as a defendant a Negro whose complexion was white or nearly white.[15] Plaintiff was "of mixed Caucasian and African blood, in the proportion of one-eighth African and seven-eighths Caucasian, the African admixture not being perceptible."[16] Criticizing the arbitrariness of a railroad conductor determining Homer Plessy's race, Tourgée argued:

> The Court will take notice of the fact that, in all parts of the country, race-admixture has proceeded to such an extent that there are great numbers of citizens in whom the preponderance of the blood of one race or another, is impossible of ascertainment, except by careful scrutiny of the pedigree. . . . But even if it were possible to determine preponderance of blood and so determine racial character in certain cases, what should be said of those cases in which the race admixture is equal. Are they white or colored?[17]

Tourgée's strategy was controversial because darker members of the African-American community thought that it would only benefit those who were nearly white or wanted to pass for white.[18] It might move the color line so that light-skinned "blacks" could sit in the white car but not eliminate segregation. The question that his strategy raised was whether alleviating discrimination for light-skinned blacks who could "pass" as white would really rid society of its most invidious forms of discrimination.

The color strategy was eventually dropped from the *Plessy* case so we will never know what would have been the effect of raising the arbitrariness of the racial classification system. Moreover, Homer Plessy lost his case, thereby reinforcing the constitutionality of "separate but equal." When *Plessy* was overturned more than fifty years later, the issue of racial classification was never raised. Hence, the law has become "separate cannot be equal" without attention to how we define the racial categories themselves.

Although *Plessy* did not challenge the system of racial classification, other multiracial plaintiffs in Louisiana did have limited success in challenging their racial classification. In a 1910 decision by the Louisiana Supreme Court, *State v. Treadway*,[19] the court concluded that defendant Treadway,[20] who was one-eighth black, could not be classified as "negro or black" to be convicted for violating the state's anti-miscegenation statute. In holding for the defendant, the Court distinguished between "negro" and "colored," concluding that the term "colored" refers to individuals who have any "traceable" "negro blood." Because the legislature used the word "negro" rather than the word "colored" in its anti-miscegenation statute, the court concluded that defendant could not be classified as a "Negro." It ruled that the legislature "meant negro, plain negro, or persons black as negroes and having the characteristics of negro, and not these other persons not coming within that description."[21] The court's decision therefore made it possible for "mulattoes, quadroons, and octoroons" to evade prosecution for cohabitating with whites but left intact prosecutions against the "plain negro." Legally-sanctioned discrimination remained alive.

(Not all courts at the time, however, agreed with the Louisiana Supreme Court's restrictive definition of a "negro." A New York State court in 1937 concluded that a woman who was one-eighth black was a "negro" for the purpose of interpreting a racially restrictive covenant.[22] This court concluded that the term "negroes" was synonymous with "colored," thereby precluding plaintiff and her husband, who was three-fourths black, from purchasing property in a residential neighborhood in Westchester County, New York. Thus, Mr. Treadway would be reclassified from "colored" to "negro" if he moved from

Louisiana to New York in 1937 and attempted to move into a white neighborhood.)

By the mid-1970s, it appeared that the Louisiana courts might conclude that racial classification was wholly arbitrary. In *Thomas v. Louisiana State Board of Health,*[23] the state court of appeals affirmed a lower court judgment ordering the state census bureau to change the designation from Negro to white on the birth certificates of Norma Gravolet Thomas and her two children. Racial designation had been made in this instance through a review of previous classifications of plaintiffs' ancestors as "mulatto" or "quadroon." The court rejected the reliability of that kind of classification system noting:

In absence of definitions accurately applied at the time race determinations or designations are made on records, there are no legal means by which a person's racial content can be computed where the records bear such description names as mulatto, quadroon, colored, personne de couleur, F.M.C. or F.C.M. Without a legal definition to be applied to such terms, these terms mean various things to different people. Under such circumstances no accurate mathematical percentage can be computed to comply with the provisions of [Louisiana law].[24]

The Louisiana Supreme Court, however, resisted concluding that the racial classification statute was unconstitutional on the grounds of vagueness. In a similar case involving racial classification on a birth certificate, the Louisiana court of appeals concluded that it was unconstitutional for a statute to define only the term "negro" and to do so through ambiguous requirements. The Louisiana Supreme Court, with one dissenting opinion, rejected that argument finding the statute constitutional because it was not "so vague that it cannot be administered" and was not void "because of invidious racial discrimination."[25]

In a strong dissent, Justice Barham disagreed. He noted that the statute only defines who is considered to be a "Negro" and instructs the Bureau of Vital Statistics to withhold a birth certificate for such a person if he attempts to classify himself as white. "No comparable statutes exist for the Caucasian and Mongoloid races. . . . Citizens of other races do not have to endure this administrative procedure. . . . The jurisprudential 'traceable amount' formula applied only to the Negro race is equally as repugnant as is the act which we consider."[26]

Justice Barham's dissent goes as far as any opinion in throwing out racial classification, but even he would not abandon it entirely. He argued that "it is the legislature's responsibility to produce a formula that may be equally applied to Negro, Caucasian and Mongoloid races if they wish to have preciseness of race determined objectively."[27] He accepted the idea that race has an "objective" component which was not reflected in the Louisiana classification system.

Even though the court did not find the statute unconstitutional, it did order the Bureau of Vital Statistics to issue a birth certificate for the plaintiff indicating that she was white, thereby upsetting established practice at the Bureau. Similarly, in numerous other cases,[28] appellate courts concluded that the Bureau had not met its burden of establishing that an individual was "Negro" and the person should be classified as white. The color line was moving but still existed.

Nonetheless, in the mid-1980s, the state and federal courts laid a stronger foundation under Louisiana's system of racial classification. In a case resembling many of the other birth certificate cases, family members sought to change the race of their deceased parents. The court of appeals raised the burden of proof for petitioners who wanted to challenge their racial designation as "Negro" and concluded that petitioners had not met the required higher burden. The racial designation of "Negro" was maintained despite strong evidence that the deceased parents were of mixed-race. Both the Louisiana Supreme Court and U.S. Supreme Court refused to hear the case. The modification in the burden of proof, although a technical change, had a major effect on the law in this area. No longer does one find large numbers of claimants successfully challenging their own or a family member's racial designation as "Negro." It appears that the courts could not tolerate the shifting designation of race that had become commonplace under Louisiana law and put an end to it.

This history brings us back to the question—are challenges to the arbitrariness of racial classification effective? These examples support the point made by Tourgée's detractors—challenges to arbitrariness only move the color line so that more "blacks" become "whites." They do not undermine classification itself nor improve the lives of "pure" blacks. On the other hand, this history shows that repeated, successful challenges to racial classification lead to the conclusion, in the words of a Louisiana state appellate court, that the *entire system* is "wholly irrational and scientifically insupportable."[29] The Louisiana courts had to stop the successful reclassification cases for light-skinned "blacks" in order to prevent the entire system from toppling. The legislature ultimately responded by repealing the "one thirty-second" statute and allowing parents to designate their own race on the birth certificate.[30] Challenges by mixed-race individuals may therefore have an incremental effect, although in the short term they are unlikely to topple the system.

II. Ameliorative Treatment

At Bank X, once a target of a case on which I was working, dark-skinned blacks were often hired to perform jobs away from public view, such as sorting and counting money in the vault, whereas light-skinned blacks [31] were occasionally hired as tellers. The light-skinned blacks were not usually passing; they were benefiting, as compared to darker-skinned blacks, from an overt appeal to the values of a color conscious society.[32] Nonetheless, light-skinned blacks were less likely to be hired as tellers than similarly qualified whites. If they were hired as tellers, they were less likely to be promoted to managerial position. To label all the blacks as "black" would not have dismantled the racial classification system in that workplace. Only by acknowledging the cultural significance attached to the points along the spectrum of race could one begin to fully address discrimination in the workplace. Failing to recognize the significance of color in fashioning a remedy causes the problems noted by Tourgée's critics—that only light-skinned blacks benefit from a remedial order. Unfortunately, the voluntary and private settlement of this case was not attentive to these problems of color and thereby diminished race discrimination without dismantling color discrimination.

Cheryl Harris tells a story that reflects the importance of being conscious of color when responding to problems of discrimination. Her light-skinned "black" grandmother passed as a "white" in order to work in a department store during the Depression.[33] Her light skin thus had a property value. Harris's grandmother was able to obtain employment while her grandfather, presumably darker-skinned, "was trapped on the fringes of economic marginality."[34] The story of her grandmother "passing" is a story about the range of experiences that "blacks" may endure, depending on their skin color. It reflects our society's consciousness of color along a spectrum, rather than its consciousness of race only at two bipolar points.[35]

These two stories demonstrate that we need to be careful about describing race discrimination too monolithically. Compounding variables such as color may ameliorate some of the effects of racism. Nonetheless, we have typically developed ameliorative programs to remedy our history of race discrimination simply by giving preferences to "blacks." Rarely do we consider which blacks may be most deserving of such ameliorative treatment and, in particular, whether mixed-raced or light-skinned individuals should be treated as "black" for ameliorative purposes.

This problem is made more difficult when we ask the more general question, when is race used for an ameliorative purpose? Can racial classification serve an ameliorative and a subordinating purpose? Affirmative action policies are somewhat easy to classify because their purported purpose is benign. Nonetheless, racial stereotyping [36] and stigma [37] might accompany this benign purpose. A focus on affirmative action for multiracial individuals adds a new level of difficulty to this problem, because the ameliorative results of race-based affirmative action become more ambiguous.

Racial preference policies in the context of transracial adoption are harder still to classify. The National Association of Black Social Workers, for example, believes that racial classification serves an ameliorative purpose [38] whereas other leaders in the black community, such as Randall Kennedy, argue that racial placement policies harm the well-being of black children and perpetuate racial stereotypes. [39] A focus on the adoption of multiracial children, historically categorized as "black," adds a further dimension to this tension because the ameliorative purposes of race-conscious placement become more ambiguous.

A. Affirmative Action

Classification

In 1977, the federal government issued "Directive No. 15" to standardize the definition of race used by the public and private sectors. This Directive is still in use and does not include a multiracial category; instead, it categorizes multiracial individuals into a monoracial category. "The category which most closely reflects the individual's recognition in this community should be used for purposes of reporting on persons who are of mixed racial and/or ethnic origins." [40]

The Directive's handling of multiracial individuals is troublesome in three respects. First, it perpetuates the *community's* right to define race, rather than to allow individuals to define their own race. Second, it renders the category of multiracial invisible. Third, it lumps together quite different national groupings and confuses race with national origin with respect to people with Latino backgrounds.

The problems with this directive can be seen in an early affirmative action controversy in New York City.[41] After the City of New York instituted an affirmative action program for promotion from police officer to sergeant, six officers came forward and asked to be reclassified from white to black or Hispanic. One officer indicated that he had originally checked both black and white on the application form but that the department computer had arbitrarily classified him as white.[42] A similar problem occurred in Boston when two firefighters, the Malones, claimed they were black because their maternal great-grandmother was black.[43] The assertion was brought into question because they did not claim blackness until after they had taken the first exam for the position. Moreover, there was some question as to whether they held themselves out in the community as black.

The New York and Boston cases show the awkwardness of racial classification systems, even for benign purposes. In both cases, the question was whether the public safety employees could be considered "black." There was no discussion of the need for a multiracial category and whether the multiracial category should be treated differently from the "black" category.

No one asked whether these individuals had a special reason to be deserving of affirmative action protection. Had they experienced educational or economic deprivation because of their racial status? Did they have a special interest in assisting with public safety problems in minority communities? Boston and New York felt more comfortable developing and enforcing clumsy categories of black and white with all blacks benefiting from affirmative action and no whites benefiting than asking these more probing questions. As a result of such policies, the Malones of this society will have an incentive in the future, when seeking the benefits of affirmative action, to check the box "black" at the earliest possible stages of the application process and not acknowledge their multiracial background,[44] perpetuating the "one drop of blood" rule.

Despite these problems with Policy Directive No. 15, which would not allow any of these individuals to be classified as multiracial, the federal government received strong criticism when it tried to change the policy in 1988. The proposed 1988 changes would have added the racial category "other" and required classification by self-identification. Opponents of the change argued "that the present system provided adequate data, that any changes would disrupt historical continuity, and that the proposed change would be expensive and potentially divisive. Some members of minority communities interpreted the proposal as an attempt to provoke internal dissension within their communities and to reduce the official counts of minority populations."[45] Acquiescing to such arguments, the federal government decided not to make any changes at that time.

In 1994, the federal government again began to explore making changes in the racial classification system. In June 1994, it invited comments on changes such as adding an "other" category, adding a "multiracial" category and providing an open-ended question to solicit information on race and ethnicity.[46] It is not clear whether the federal government will permanently add a multiracial category, but the Census Bureau is moving in that direction. For 1996, the Census Bureau has sought reaction to including a multiracial category on its survey instrument.[47] This proposal has caused much controversy in the civil rights community. The Association for Multiethnic Americans, an umbrella group for approximately sixty multiracial groups, supports the change. Billy Tidwell, of the National Urban League, however, opposes the change because "splintering the black community between light-skinned and dark, would 'turn the clock back on the well-being' of African-Americans."[48] Tidwell's arguments sound remarkably like those made against Tourgée's strategy to challenge the racial classification system in the nineteenth century. The National Urban League wants to insist on its right to claim a large number of individuals as black who might self-identify as multiracial. Multiracial groups therefore criticize such groups as the National Urban League for "clinging to racial differences and a zero-sum mentality."[49] They argue that Tidwell's position is disrespectful to multiracial people who suffer emotionally when there is no fitting box for them to check.[50] It is ironic that the same groups who have criticized white society for defining them stereotypically are not more tolerant of the desire of multiracial groups to be able to define themselves more accurately. Their lack of tolerance, however, does not stem from racial stereotypes. It stems from the political awareness that modification in how we count the number of "blacks" in society could have profound repercussions in resource allocation as well as the structure of voting districts. As will we see in chapter 8, the Census controversy does not lend itself to easy solution since this is one area of life where categorization is presumed essential.

Although the federal government has been slow to recognize multiracial individuals, some private institutions have begun to try to change this practice of insisting that people classify themselves within rigid categories. Columbia Law School, for example, asks student applicants who wish to have their racial or ethnic background taken into account for admission to submit personal statements. In addition, the application invites students to check off more than one racial or ethnic category if appropriate.[51] This question makes some people feel uncomfortable because they interpret it as asking how closely they fit racial stereotypes.[52] But transgressing boundaries to acknowledge a multiracial category is a step toward creating a more individualized sense of the meaning of race to each person. Such ethnic statements might make us feel uncomfortable, but they may be a more respectful way to acknowledge the socially constructed and individualized experience of race in our society.

Nonetheless, the Columbia Law School policy of seeking personal narratives is problematic. It presumes that the only purpose of affirmative action is to assist individuals in overcoming disadvantage by asking students to comment on their personal histories. Affirmative action for African-Americans in law school admissions also serves other forward-looking purposes such as diversifying a student body, educating African-Americans who can serve as role models for the next generation, and increasing the quantity and quality of legal services available to the black community. The Columbia approach does not facilitate affirmative action for those other purposes. In order to construct appropriate admissions questions, we need to understand better why we use affirmative action and what programs would best achieve its purposes.

B. Purposes of Affirmative Action

Naomi Zack, author of *Race and Mixed Race*,[53] shares with the reader her own story of benefiting from affirmative action. Zack explains that her mother was a white Jewish immigrant with whom she grew up. Her father, who was not identified to her as her father until she was sixteen, was a black man. Race did not become a preeminent occupation in her life until she returned to academia in 1990 at the age of forty-six. After doing some adjunct teaching, she obtained a tenure-track position in the Department of Philosophy through a university affirmative-action recruitment program for racial minorities called Target of Opportunity ("TOP").[54] She rationalizes acceptance of this position by noting that only seventy-five out of ten thousand academic philosophers in the United States are "of African descent."[55]

Zack's story sharply raises the question of why we have affirmative action. As someone who was not aware of her African heritage until the age of sixteen and did not strongly identify with that heritage until the age of forty-six, should she qualify for affirmative action for people of African descent?

Four rationales for affirmative action are often offered and can help us answer that question:

Diversity of Ideas. Because racial minorities have had a distinctive life experience which can be reflected in their perspectives, affirmative action can increase the diversity of ideas at an institution.

Role Models. Affirmative action provides racial minorities with examples of success. These examples, in turn, will help shape high goals and aspirations for racial minorities.

Overcoming Disadvantage. Prior victims of racial injustice are entitled to "reparations" to put them in their "rightful place."

Overcoming Stereotypes. Diversifying opportunities on the basis of race will help overcome stereotypes about racial minorities thereby helping to overcome disadvantage in the future.

Zack's appointment reflects two of these rationales. She contributes to the "diversity of ideas" because of her multiracial heritage. She is an outspoken member of the multiracial community, and serves as an excellent multiracial role model. Zack's personal history, to the extent that she recounts it for the reader,[56] however, does not seem to reflect much race-based disadvantage. She did not grow up in a household defined by racial adversity nor would she help overcome stereotypes by virtue of being visibly black. Should the diversity or role model rationales be used as a justification without concrete evidence of disadvantage stemming from race? Should race have been an explicit consideration in Zack's appointment?

Diversity of Ideas

The "diversity of ideas" rationale has received the strongest support from the U.S. Supreme Court. In *Regents of the University of California v. Bakke,*[57] a white applicant for admission to the Medical School of the University of California at Davis challenged the "special admissions program" which was open to "disadvantaged" special applicants. Because no white had ever been admitted through this special program, plaintiff successfully characterized it as a race-based affirmative action program. The University defended the program through reference to each of the rationales listed above.

Justice Powell accepted the diversity rationale in an opinion that served as the "swing" vote. He found that such a rationale could even pass muster under strict scrutiny:

Academic freedom, though not a specifically enumerated constitutional right, long has been viewed as a special concern of the First Amendment. The freedom of a university to make its own judgments as to education includes the selection of its student body.... The atmosphere if 'speculation, experiment and creation'—so essential to the quality of higher education—is widely believed to be promoted by a diverse student body.[58]

Although Justice Powell approved of the diversity rationale as meeting the "compelling state interest" test which is required under strict scrutiny, he rejected the argument that the race-specific means chosen by the University were necessary. Powell concluded that although race could be a "plus" along with other diversifying factors such as being raised on a farm, a university could not assign a fixed number of places to a minority group.[59] Moreover, the "plus" would not "insulate the individual from comparison with all other candidates for the available seats."[60]

It is not clear from Justice Powell's opinion whether he thought that all racial or ethnic minorities should receive such a "plus," whether there should be a rebuttable presumption of diversity, or whether diversity must be established on a case-by-case basis. He simply stated that race or ethnic background "may" be deemed a "plus" without explaining why it may provide such a "plus."

Other legal scholars, such as Randall Kennedy,[61] have questioned whether there should be any presumption at all that racial or ethnic minorities bring a "plus" to the educational process. What exactly is the basis of this "plus"? Is it a "plus" based on life experience or ideology? If it is a plus based on life experience, then it is the same as the disadvantage rationale. If it is a plus based on ideology, it is problematic. As Clarence Thomas's presence on the Supreme Court highlights, there is not a monolithic "black" perspective on any issue.

The diversity rationale often is applied in the context of academic appointments, but it is inappropriate to assume that members of racial minority groups have an inherently distinctive way of thinking about race or a specialty in that area. If we want to hire someone to teach and write about race issues, then we should redefine merit by identifying an opening in the field of race relations or African-American history. Then, when someone like Naomi Zack applies, we might hire her because of her proven expertise in that field, not simply because she is of African heritage.

Clumsy uses of affirmative action in the hiring or promotion context often circumvent probing discussions of the definition of merit. One of the best examples of this phenomena is *Johnson v. Transportation Agency*,[62] in which the Santa Clara Transportation Agency successfully defended an affirmative action program in which it promoted a woman, Joyce, over a man, Johnson. Joyce had been one of the first women hired in a road maintenance position and led the way for other women by, for example, persuading the employer to issue her coveralls (as it had the men) so that she would not keep soiling her own clothes. Rather than get credit for this activism, she was labeled as a troublemaker. (One panel member described her as a "rebel-rousing, skirt-wearing person.")[63] Johnson was initially selected for the position over Joyce because he scored a 75 as compared to her 73 on the interview. That decision was reversed when Joyce complained to the affirmative action officer about interview bias. The employer ultimately promoted Joyce and then had to defend itself in a reverse discrimination lawsuit brought by Johnson. The employer defended Joyce's promotion as a lawful example of affirmative action, and prevailed. Rather than defend her selection as lawful affirmative action, it would have been more appropriate to defend her selection under the principle that a redefinition of merit showed that she was more qualified than Johnson. Joyce was entitled to be told that she was selected, in part, because her advocacy on behalf of women was valued and that the interview had suffered from gender bias.

Affirmative action as a justification can be a mechanism that allows white men to avoid confronting their inadequacies. Allan Bakke, for example, insisted in the U.S. Supreme Court that his race (white) was the reason he was not admitted to medical school. The Supreme Court accepted that rationale with little question. Bakke, however, was refused admittance to dozens of medical schools, many of which were not using race as a positive factor in the admissions process.[64] More likely, Bakke's age and poor interviewing combined to render him less qualified than many other applicants. When a white person fails or when a minority or female succeeds, we are quick to use "affirmative action" as the explanation.[65] We need to find ways to use affirmative action that make clear the positive attributes that women and minorities bring to an employment or educational setting; similarly, we need to make it clear how and why white men may not be competent for a particular position. We need to question and make *them* question their quick reflex of blaming "affirmative action" for their failures.

I have often been the beneficiary of the "diversity" rationale but grow tired of its mechanical application to my situation. Each time that I have been hired at an academic institution, I am surprised to find out how few members of the faculty bothered to acquaint themselves with the *quality or substance* of my scholarship. It is easier to say that I diversify the faculty because of my gender or sexual orientation rather than to ask the more probing question of whether my gender or sexual orientation have affected my scholarship in ways that are original and thought-provoking. By contrast, when I have observed the hiring deliberations for white men, I have seen close attention paid to the quality of their work. When they are hired, they receive very positive feedback about their qualifications. Anita L. Allen has written: "White men, who predominate in higher education, have frequently failed to communicate confidence in the possibility of minority achievement. Snap judgments made on the basis of skin color alone are not uncommon; nor are begrudging affirmative action appointments. Black women have been made to feel inferior and out of place in higher education." [66] As a white woman, I would add that white male academics have rarely taken my scholarship seriously and made me feel valued or welcome. The scholarship of women and minorities deserves serious attention as part of the appointment process.

Role Models

Anita L. Allen has offered the fullest explanation for what constitutes the "role model" theory. The role model theory, she argues, presumes that an individual will serve as one or more of the following:

(1) an *ethical template* for the exercise of adult responsibilities;
(2) a *symbol* of special achievement;
(3) a *nurturer* providing special educational services.[67]

Put more simply, the theory presumes that "if students are to realize their full potential as responsible adults, they need others in their lives whom they can emulate and by whom they will be motivated to do their best work."[68] This argument was put forward most strongly in the academic context when Derrick Bell, a tenured black professor at Harvard Law School, took an unpaid leave of absence until the law school tenured a black woman. Bell, and others who supported his position, argued that black female law students need black female law teachers as role models.[69] After his leave of absence extended for several years, and Harvard Law School failed to tenure a black woman, Bell resigned his position. His political stance raises the question of whether all students need "same-kind" role models.[70]

The role model theory was proposed and rejected by the U.S. Supreme Court in *Wygant v. Jackson Board of Education*.[71] The district court and court of appeals had approved the role model theory, concluding that "teaching is more than just a job. Teachers are role-models for their students. More specifically, minority teachers are role-models for minority students. This is vitally important because societal discrimination has often deprived minority children of other role-models."[72] This theory has also been accepted as a basis for affirmative action by many academics who argue that it has engendered "the expansion of a professional class able to pass its material advantages and elevated aspirations to subsequent generations."[73]

The Supreme Court rejected the role model theory because it relies on the existence of "societal discrimination" rather than the existence of discrimination at a particular institution. Because it was not tied to a particular institution's actions, the Court found that it has "no logical stopping point."[74]

The role model theory may have no logical stopping point, but only because it is forward-looking rather than backward-looking. The premise of the role model theory is that we train students to be high achievers *at all institutions* irrespective of whether those institutions engaged in egregious discrimination in the past. It is not a reparations theory; it is a theory about the future we want to create.

The role model justification has also received strong criticism from minority academics. Anita L. Allen offers many arguments for not relying primarily on the role model argument for affirmative action; one of her arguments relates to the application of the theory to multiracial individuals. She argues that the role model justification presumes that one must be recognizable as belonging to a specific group. A role model theory, she suggests, might preclude a light-skinned black from being considered for affirmative action purposes yet "throughout American history black communities have embraced high-achieving blacks of whatever hue as symbols of special achievement for the race" irrespective of how discernable is their black appearance. "Indeed, a number of historically important black political leaders have been men of mixed-race ancestry who 'looked white,' but opted against 'passing.' "[75]

Allen recognizes the value of black female students having black female role models but does not believe that this end should be pursued through role model justifications. Role model arguments, she contends, "treat minorities like inferiors."[76] She would prefer to achieve same-kind role models through "a search for talent in its many and diverse forms."[77] In other words, she prefers the diversity justification while recognizing that it accomplishes the same role model result.

Like the diversity rationale, the role model theory could benefit from a redefinition of merit. It is typical in higher education, for example, for women and racial minorities to serve an enhanced advising function on a faculty because of their underrepresentation in comparison to the student body. At tenure time, however, the qualifications for tenure usually focus primarily on scholarship with some attention to classroom teaching. Hours spent inside or outside of the office advising students or attending functions usually are not included in the definition of merit for tenure. If we are going to embrace the role model theory in our affirmative action programs then we have a responsibility to the individuals we hire to value the work they do in the community and as role models.

But we need not abandon the role model justification for affirmative action entirely. White men often make black women "feel inferior and out of place in higher education."[78] The role model theory lets white men off the hook by making them think they have no responsibilities toward women or minorities. We should respond to that problem by insisting that *everyone* be willing to serve as a role model rather than by not valuing the important role model work that is usually done by women and minorities.

If we insist that everyone has the obligation to serve as a role model, then there is no problem in deciding how to deal with individuals who are multiracial. They, like everyone else, can agree to take on the commitment to be a positive role model. If they seem uninterested in that commitment, then that fact should be a negative factor in the appointment process. But, of course, we cannot ask questions about role model commitments only to multiracial or minority candidates. We have to ask those questions of everyone.

Overcoming Disadvantage

The disadvantage theory was raised by the University of California at Davis in *Bakke* and accepted by Justice Brennan, in an opinion joined by Justices White, Marshall, and Blackmun. As applied to the medical profession, the Brennan opinion found that "the problem of underrepresentation of minorities was substantial and chronic and that the problem was attributable to handicaps imposed on minority applicants by past and present racial discrimination."[79] Moreover, the Brennan opinion concluded that this pattern would continue if a single admissions standard were continued: "Massive official and private resistance prevented, and to a lesser extent still prevents, attainment of equal opportunity in education at all levels and in the professions."[80]

The lower court had rejected the disadvantage rationale concluding that race-neutral rather than race-specific means should have been used to achieve that objective. The Brennan opinion responded that a race-neutral approach would not have been effective because *economic* disadvantage and *racial* disadvantage are not synonymous: "While race is positively correlated with differences in GPA and MCAT scores, economic disadvantage is not. Thus, it appears that economically disadvantaged whites do not score less well than economically advantaged whites, while economically advantaged blacks score less well than do disadvantaged whites."[81] In other words, even economically advantaged blacks often require affirmative action to be admitted to medical school when in competition with economically disadvantaged whites. A race-neutral solution might benefit economically disadvantaged whites but would have little impact on the historical disadvantage faced by blacks of any economic background.

Justice Powell rejected the disadvantage theory concluding that it was not fair to impose disadvantages on individuals such as Allan Bakke "who bear no responsibility for whatever harm the beneficiaries of the special admissions program are thought to have suffered."[82] The Brennan opinion refused to accept the categorization of Allan Bakke as an "innocent white":

If it was reasonable to conclude—as we hold that it was—that the failure of minorities to qualify for admission at Davis under regular procedures was due principally to the effects of past discrimination, then there is a reasonable likelihood that, but for pervasive racial discrimination, respondent [Bakke] would have failed to qualify for admission even in the absence of Davis' special admissions program.[83]

Because Justice Powell would not go along with the Brennan group, the disadvantage theory only garnered four votes in *Bakke*.

Nonetheless, the disadvantage theory continues to shape much of the legal discourse surrounding affirmative action. Most recently, the U.S. Supreme Court considered whether a disadvantage theory could justify a race-based subcontractor compensation clause in *Adarand Constructors, Inc. v. Pena*.[84] The programs at issue in this case were shaped with the disadvantage theory in mind. Instead of calling the favored companies "minority" business enterprises, as they had been called in earlier cases, they were called "disadvantaged" business enterprises. Designation as a DBE varied from program to program but generally consisted of a rebuttable presumption that members of a racial minority group (and women, in some cases) were disadvantaged unless there was contrary evidence; whites were permitted to qualify for the program if they could establish disadvantage (but did not get the benefit of a presumption). Because the factual record was unclear as to how individualized were the findings of disadvantage, and the role that race played in those deliberations, the Supreme Court remanded the case back to the trial court for further findings. Interestingly, the same dispute existed in *Bakke* concerning how individualized the program was in practice. The University argued, and the Brennan opinion concluded, that "Davis considers on an individual basis each applicant's personal history to determine whether he or she has likely been disadvantaged by racial discrimination."[85] The Powell opinion rejected this nonracial explanation, finding that no disadvantaged whites received an offer of admission through the special admission process, although many applied. In *Adarand,* the program clearly applied to whites who could demonstrate disadvantage;[86] the key factual dispute concerned whether some minorities were actually disqualified under the rebuttable presumption.[87]

Although the issue remained the same—how individualized was the finding of disadvantage—the factual predicates shifted from *Bakke* to *Adarand.* In *Bakke,* the Brennan opinion argued that we should not conflate economic and racial disadvantage. Even economically advantaged blacks face serious educational and economic barriers to advancement in society. Nearly twenty years later, attempts to describe the distinctiveness of racial oppression have largely ended in judicial opinions. The dissent by Justices Stevens and Ginsberg in *Adarand* focused on the individualized nature of the programs at issue. It stressed that race played only a part in the decisionmaking process; the racial presumption was rebuttable. The dissent emphasized that the Small Business Administration was instructed to periodically review the status of DBEs. "Such review prevents ineligible firms from taking part in the program solely because of their minority ownership, even when those firms were once disadvantaged but have since become successful. The emphasis on review also indicates the Administration's anticipation that after their presumed disadvantages have been overcome, firms will 'graduate' into a status in which they will be able to compete for business, including prime contracts, on an equal basis." [88] Whereas the Brennan decision in *Bakke* was premised on the notion that racial disadvantage is a lifelong experience, the Stevens and Ginsburg decision in *Adarand* was premised on the notion that one could "graduate" from racial disadvantage in a relatively short period of time. The Stevens and Ginsburg view was possible, because their opinion conflated racial and economic disadvantage. Once economic resources are acquired, racial disadvantage presumably disappears.

The empirical literature on black and white poverty, however, suggests that the Supreme Court was wrong to conflate racial and economic disadvantage. As Andrew Hacker has noted: "To be black in America is to know that you remain last in line for so basic a requisite as the means of supporting yourself and your family. More than that, you have much less choice among jobs than workers who are white. . . . entire occupations still remain substantially closed to people who were born black." [89]

The disparities between blacks and whites is starkest in the business world. Robert Suggs has documented this disparity:

The black participation rate [in business] is only about one-quarter of the national average. While blacks make up twelve percent of the population, they own only two percent of all business firms. Only $16 of every $10,000 in business receipts, less than 0.2%, comes from black-owned firms. Black business receipts would have to increase seventy-five fold before they would be proportionate to the black share of the total population.[90]

These disparities are due, in part, to racism. As Suggs notes:

Negative stereotyping of blacks still remains a significant feature of black-white relations. So long as continuing discrimination can be identified in housing and employment opportunities, it seems fair to infer its persistence in the business world. . . . The sheer volume of current legal decisions finding discrimination in these areas suggests that race and ethnicity are pervasive in their effects in American society. Absent some compelling evidence to the contrary, it would be disingenuous to assume that these factors play no role in business decisions and that they do not affect a firm's choice of its suppliers.[91]

Nonetheless, disregarding the evidence of racism throughout our society, the Supreme Court is moving affirmative action to a purely economics model of disadvantage. As the Brennan opinion noted in *Bakke:* "With respect to any factor (such as poverty or family educational background) that may be used as a substitute for race as an indicator of past discrimination, whites greatly outnumber racial minorities simply because whites make up a far larger percentage of the total population and therefore far outnumber minorities in absolute terms at every socio-economic level."[92] If we eliminate considerations of race in defining disadvantage, we will have affirmative action primarily for disadvantaged whites. That will do nothing to overcome the pervasive inequality faced by racial minorities in our country. If anything, it will magnify it by improving yet another group's situation while leaving racial minorities behind.

One must also wonder if the move toward individualized inquiries reflects a genuine commitment to affirmative action because it so impractical. As the Brennan opinion noted: "A case-by-case inquiry into the extent to which each individual applicant has been affected, either directly or indirectly, by racial discrimination, would seem to be, as a practical matter, virtually impossible, despite the fact that there are excellent reasons for concluding that such effects generally exist." [93]

Affirmative action should not be entirely reshaped into an economic disadvantage theory. We need to be mindful that racism as a historic practice and current reality still exists. Poor whites do not face racism. Supreme Court jurisprudence cannot be used to erase the existence of racism. As Robert Suggs has argued, blacks can become "temporary whites" when they succeed within one employment sphere. However, they cannot transfer their social capital from one employment situation to another.[94] Similarly, middle-class black parents can provide their children with the comforts of life and a good education but cannot shield them from the racism that is endemic in the commercial sector. Their children will face a much higher likelihood of slipping back into poverty than will the children of middle-class white parents. Irrespective of how much economic capital blacks bring with them, they face barriers not faced by whites when entering new industries or situations.[95] This lack of transferability of social capital is consistent with the empirical literature from social cognition theory—strangers will always first see a black person as "black" with all of the attendant stereotypes. Many blacks, for example, find that when they patronize expensive stores, restaurants, or other settings where blacks are infrequent participants, they are often subject to discriminatory and even hostile treatment, ranging from avoidance to police confrontation.[96] Economic success does not erase blackness.

With the advent of the Civil Rights Act of 1964, some social scientists, most notably Richard Freeman, thought that labor market discrimination against blacks would virtually collapse,

thereby precluding the need for affirmative action.[97] Other social scientists thought that the disparities between whites and
blacks would disappear over time as young blacks benefitted
from educational opportunities not available to their older relatives. (This was called the "vintage" theory.)[98] Unfortunately,
both schools of thought have been proven wrong:

Labor market discrimination did not "collapse" with the passage of
civil rights legislation; instead it underwent a metastasis, living on,
one suspects having received considerable nourishment from the past
Reagan administration.

The vintage hypothesis is also wrong. Before it can be taken seriously, it must explain why black and white youths whose skill levels
are supposedly converging have such disparate employment opportunities.[99]

Civil rights legislation and increased educational opportunities
for blacks have not been able to end the pattern of labor market
discrimination.

But what happens to the disadvantage theory when applied
to multiracial individuals? As the many autobiographies of such
people reveal, even when they look "white," they still live an
existence defined by their minority racial status. For those who
are multiracial yet look black, society is unlikely to consider
them anything other than "black" irrespective of how they
might self-identify. The presumption of disadvantage would
appear to exist for all persons of any discernable African heritage, because economic opportunity in the United States has
been created under the "one drop of blood rule." A rebuttable
presumption (i.e., a presumption that could be overcome with
evidence that the disadvantage rule should not apply) could
certainly uncover individual cases in which such individuals
have spent their entire lives "passing" as white and living in
"white" households, thereby avoiding racism. In fact, it appears

that in some of the cases in which the Small Business Administration successfully challenged claims of "disadvantage" by "minorities," the individual was, in fact, someone who "discovered" a minority ancestor for the purpose of obtaining the benefits of the set-aside program.[100] A rebuttable presumption may therefore be an excellent way to resolve the variation in experience among multiracial individuals.

It is important to insist that multiracial individuals have grown up in a minority, rather than white, household if we are to be true to the literature which distinguishes racism from poverty. If it is true that whites, in general, have more social capital than blacks to help them attain economic development, we should not lump poor whites with blacks for affirmative action purposes. If Greg Williams truly passes as white, then we have to contend with whether we want to have affirmative action for poor whites. But we should not taint that decision by classifying him as black. Greg Williams's children (who have a white mother), for example, most likely would not qualify for affirmative action under the disadvantage theory. If, like Greg, they decide to devote their attention and scholarship to racial issues, then they might qualify under a diversity rationale.

Nonetheless, by accepting the disadvantage rationale, we should not preclude ourselves from making distinctions among blacks so that, if possible, we can try to help the most disadvantaged. An example which illuminates this point emerges from a conversation I had with my colleague, Jody Armour. Jody described an educational program in which he has participated that tries to help disadvantaged blacks get a "better chance" by attending high-achievement high schools. Originally, the program primarily benefited blacks from inner-city segregated schools. Today, he has seen an increasing number of black children who apply to the program who come from middle-class backgrounds. It is tempting for the organizers of this program to pick such children because, given their lesser disadvantage, they are less at risk of failure in the "better chance" program, thereby making the program appear "successful." When we devise a program for the explicit purpose of assisting disadvantaged individuals in our society, we should stay mindful of that original purpose in selecting beneficiaries even within the group of blacks.

Stephen Carter has made a similar point in arguing that we should reserve affirmative action for the most needy blacks in our society:

Because the principal battleground is affirmative action, which benefits mainly those least in need of society's aid, there may be a tendency for all of us to forget who it is that is suffering as the rest of us toss our brickbats: for it is our people, black people, those on whose behalf all of us claim to be laboring, who are withering in the violent prisons that many of our inner cities have become.[101]

Carter is correct to argue that the most needy blacks especially require our assistance but that argument should not obscure the fact that, unfortunately, even the children of middle-class blacks often need affirmative action to overcome the racism that is endemic in our society. We should not fail to admit the children of middle-class blacks to medical school under a special admissions program when more impoverished blacks are unavailable for those slots. Blacks, like whites, benefit from education and class background. The children of blacks who have recently entered the middle-class need affirmative action so as not to slip back into poverty in the next generation. We cannot delude ourselves into thinking that racism is solved in one generation because we "graduate" from racism. Carter's approach, unfortunately, would risk the loss of the modest gains made by the emerging black middle class. Thus, we should make distinctions among blacks while also remembering that racism can touch even the children of Harvard and Yale law professors.

Overcoming Stereotypes

The University of California argued in *Bakke* that one justification for its affirmative action program was to "dismantle pernicious stereotypes."[102] That argument, however, was not considered seriously by any member of the Court. Since *Bakke,* that theory rarely has been raised. Justice Stevens used the theory in his dissent in *Wygant* arguing that: "It is one thing for a white child to be taught by a white teacher that color, like beauty, is only 'skin deep'; it is far more convincing to experience that truth on a day-to-day basis during the routine, ongoing learning process."[103] No other member of the Court, however, joined his opinion.

The stereotype justification should be an important justification in light of the social cognition research on prejudice. An important component to racism is stereotypical thinking which cuts across the socioeconomic status of blacks in our society. For example, one study found that when an individual "bumped" someone in the hall, the reaction of the person being bumped varied depending on the race of the person who bumped them. When they were bumped by a black person, they felt that the person was hostile or violent; when they were bumped by a white person they felt that the individual was merely playing around or dramatizing. When they were bumped by a white person, they excused the behavior as unintentional and harmless.[104] The employment of more black physicians, lawyers, or even Supreme Court justices, might help overcome those stereotypes. Having a black teacher will make black *and* white students put aside their stereotypes about the incompetence of blacks. Especially, as affirmative action moves beyond tokenism, a substantial influx of minorities into positions of respect and authority might help overcome stereotypes about incompetence.

The stereotype theory, however, is difficult to apply in the multiracial context. The issue is really one of identifiability rather than mixed-race. If Naomi Zack, Greg Williams, Maria O'Brien Hylton, or Judy Scales-Trent are walking down a hall and bump into a stranger, what will that stranger think? Will that stranger think that he or she was bumped by a "white" person or by a "black" person? Being able to "pass" as white when, metaphorically speaking, walking down the hall can be a real privilege when it is extended to business meetings and social gatherings. A dark-skinned person does not have the option of moving back and forth across the color line. A light-skinned person exercises that option, even without trying. If our primary goal is to help overcome racial stereotypes, then it is hard to see how hiring multiracial individuals who are light-skinned furthers that purpose.

So Where Does This Leave Us?

This discussion of the various rationales for affirmative action creates much confusion. Some justifications work well for multiracial individuals; other rationales do not. There are, simply, no easy answers or blanket solutions. The important point is that we recognize the range of ways that affirmative action can be justified for multiracial individuals. In applying these justifications, we need to be mindful of the utility of these justifications. If a hiring decision comes down to two blacks—one who is light-skinned and who has often passed as white and the other who is dark-skinned and has lived a life defined by racial prejudice—we should prefer the dark-skinned over the light-skinned individual (assuming all other factors are equal). On the other hand, if a hiring decision comes down to a white person and a mixed-race black person, we should favor the mixed-race black over the white, knowing that economic disadvantage for whites is more easily overcome than it is even for advantaged blacks. Having a sensitivity to race and color as well as the justifications for affirmative action might permit us to use our limited resources more fairly and effectively.

Returning to Greg Williams's story about being considered for the sheriff position in Indiana can highlight the usefulness of this discussion. Greg's relative who commented that Greg deserved to be the beneficiary of affirmative action because he had not received any "breaks" in life was referring to the disadvantage theory. Greg's childhood, after he went to live with his black relatives, was defined by his minority racial status. Greg deserves reparations for those experiences. The black minister, however, was also correct to note that Greg would do little to overcome stereotypes about blacks when he walks on patrol in the neighborhoods. The community would view him as another "white" police officer. If a more visible black were available for the position, who could also meet the reparations theory, then that other person may be more deserving (assuming all other factors are the same). But, if the alternative is another white sheriff, then clearly Greg is the more deserving candidate. No matter how disadvantaged was Greg's life experience, he will always have the privilege of "passing" that is not accorded to many dark-skinned blacks. As Albion Tourgée noted, and Cheryl Harris has reiterated, there is a property value in whiteness, even for "blacks."

C. Transracial Adoptions

The National Association of Black Social Workers (NABSW) strongly influenced our adoption and placement policies by its 1972 position paper in which it strongly argued against the adoption of black children by white families.[105] Although the NABSW may have made an important contribution to our understanding of the best interest of black children seeking family placement, it has also perpetuated stark black/white thinking about society. Its position paper states: "Our society is distinctly black or white and characterized by white racism at every level. We repudiate the fallacious and fantasied reasoning of some that whites adopting Black children will alter that basic character."[106] Unfortunately, in trying to protect the interests of black children, the NABSW ignored the interests of the growing number of multiracial children by assuming that we can easily divide society into black and white categories.

The NABSW position paper has generated extensive discussion of transracial adoptions.[107] Will blacks face cultural genocide if black children are made available for adoption by white couples? Do black children suffer so much from the foster care system that they are better off placed with a white family than allowed to languish in the foster care system?

Many voice concern about preserving "black culture" and serving the best interest of "black children," but give little attention to how we define "black." In particular, they ignore that many children available for adoption are multiracial rather than exclusively white or black.[108] Multiracial children[109] are usually lumped into the category "black" on the assumption that steps need to be taken to preserve their black heritage without any consideration of whether we are using family law to *create* rather than preserve cultural heritage.[110] Consider:

A biracial youngster whose birth mother is White and whose father is unknown was classified as Black. His foster family was then classified as White, even though the White foster mother was married to an African American. The foster child thus became a candidate for removal.[111]

When we assume that all children with a white parent and a black parent should be treated as if they are black in the context of family placements, we are sending the message that these children should be classified and treated as if they are black, thus increasing the likelihood that they will languish in foster care.

We generally ignore what the family composition of these children would be without adoption. In many of the reported cases of biracial children, the biological mother is white and the biological father (who is not the mother's husband) is black.[112] Given our gendered system of childrearing, the child would most likely have been raised in a white household absent adoption. Ironically, when we classify these types of mixed-race children as black and place them in a black family, we have transported the children to a different family situation than they would have experienced absent adoption. Those who consider "transracial adoptions" to be cultural genocide for black children often ignore the weaknesses of the cultural genocide argument when children with white mothers and black fathers are placed in white families. By lumping together all children with at least one biological black parent into the category "black" for adoption purposes, we help construct a larger category of "black" than would exist absent adoption.[113]

In one case, *Reisman v. State of Tennessee Department of Human Services*,[114] the court recognized the mixed-race background of a child and searched for a "mixed-race" couple to adopt the child.[115] But the court never defined exactly what it meant by a "mixed-race" couple. Ordinarily, if no adoption takes place and the nuclear family stays intact, a mixed-race child is raised by parents of two different races (let's assume white and black for this discussion). Those parents do not have the same racial make-up as the child, who is half white and half black. The only way that child would share the racial make-up of his or her parents is if the parents were each half-white and half-black (possible but unlikely). In what sense, one must wonder, is it better for a "mixed-race" child to have parents of two different races than two parents of the same race? In neither case does the child really share her racial heritage fully with her parents.[116]

Other courts have used the term "biracial," failing to appreciate that nearly all blacks (as well as many whites) are of "mixed-race" background in the United States.[117] The term "biracial," as used by the courts seems to be limited to an instance where a child has a white and a black parent. What happens, one must wonder, when a biracial child who grew up in a white household grows up and bears a child. If she bears a child with a white man is her child still biracial? What if she bears a child with a black man? Is the child still biracial or will social convention cause it to be considered black? The biracial category, as used by courts and commentators, seems to only reflect the situation where a child is exactly 50 percent white and 50 percent black. It is not a term that reflects a spectrum; it simply designates a new point—the middle—on the bipolar racial scale. Ironically, that middle point probably does not even exist in the cases to which it is being applied because the parent who is labeled as "black" probably is the product of a mixed-race heritage. Thus, although it might make sense abstractly to recognize the category "biracial" and use that category to find homes for biracial children, the category is actually unworkable. Nearly all of us are, in fact, multiracial, and it distorts reality further to consider only the child with one "white" and one "black" parent to be biracial.

These classification questions are challenging, because the courts do not define the race of a child in a vacuum. The fact that a court recognizes a child as multiracial will not necessarily cause society to treat the child as multiracial. Society may still choose to treat the child as if she is black. If a court, for example, insisted on giving no racial preference to black parents over white parents in the adoption of a multiracial child, and the child was eventually placed with white parents, the child may still face unfavorable treatment by friends, classmates, teachers, employers, and health care workers who consider the child to be black. Some people may therefore argue that we should try to place the multiracial child with a black family so that the child will learn how to deal with a racist society.[118] But such a preferential policy makes the assumption that the best way to learn to deal with society's classification scheme is to adopt it as part of one's self-identity. That is a dangerous presumption because it puts the courts and social service agencies in the position of helping to perpetuate an arbitrary classification system. While some people may consider such a racial classification system in the adoption context to be ameliorative, it also helps perpetuate the subordinating "one drop of blood" rule for racial classification under which a person with a known trace of African ancestry is considered to be black.[119] Racial preference policies for adoption of multiracial children therefore do not present exactly the same problems as they do for "black" children. Classifying a multiracial child as "black" and thereby preferentially placing her in a black home promotes a racist and subordinating classification system.

We get a different perspective on the transracial adoption

controversy when we examine it from the context of a multiracial child. First, we see that many of the children who the courts
and social agencies have unreflexively labeled as "black" for
adoption purposes are, in fact, multiracial. It is therefore too
simplistic to say that these cases raise issues of "transracial"
adoption only when a white couple or individual tries to adopt
a multiracial child. Second, we see that our goal should be to
respect an individual's full racial heritage rather than distort
one aspect of that racial heritage. When courts or social agencies distort one aspect of that racial heritage, they help perpetuate our racist "one drop of blood" rule. Nonetheless, as we
should stop applying to the context of multiracial children what
is considered by some to be good social policy for black children, we should also be careful not to transfer these lessons
from cases involving multiracial children to cases involving
black children. Our policy of preferring black parents for a
black child may be beneficial in terms of preserving racial heritage and even teaching a child how to deal with the racism of
our society.[120] Stretching that policy to include all multiracial
children with a "drop" of African-American blood reinforces
racism rather than the best interest of the child. By taking that
step, we are helping to construct a bipolar racial model which
is disrespectful to the genuine mixed-racial heritage of that
child. Children should not be the instruments of such social engineering.

How then could we really move toward a spectrum of race
rather than false polarities? We could begin by truly investigating our racial heritage. The assumption would be that we all
are of mixed-racial heritage and the challenge would be to
discover as much of that family tree as possible. If the child in
the Reisman case, for example, could be determined to have
ancestry from Africa, Europe, and North America, then we

could hope the child would be taught to honor and value that mixed-racial heritage. It is wrong to assume, however, that only parents who shared that identical racial background would try to honor and respect a child's racial heritage. Outside the adoption context, adults who marry someone of another race and bear children together routinely raise multiracial children. We expect them to honor and respect a heritage to which they do not directly belong. By only sending the multiracial child to a multiracial household, we attempt to do the impossible—give each of us parents with racial backgrounds identical to our own. That does not always happen outside the adoption context, and there is no reason to impose it artificially onto the adoption context.

A problem with this thesis is that much African heritage was lost through forced deportation and enslavement. Whereas many people of European heritage can trace their families back to a specific country, many people of African heritage cannot because of the coercive nature of their voyage to the United States. For the child with African heritage, the task of tracing back ancestry may become a lesson in the trials of forced enslavement. And, for a multiracial child, it may lead "a descendant to an irreconcilable slave and slave-owning genealogy." [121] As we begin to acknowledge the multiracial category, we may also take the opportunity to break down the monolithic category of "Africa" and discuss the many countries of that continent. Such discussions may not only help children of African heritage to learn more about their heritage but may help all of us to move beyond our monolithic thinking about Africa.

A final difficulty is confidentiality. Children who are adopted often have special problems in tracing their heritage because of the confidentiality of the adoption proceedings. Nonetheless, if their racial heritage is to be meaningfully honored and respected, it would seem important for the adoption agency to collect as much information as possible while the birth mother and father are known to them. Rather than classifying a child as "black" or "multiracial," it would be helpful to learn as much as possible about what kind of African heritage the child may have (as well as what kinds of other heritage the child might have). If this information is communicated to the adoptive parents, then they can try more faithfully to learn about that heritage and to imbue in the child a sense of pride about that heritage.

Adoption, by definition, is a highly individualized process to which we devote considerable social resources. There is no excuse for social agencies and courts to blindly perpetuate the "one drop of blood rule" without fully investigating the best interests of the child.

In sum, the invisibility of multiracial individuals is subtly enforced, through Census rules, affirmative action programs, and adoption policies. Clumsy policies have unconsciously preserved a "one drop of blood rule" that results in nearly all people of mixed-racial heritage being labeled "black." It is time for us to consider *why* we engage in racial categorization so that we can develop rules that achieve ameliorative rather than subordinating purposes. I will present a modest proposal for how to achieve respectful Census categorization in chapter 8, and hope that others will join me in beginning the journey toward respectful racial categorization in the context of other issues.

Disability

· · · · · · · · · · · · ·

"Transvestism, transsexualism, pedophilia, exhibitionism, voyeurism, gender identity disorders not resulting from physical impairments, or other sexual behavior disorders"[1] were excluded from coverage under the Americans with Disabilities Act (ADA) in order for the statute to avoid defeat. The definitional fight about which disabilities should be covered by the ADA has had the same moral overtones as the controversies surrounding whether Title VII should cover transsexuals and transvestites. Citing the repugnance of an employer having to tolerate a transvestite wearing a dress, Senator Helms commented from the Senate floor during the ADA debate: "Do we really want to prohibit these private institutions from making employment decisions based on moral qualifications?"[2] The ADA's "per se exclusion from its definition of a disability of what it calls 'sexual behavior disorders' reifies the moral grid that lies beneath the notion of a disability. Rather than changing the ethical significance of disabilities, the Act carves out a new class of untouchables defined by sexuality and sex behaviors."[3] The ADA reinforces the case law we examined under Title VII by condoning discrimination against transsexuals and transvestites even when they are qualified to perform their employment.

Despite this moralistic limitation on the definition of disability, the ADA still is criticized for being too inclusive, for not being limited to the "worthy" disabled. As one commentator has stated, "the definition of disability is so broad that it may be raised by many people who are unable to or unwilling to work but who will hide behind the claim of disability."[4] ADA cases, however, rarely arise because people are "unable" or "unwilling" to work. They usually arise when employers perceive people as being unfit for a job based on an irrelevant physical characteristic.

The controversy surrounding so-called sexual disorders was played out during the drafting and passage of the ADA. Obesity, learning disabilities, bad backs, allergies, and alcoholism are currently at center stage. Ridiculed, stereotyped, coerced, and mistreated, the "obese" can serve as a metaphor for individuals who are not seen as "worthy" of protection under the Americans with Disabilities Act. They receive little protection under the ADA and much social castigation. As the *Wall Street Journal* quipped: "There is little question that most people would give generously to ease the way of the truly disabled into mainstream America. But people with lower back pain? Sinusitis sufferers?"[5] (These same *Wall Street Journal* editors, however, also oppose mandatory curb cuts which are essential to the mobility of people who use wheelchairs—a group that is usually considered "truly disabled.")[6] One must wonder why such institutions as the *Wall Street Journal* that have a professed commitment to the "truly disabled" consider it fair game to ridicule people they consider undeserving of ADA protection. Their loud contempt provides some of the strongest evidence for why expanded protection is needed.

Deciding to cover disabilities such as obesity under federal anti-discrimination law, however, presents difficult definitional questions. Because disability law is bipolar, the courts have had to provide stark yes or no answers—either obesity is a covered disability or not. Body weight and obesity, however, exist on a spectrum. There are the "overweight," the "medically significant obese," "gross obesity," and the "morbidly obese." [7] These terms are defined in comparison with "ideal" weights which are taken from insurance company tables rather than medical determinations of body fat. Thus, a muscular body builder might fit any of these definitions although his or her body fat is quite low; or a frail individual with poor muscle tone and conditioning might be considered to be in the "normal" range although he or she has a high percentage of body fat. Moreover, people's weight varies over time so that "obesity" is not even a static condition for a given person. Embedded with much social significance, obesity remains an elusive category. How then can we create legal protections for such an unruly category?

I. Body Size

Even research suggesting there is an "obese" gene does not lessen the castigation of the obese. A recent political cartoon featured a woman walking with a man, who was eating a triple-decker ice cream cone; on the woman's shirt was a sign saying "I'm with ~~FATSO~~, MR. HORMONALLY CHALLENGED" and an arrow pointing to the man.[8] The message is clear—the obese will be the subject of ridicule irrespective of whether their obesity is caused by overeating, hormones, or genes.

One of my mother's favorite expressions, usually targeted at my sister and myself, is, "You can't be too rich or too thin." Social scientists illustrate this familiar saying with empirical evidence that women who are obese during their adolescent years are likely to have lower socioeconomic status in later life.[9] Additional body weight seems to limit women's upward economic mobility; working class communities as well as the black community seem less obsessed with women's weight than middle-class communities.[10] My mother's statement was reflective of her race (white), and class (middle-class) as well as the gender of her daughters since standards for women's appearance are more stringent than for men's appearance. Obesity therefore correlates with gender, race, socioeconomic status, and disability; yet obesity discrimination is often beyond the reach of anti-discrimination law.

Even when obesity discrimination does receive legal protection, favorable court decisions are heavily criticized and even ridiculed by the media. A *Wall Street Journal* editorial commented disdainfully that "the morbidly obese are just some of the many mysterious subgroups finding space in the ADA's expanding tent."[11] Other media reports criticized Deborah Birdwell, who weighs 250 pounds, for claiming that she should be able to bring her own folding chair to a movie theater so that she could watch a movie with her niece. The obese should "choose" to diet, should stay out of public view, and should stay out of the labor force, although we do not want to offer them public assistance if they are unemployed. As Betsy Hart, a former White House spokesperson and press secretary to the House Republican Policy Committee has said, Deborah Birdwell should not be able to recover under the Americans with Disabilities Act because she "can't pass by the Ho-Hos in the grocery store without partaking."[12] Even if Birdwell has a genetic predisposition toward obesity, Hart argues, "it doesn't mean that one should give in, or that such a person has a moral claim to my sympathies, pocketbook, or job."[13]

Dozens of law review articles have been written in the last several years arguing that "obesity" should be covered by the

Americans with Disabilities Act.[14] Although some attention has been devoted to the fact that society has more stringent rules for women's body weight than for men's and that obesity correlates with socioeconomic status, little has been made of the fact that obesity disproportionately affects *black* women. A pure disability focus on obesity misses the gender and race implications of this societal category. Further, because obesity exists along a spectrum of body weight, we only get a proper picture of society's treatment of obesity if we examine the range of arbitrary, weight-related restrictions that have been imposed by employers and other institutions on people who are purportedly underweight as well as overweight.

A. Underweight

I was not particularly conscious of my bodyweight until I was at a party with some girlfriends when I was around twelve years old. The conversation turned to who was the "skinniest" and all eyes soon converged on me. I immediately protested that I was certainly not the smallest and turned an accusatory finger to my best friend, Meg, whom I considered to be much skinnier. Before I could count to ten, someone had found a bathroom scale and insisted that we each weigh ourselves. To my chagrin, I was the only girl who was still under 100—a marker that soon became my secret goal. For us, moving past the 100 pound mark was a watershed in the transition out of girlhood into womanhood. It was a transition my body was slow to make.

The days of weighing under 100 pounds are a distant memory for me, but many other women find themselves to be quite small even in adulthood. They complain that they are infantilized and not taken seriously in a society that uses norms for men's height and weight for respect. As the National Association of Professional Baseball Leagues argued in defense of its inflexible standard of 5 feet 10 inches and 170 pounds for baseball umpires: an umpire "must be a person who commands respect of big fellows, big men." [15]

Unfortunately, these standards for respect are not limited to Major League Baseball umpires. The New York City Department of Parks and Recreation was at a loss to provide any explanation for its requirement that lifeguards be 5 feet 7 inches with a minimum weight of 135 pounds: "the real basis for those standards was just that it was felt that there had to be some line of demarcation." [16]

When hiring police officers, cities have been slow to eliminate minimum height and weight requirements. In one of the first cases successfully challenging such requirements under California state anti-discrimination law, the concurrence expressed its uneasiness with replacing such requirements with physical performance tests of actual ability: "A factor upon which there is neither evidence nor discussion here is that of public confidence. The police arm functions not only to protect the public, but to instill in that public confidence that it is being protected—an increasingly difficult task in these days of rising crime rates. Some nondiscriminatory minimum size requirement is entirely in order." [17] In other words, even if a woman was physically qualified to do the job, she should be disqualified if her presence on the force would erode public confidence. The City of East Cleveland tried to defend a 150-pound minimum weight rule for police officers under the theory that a potential *assaulter* would be affected by the size of the police officer. The court readily dismissed this conclusion finding that: "The assaulter could hardly tell whether a fully clothed police officer weighs 145, or 155, pounds, even assuming that if he could such knowledge would be relevant in his decision as to whether to assault an officer or not."[18] Nonetheless, the court did uphold the 5-foot 8-inches height requirement because of the "nearly universal use of height requirements in hiring police."[19] As with the weight requirement, the offered justification was "the psychological advantage of a taller officer,"[20] which the court found rational.

The deference to the psychology of potential assaulters or criminals in maintaining height and weight requirements to exclude women from law enforcement reached a peak with the U.S. Supreme Court's decision in *Dothard v. Rawlinson*.[21] Instead of relying exclusively on the argument that size is crucial to maintaining a psychological advantage in law enforcement, the state of Alabama directly argued that being a man was essential to effective law enforcement. Because male prisoners may desire to rape female prison guards, the state of Alabama successfully argued that the female "employee's very womanhood would . . . directly undermine her capacity to provide the security that is the essence of a correctional counselor's responsibility."[22] Ironically, the Court found no support for the 5-foot 2-inches and 120-pound weight requirement for prison guards but did find support for the per se exclusion of all women.

Dothard v. Rawlinson was decided by the U.S. Supreme Court in 1977 and has never been overturned although courts have increasingly tried to confine its holding to prisons, like Alabama's, with large number of sex offenders and very volatile conditions. Prisoner psychology—not to respect people who are female or small—is not limited, however, to the prison setting. Women who are small know how it feels to face such disrespect in all walks of life. So-called prisoner psychology is just a distilled version of larger society. Empirical research confirms the hypothesis that shortness harms women's professional status and even their perceived physical attractiveness.[23] Women usually cannot reach the glass ceiling.

Sandra Bem, a psychologist who is most noted for her work on gender socialization, has noted that we exclude short people from firefighting based on the stereotype that they are incapable of fighting fires effectively. At four-feet nine-inches, she asks how we would structure society if *everyone* were her size. "Would all the houses in this community of short people eventually burn down?"[24] No, she answers, we would construct a world around that norm for height. She argues: "The moral here should be obvious: shortness isn't the problem; the problem lies in forcing short people to function in a tall-centered social structure."[25] The norm that is chosen for professions such as firefighting is based on the average physique of white men; our homes would probably be equally safe from fires had we chosen a norm more closely centered around the average height for women. But we rarely question whose norms are chosen.

B. Overweight

Diatribes against people who are obese have a long tradition within American culture. Dating back to the Biblical injunction that the "glutton will be reduced to poverty,"[26] Western society continues to affirm the stereotype that people who are obese are slovenly, lazy, and lack energy.[27] Small children rate an obese child as less likeable than a child with no visible physical handicap, a child with crutches and a brace on the left leg, a child sitting in a wheelchair with a blanket covering both legs, a child with the left hand missing, or a child with a facial disfigurement on the left side of the mouth.[28] By college, students report that they would rather marry someone who is an embezzler, ex-mental patient, cocaine user, or shoplifter than someone who is obese.[29] Overweight adults report that they experience constant public humiliation with people snatching food out of their grocery baskets, giving them dirty looks, or offering rude remarks.[30]

Abstractly, one would think that maximum weight rules would impact more harshly against *men* than women, because men, on average, are bigger than women. In fact, the opposite result occurs because maximum weight requirements are imposed through a gender-specific lens. In other words, we do not have the same maximum weight rules for women and men, even for women and men of the same height. Thus, both minimum *and* maximum weight rules have a disparate impact against women because minimum weight rules are gender-neutral and maximum weight rules are gender-specific. Women, therefore, only avoid discrimination if they fit a narrow band of acceptable body weight.

Stricter weight standards for women than men have an enormous impact in women's lives. Researchers have found that for both black and white women being overweight inversely correlates with family income.[31] Obesity does not play the same role in the lives of men. Men who are overweight are less likely to marry but do not fare worse on measures of education and family income. Overweight women live in households that average $6700 less in yearly income, complete one-third of a year less in school, remain 20 percent less likely to get married, and have higher rates of household poverty than their less heavy counterparts.[32] These rules often have a particular disparate impact on black women who are, on average, heavier than white women after the third decade of life.

The commonly recognized notion that appearance rules are more rigid for women than for men is played out in the cases involving weight requirements, nearly all of which are brought by women. As feminists have long said, "fat is a feminist issue."

Despite the disproportionate effect that maximum weight rules have on women's employment opportunities, few of these rules are susceptible to legal challenge. A successful legal challenge under a disparate impact theory requires a large workforce where statistically significant comparisons can be made between the employment opportunities for women and men. Moreover, the weight policies must be explicit so that plaintiffs can prove that gender-specific weight rules are the cause of the disparate impact. An office with thin female receptionists and chubby male file clerks would be unlikely to be legally challengeable because the workforce would be too small for statistical significance and the policy is unlikely to be explicit. The airline industry, however, has been a perfect forum for challenging more stringent rules for women than for men. In a 1994 case against USAir, a federal court found that the airline had more stringent rules for women than for men.[33] In an earlier case against Continental, a federal court found that the airline had *no* weight standards at all for men and stringent standards for women.[34] As with the minimum weight rules in prisons and police departments, the justification was public relations. This time the weight rule was needed "to create the public image of an airline which offered passengers service by thin, attractive women, whom executives referred to as Continental's 'girls.' "[35] None of these rules mentioned race although it seems clear that the employer's idea of a "thin, attractive woman" was race-based.

Plaintiffs who have challenged maximum weight rules under Title VII have typically been women who were slightly over a gender-specific standard. In the airline cases, for example, the female plaintiffs had been hired in accordance with the maximum weight standard but were disciplined or terminated when they could not maintain the required weight. These women could not be characterized as "obese" as they were only a few pounds over the norm for women. Women who are characterized as "obese" have generally brought their claims under the Americans with Disabilities Act rather than Title VII. Instead of challenging weight rules at large workforces where the rules are explicit and gender-specific, these women have challenged maximum weight rules at smaller institutions where the rules are more subtle. The ADA cases therefore move us along the spectrum from the underweight and mildly overweight cases that have been brought under Title VII to the obese. If we remember that women who are small as well as women who are mildly "overweight" have faced gender-based discrimination, it should not surprise us that women who are "obese" face substantial employment discrimination. As we advance along the weight spectrum, societal treatment worsens.

C. Obese

Toni Linda Cassista, who was 5-feet 4-inches tall and weighed 305 pounds, applied for repeated openings at a local health food store.[36] Her prior work experience fit the qualifications that the store stated it sought in a new employee. Despite evidence that Cassista's weight had been an explicit factor during the hiring process, the jury returned a unanimous verdict in favor of the defendant, a health food store. On appeal in state court, one issue was whether obesity was a covered disability under the California Disability Discrimination statute. The California Supreme Court concluded that obesity is only a covered disability if there is a "physiological or systemic basis for the condition."[37] Because Cassista could not meet that standard, she lost.

Cassista had argued that her situation should be covered by California state law if the employer *perceived* her as being disabled, even if she considered herself to be able-bodied. Applying that argument, she noted that the employer had presumed that she lacked physical stamina, could not lift heavy boxes, and could not use certain equipment at the workplace because of her weight. The California Supreme Court rejected her argument, concluding that the employer must have regarded her as having a physiological disease or disorder which rendered her unqualified; it was not sufficient for the employer simply to regard her weight as rendering her unqualified. Because Cassista as well as the defendant had maintained at trial that she was a healthy and fit individual, she lost under California law.

Bonnie Cook, who was 5-feet 2-inches tall and weighed over 320 pounds, applied for a position as an institutional attendant at a residential facility for people with mental retardation.[38] Like Cassista, Cook clearly was qualified for the position. She had held the position for seven previous years, had departed voluntarily, and had a spotless work record. The employer refused to rehire her, claiming that her obesity compromised her ability to evacuate patients in case of an emergency and put her at greater risk of developing serious ailments and filing worker's compensation claims. It testified that it would only rehire her if she reduced her weight to 190 pounds. A jury awarded the plaintiff $100,000 in compensatory damages under federal anti-discrimination law despite the fact that the trial court instructed the jury that "a condition or disorder is not an impairment unless it . . . constitutes an immutable condition that the person affected is powerless to control." [39] In other words, Cook like Cassista was only able to prevail if she convinced the jury that her obesity was "innate" and "immutable." Cook met this burden of proof whereas Cassista did not.

Cook also was more successful than Cassista under the "regarded as" prong of anti-discrimination law. Cook, like Cassista, had argued that she was a healthy and qualified individual but that the defendant-employer had treated her as if obesity were a physical impairment. The federal court of appeals accepted this argument, concluding that the employer "treated plaintiff's obesity as if it actually affected her musculoskeletal and cardiovascular systems." [40] That conclusion was possible in *Cook* because the employer specifically said that her obesity would preclude her from performing many of the physical aspects of the job.

Unanswered by the court's reasoning in *Cook*, however, is whether an employer could simply say that it thinks that the public would object to an obese person working in a health food store or working with mentally retarded people but that it, the employer, does not consider the individual to be physically impaired due to obesity. If both the plaintiff and defendant maintain that the plaintiff is healthy, but defendant disputes her good "public image," can a plaintiff prevail under the reasoning in *Cook*? I suspect not. Employers therefore may be better off revealing their real, stereotypical reasons for rejecting people who are obese for employment rather than hiding behind apparent, objective, physical facts. Although federal anti-discrimination law may provide some relief in employment cases for people who are obese, it is unlikely to be a panacea against such discrimination. As we move from the underweight, to the overweight, to the obese, we see federal anti-discrimination protection evaporating except for the rare case in which the employer acknowledges that it considered the plaintiff's obesity to be a physical disability.

The ADA is a bipolar model, causing the courts to determine whether an individual is entitled to protection based on whether he or she fits the category "disabled." A recent example which highlights the inappropriateness of the bipolar framework under the ADA involves Deborah Birdwell. Birdwell is obese and had wanted to see a movie with her niece. Knowing that she could not fit into a movie theater seat, she called ahead to ask if she could bring her own chair and use it in the wheelchair section.[41] She was told that she could. But when she went to the theater with her chair, she was rudely told that she would not be able to use it. Birdwell sued under the public accommodations provision of the ADA and the case was settled. Had Birdwell's case gone to trial, the outcome of the case would have depended upon whether Birdwell's obesity was considered to be a "disability." In the language of the ADA: Did it substantially affect a major life activity? Since going to a movie theater is unlikely to be considered a "major life activity," Birdwell would probably have had to argue that her obesity affected her life more generally. Not having any specific information about her life, it is impossible to evaluate whether she could have made that claim successfully. But why must Birdwell's obesity have to globally be a "disability" for a theater owner to allow her to bring her own chair to sit in the wheelchair section? Birdwell was politely making a reasonable request to a theater owner in order to patronize the theater. She suffered disadvantage because of her obesity. If we viewed disability in terms of the disadvantages that it causes in concrete situations rather than on a bipolar scale, we would easily recognize that Birdwell has a legitimate claim of disability-related discrimination, and that both Cassista and Cook had valid claims since they were denied employment despite their qualifications.

A less bipolar model might attain better justice. Since the term "obesity" does not have a standard definition, it makes little sense to try to distinguish between the "overweight" and the "obese." If we viewed disabilities in terms of disadvantage, then we would not be concerned with that line-drawing. Women and men who cannot meet the arbitrary weight restrictions of the airlines[42] would have as valid a claim as Deborah Birdwell who is classified as "morbidly obese." In both cases, they have been forced to suffer disadvantage due to their body weight. In both cases, these imposed disadvantages had nothing to do with their actual abilities. They should be entitled to make an individualized showing of disadvantage due to body size. The issue should be disadvantage rather than bipolar classification.

The obesity cases also raise the issue of how much significance should be attached to the criterion of "voluntariness." One argument against covering obesity under the ADA is that people who are obese should be strongly encouraged to lose weight rather than to receive societal protection. The most paternalistic version of this attitude is that anti-discrimination law should not cover "obese" people because we should provide them with every possible incentive to lose weight *for their own good*. (Nonetheless, some studies show that dieting is ineffective and sometimes physically dangerous for people who are "overweight.")[43] Similarly, some commentators have argued that people who are bisexual should be strongly encouraged to express their heterosexual side rather than be protected in their freedom to choose a sexual partner. Some people have also suggested that light skin "blacks" such as Greg Williams should "pass" as white rather than be protected for their decision to embrace their African-American heritage. Society is suggesting that people who are obese, bisexual, or multiracial should change their behavior to conform to society's norms for the most valued members of society. Rarely does society contemplate its own role in making these people's lives difficult and unvalued. What needs to change is the attitude of the viewer rather than the actions of the person being viewed.

Irrespective of whether a particular individual's obesity has a genetic component, voluntariness should not be relevant to statutory coverage. As bisexuals, who have the capacity to experience sexual relations with people of either gender, should be able to choose partners of either gender, individuals, who have the capacity to be thin or obese, should be able to choose to be obese. Being obese and being bisexual stand in opposition to the cultural norms for heterosexuality and physical appearance. (In fact, these cultural norms are interrelated as we have higher standards for women's physical appearance than men's.) The ADA and Title VII should challenge the imposition of those cultural norms in the workplace when they conflict with an individual's qualifications to perform a job. Voluntariness should not be an excuse to coerce "choices" of sexuality or physical appearance. Although being obese may correlate with certain adverse health conditions, we allow cigarette manufacturers to display billboards associating their products with sexual prowess. It is not fair to single out the obese for their purportedly unhealthy lifestyle while we look the other way regarding the far more serious threats to health caused by other lifestyle choices.

One of the most dramatic and coercive extensions of the "voluntariness" principle were the laws against interracial miscegenation. We sent "blacks" to prison who "chose" to date "whites" in violation of anti-miscegenation law. We criminalized behavior to compel socially acceptable sexual expression. It was not until the U.S. Supreme Court overturned such laws in the 1970s that we saw a dramatic rise in the number of interracial marriages and an increase in the number of births of multiracial children. Unfortunately, we have not overturned the voluntariness principle in the context of gender, sexual orientation, or disability discrimination. We still expect transsexuals to "choose" to express only their socially acceptable gender, for bisexuals to "choose" to be heterosexual, and for people to "choose" to diet to thinness. Senator Helms's bold statement that employers should be able to impose "moral qualifications" on individuals who are qualified to be employed still rules disability law.

II. Other Disability Hybrids

The bipolar legal category reflected in the label "obesity" is not unique to disability law. People who have suffered job losses due to poor vision,[44] allergies,[45] cross-eyedness,[46] bad backs,[47] and mental depression[48] have sometimes fallen on the "able-bodied" side of the bipolar divide and thereby been deprived of any recovery under the ADA. Similar problems exist under the Individuals with Disabilities Education Act,[49] a broad-based statute for children with disabilities who have special educational needs. Like the ADA, the IDEA is based on a bipolar model—disabled children are entitled to certain benefits and nondisabled children are not.

A. Alcoholism

Like obesity, alcoholism eludes definition. Drinking alcohol is legal in the United States, and most adults partake of alcohol during their lives. The United States ranks fifteenth in the world in annual consumption of alcohol with each person drinking the equivalent of 5.3 gallons of 80-proof liquor.[50] "Alcoholism" is usually considered to be the "abuse" of alcohol although there is not one accepted definition of how much is too much.[51]

People who seek treatment for "alcoholism" and companies that try to exclude "alcoholics" from employment sometimes apply clumsy rules that do not always reach people with serious alcohol abuse problems. For example, after the Exxon Valdez incident, Exxon Shipping Company adopted a new policy "barring any employee who had ever participated in an alcohol rehabilitation program from holding designated jobs within the company."[52] Theodore Ellenwood, a chief engineer of an oil tanker, was removed from his position pursuant to this policy because he had participated in a month-long alcohol rehabilitation program a year before the Valdez incident. Ellenwood had never had an on-the-job problem with alcohol and a psychiatrist testified that Ellenwood had never been an alcoholic.[53] Because Exxon was operating under the misconception that it could best protect its workplace by excluding the static category of "alcoholics," it both reached too broadly and not broadly enough. It reached Ellenwood, who was seeking treatment before his use of alcohol became problematic, and did not reach other employees who had an alcohol problem for which they were not seeking treatment. Had Exxon created a policy based on alcohol *abuse* rather than the label of alcoholism, it would have better protected the public from alcohol-related problems.

Alcoholics are generally considered to be poor employees. When their alcoholism affects their job performance, employers are particularly reluctant to accommodate them, as they might other disabled employees. The stereotypes and prejudices about alcoholics have been reflected in the federal anti-discrimination laws. Section 504 of the Rehabilitation Act of 1973, the precursor of the ADA, initially provided protection for alcoholics alongside other people with disabilities in programs that received federal financial assistance. So long as they were "otherwise qualified" to perform their job, they could not be subjected to job discrimination. Moreover, like other potential employees, they deserved "reasonable accommodations" to assist them in being otherwise qualified.

When the federal government issued regulations under the Rehabilitation Act in 1977, it took a somewhat more narrow view of the coverage for alcoholics than for other people with disabilities. The Attorney General stated that alcoholics were covered by the Rehabilitation Act, and could not be denied employment solely because of their status as alcoholics. On the other hand, the Attorney General stated that an alcoholic could be terminated if his alcoholism interfered with his ability to perform his job.[54]

Although the Attorney General had been trying to achieve a compromise principle, many people in Congress were unsatisfied. An amendment was added to the Rehabilitation Act in 1978 stating that a handicapped individual "does not include any individual who is an alcoholic ... whose current use of alcohol ... prevents such individual from performing the duties of the job in question or whose employment, by reason of such current alcohol ... abuse, would constitute a direct threat to property or the safety of others."[55] This rule was more restrictive than the one offered by the Attorney General because of its "direct threat" language. Alcoholics and drug abusers were singled out for the "direct threat" rule; other people with disabilities were not subjected to that requirement.

Part of the controversy surrounding the coverage of alcoholism was definitional—was alcoholism a disease or a behavioral disorder that an individual could control? Many medical experts classify alcoholism as a disease; others label it as a behavior disorder. Two authors summarize the views on causation: "excessive drinking . . . result[s] from a complex cluster of influences: cultural rules, parental and peer influences, easy availability of the abused substance, desire for a change in mood or feelings, ignorance, inadequacy of social skills, lack of satisfying alternatives, and perhaps to a minor degree some biological predisposition."[56] The federal government took the behavioral view which was upheld by the U.S. Supreme Court. The Veterans Administration denied recovered alcoholics an extended period to utilize veterans' benefits, because their failure to use benefits in a timely fashion was considered to be "willful misconduct." Recovered alcoholics argued that this rule violated the Rehabilitation Act because alcoholics could not receive extensions that were routinely awarded to other people with disabilities. Finding that benefits were denied as a result of "willful alcohol abuse" rather than "solely" because of alcoholism, the Supreme Court upheld the regulation as consistent with section 504.[57] Despite section 504's coverage of alcoholism, it was appropriate to discriminate against people because of their alcohol-related conduct. Had the plaintiffs been individuals with other kinds of disabilities, the Veterans Administration would have had to provide a reasonable accommodation, such as a time extension. The Supreme Court was moving in the direction of erasing the reasonable accommodation requirement for alcoholics.

Lower courts, however, have not always interpreted section 504 to conform to the behavioral theory. The case that best reflects this rejection is *Teahan v. Metro-North Commuter Railroad Company*.[58] John Teahan was employed as a telephone and telegraph maintainer for five years during which he was unexcusably absent from work on many occasions. When his employer began to reprimand and suspend him for his excessive absences, he informed his employer of his substance abuse problem and entered a substance abuse rehabilitation program before receiving his final notice of discharge. The substance abuse program was successful and Teahan was not absent from work for the four months preceding his discharge. The district court granted summary judgment for the defendant concluding that Teahan was fired on the basis of his *conduct* not his alcoholism. The Second Circuit reversed, concluding that Teahan was covered by the Rehabilitation Act, because he was not a current user of alcohol at the time of his discharge. The court stated that he should prevail under section 504 so long as his absenteeism was caused by his alcoholism.[59] On remand, the trial court reinstated its judgment, now under the theory that Teahan was not otherwise qualified because of the likelihood of a recurrence of his alcoholism.[60]

The Second Circuit decision in *Teahan* is unlikely to be repeated under the Americans with Disabilities Act. The ADA contains the same language as section 504 regarding the exclusion of current alcoholics from coverage but then, even for the former alcoholic who is covered by the statute, the ADA provides a rigid standard: An employer "may hold an employee who . . . is an alcoholic to the same qualification standards for employment or job performance and behavior to which the entity holds its other employees, even if any unsatisfactory performance or behavior is related to the employee's drug use or alcoholism."[61] Under this rule, Metro-North would not be required to accommodate Teahan's absenteeism. Even if absenteeism or other problems are not tolerated for alcoholics but are tolerated for other employees, there is no violation of the ADA. In other words, recovered alcoholics (who are usually invisible) are covered by the ADA if they are not hired or discharged simply based on stereotypes about their condition. "Practicing" alcoholics can be treated more harshly than other employees so long as their behavior is being affected by current use of alcohol. The law's construction of a hybrid category, the "recovered alcoholic" is for the purpose of having a reference point so that "real alcoholics" can be openly maligned.

Part of the difficulty with the zero tolerance level for alcohol use that is embedded in the ADA is that it is inconsistent with developing theories regarding treatment for alcoholism. The current trend in treatment is moderation rather than abstinence. Under moderation theory, an alcoholic strives to develop a healthy and controlled relationship to alcohol. He or she strives to become what is called a "successful drinker."[62] As the proponents of the moderation philosophy acknowledge, some long-term alcohol abusers can only cure their drinking problems with total abstinence. Rejecting a bipolar approach to alcoholism, however, they note: "But our studies also show that not all serious abusers are alike. Remember, we measure abuse as a matter of degree and not as an after-the-fact, all-or-none, alcoholic vs. nonalcoholic determination."[63] The ADA, however, allows an employer to distinguish between employees through a bipolar distinction between alcoholics and nonalcoholics, imposing a zero tolerance level exclusively on the recovering alcoholic. It may therefore force upon the recovering alcoholic an inappropriate treatment program as a condition of maintaining employment.

B. *The IDEA Bipolar Model*

Another statute with a rigid bipolar disability model is the Individuals with Disabilities Education Act. A child who quali-

fies as "retarded" under the IDEA gets special educational benefits whereas another child, who might have a below normal I.Q.
but is not technically "retarded," gets no benefits at all. Further,
children have to suffer the stigma of being classified as "disabled" to receive special benefits.[64] The IDEA recognizes the
stigma associated with the classification of "disabled" which is
why there is special attention to how classifications can be made
inappropriately due to racial or ethnic bias. Similarly, the IDEA
supports an integrated education where feasible, in part to
lessen the stigma associated with separate education. On the
other hand, the IDEA forces a parent or guardian to seek to
have his or her child categorized as "disabled" to receive special services.

This bipolar model seems unnecessary in light of the individualized model underlying the IDEA. The IDEA uses individualized determinations to create appropriate educational programs
so that a child need not be classified as "disabled" to argue for
special services. One could, for example, say that all children
who have special disability-related needs should be able to seek
individualized services. A child may not be disabled with respect
to his intellect but may be disabled with respect to his vision.
His or her vision might not be so poor as to render the child
"visually impaired" or "blind." Nonetheless, the child might
benefit from some individualized attention to his or her vision
ranging from a seat near the front of the classroom to special
equipment for certain science exercises. Aside from cost, there
is no reason not to make available to all students whatever
assistance they need in overcoming particularized disabilities
they may have, even if they do not fit the definition of a "child
with disabilities."

The larger problem this discussion raises is whether benefits
should be tied directly to whether one is "disabled." By em-

ploying the category "disabled" to determine who qualifies for legal protection, we promote stereotypes about the "disabled" that they inherently need special assistance. The issue should not be whether a person is "disabled" as that term is defined under the IDEA. Instead, the issue should be whether a person is not able to receive an appropriate education because of a disability. In other words, does the so-called disability actually disadvantage an individual? If the disability does not disadvantage an individual then an individualized analysis of special needs is not necessary; if a disability does disadvantage an individual, then an individualized analysis is necessary even if the person does not technically fit the definition of a child with a disability. We contribute to the stigma associated with disability by assuming that all children with disabilities have special educational needs, and that no child who is technically "able-bodied" has special educational needs related to a disability.

A more concrete example may illuminate this discussion.[65] Three children are in a science classroom. Child *A* is blind. Child *B* has strabismus (commonly known as "crossed eyes") which leaves her with vision that is correctable to "normal" although she does not have stereoscopic vision (the ability to use both eyes at the same time, thereby gaining "depth perception"). Child *C* does not have the use of his legs but is not otherwise disabled. Child *A* will not be able to read the class material or use a microscope without some kind of technological assistance. Child *B* will be able to read the course materials but will not be able to use a "stereoscopic" microscope to see objects in depth. Child *C* will be able to read all of the class material and use the microscope. Under the IDEA, children *A* and *C* are "disabled" and entitled to an individualized education plan; child *B* is not.

Of course, we may not be able to afford to solve all of *A, B,* and *C*'s problems of disadvantage related to disability. That, however, is not a new problem. The Supreme Court has ruled that the IDEA does not provide each child with the right to a "potential-maximizing education." [66] Instead, it provides each child with the right to "specialized instruction and related services which are individually designed to provide educational benefit to the handicapped child." [67] The Supreme Court made this decision out of the recognition that "the educational opportunities provided by our public school system undoubtedly differ from student to student, depending upon a myriad of factors that might affect a particular student's ability to assimilate information presented in the classroom." [68] The solution, however, is to use individualized assessments rather than categories. The solution for children *A* and *B* for that particular assignment in that science room may be costless—maybe they need to be paired with another student (like student *C*) who can use the stereoscopic microscope and could verbally describe what he or she is able to see. By contrast, if the only good solution for child *B* is a special, very expensive microscope, we may decide that the cost is not worth the modest gain in educational experience. Child *B* can attain educational benefit in that classroom without a special microscope for one assignment. By contrast, child *A* may need technological equipment so that she can read any of her course assignments. Because she can attain no educational benefit without such equipment, it should be provided to her. Finally, child *C* may come to school with a wheelchair and face no barrier problems in the classroom. Although he is disabled, he may have few or no special needs or costs and does not need a specialized educational plan for his substantive classes so long as the building is barrier-free. On the other hand, when we move out of the science classroom to the physical education classroom, the needs of children *A, B,* and *C* change enormously. Child *C* will then probably become a child with a disability-related disadvantage.

The lesson from these examples is that individualized assessments of disability-related disadvantage should determine our decisions about how to allocate resources to assist children, not whether children fit into certain bipolar categories. As people move from context to context, they take their range of disabilities and abilities with them; we can help remove the stigma associated with disability if we recognize the disability within each of us; and we can more effectively deal with disabilities if we assess them from the perspective of the disadvantages that they pose for us in our lives.[69]

III. Beyond Legal Hybrids

Although disabilities rights law, like the law of race, gender, and sexual orientation, suffers from the problem of being bipolar in orientation, it also offers individualized assessments within the category of "disabled." This area of the law can help us learn how to conduct respectful, individualized assessments in other areas of the law while being mindful of the administrative need to retain some group-based categories.

The ADA contains concepts such as: reasonable accommodation, undue hardship, direct threat, and otherwise qualified[70] which result in individualized determinations about people's qualifications and abilities as well as the resources of the defendant organization. To see how this individualized model works, an example may prove useful. Persons *F* and *G* are surgeons who are HIV positive. They would like to continue in their employment. An individualized inquiry may determine that Person *F* is at the early stages of infection, performs surgery that involves little potential contact with a patient's blood, and can safely avoid nearly all risk of harm to others through diligent use of the recommended barrier precautions. Person *G* is at the later stages of infection and has begun to experience some loss of stamina. Because her work requires her hands to be placed in a patient's body cavity with dim light and the use of sharp tools, it is impossible to prevent the risk of infection to others. On the other hand, Person *G* could safely practice other types of medicine such as routine check ups without risk to the patient. In such cases, the courts might conclude that Person *F* should be protected under the ADA at her current job and Person *G* should be accommodated by being moved to another safer position.[71] Although they both have HIV infection and perform similar jobs, the results are different under this highly individualized inquiry.

Such individualized assessments are foreign to Title VII jurisprudence. If Persons *F* and *G* had raised a gender discrimination case, and some credible arguments had been raised about their qualifications to perform surgery, no attention would have been given to whether they could have adequately performed *other* work. The lack of individualized assessments is even more obvious under our affirmative action jurisprudence. As we saw in the discussions concerning Maria O'Brien Hylton and Greg Williams, we either lump people into the category of racial "minority" so that affirmative action is appropriate or lump them into the category of "nonminority" so that affirmative action is inappropriate. The reasonable accommodation analysis under the ADA is much more context-specific. It would allow us to identify exactly how Hylton or Williams might bring special qualifications and abilities to their respective professions without applying such bipolar labeling.

The individualized treatment model, as reflected by the ADA, is not without its difficulties. Individualized inquiries are time-consuming and expensive. Often, group-based generalizations could avoid that expensive process. For example, in one recent ADA case, an individual was fired after he brought a gun to work.[72] Plaintiff argued that he was disabled because of a chemical imbalance and deserved reasonable accommodation in lieu of being discharged. Defendants moved for summary judgment on the assumption that no individualized inquiry could possibly lead a trier of fact to conclude that plaintiff was otherwise qualified. Following the individualized rules of the ADA, the trial court refused summary judgment. Not surprisingly, however, plaintiff ultimately lost on the merits.[73] The individualized inquiry became an expensive way to arrive at a foregone conclusion—that employers are entitled to fire people who bring guns to work. A categorical rule would have arrived at the same conclusion at much less cost.

The ADA is barely five years old. A statute with a longer history of employing the individualized model is the Individuals with Disabilities Education Act (IDEA). Despite the problems with its bipolar framework, the IDEA does offer an individualized structure that is unique to anti-discrimination law. Each disabled child[74] is guaranteed an individualized educational plan.[75] There is no automatic assessment that a child should receive an integrated, segregated, or at-home education.[76] The setting for the child's education and its structure are developed on an individualized basis.

In theory, this model is an improvement over Title VII, because it causes educational institutions to meet with parents, children, and professionals to develop an appropriate educational plan for each child with disabilities. There is no assumption that all children who are "retarded," for example, must be in a special classroom. Instead, each retarded child is evaluated to see exactly what kind of education is appropriate. One re-tarded child might be placed in a special classroom for children with substantial learning disabilities, another might be placed in a normal classroom with a special aide, and another might spend half-a-day in a special classroom and half-a-day in a normal classroom. Moreover, the plan for each of these children would vary from year to year depending upon how they prog-ress and what programs are available in their state or school district. This is quite a dramatic improvement from the days when such children monolithically received no education, or a segregated and quite inadequate one.

The procedure underlying the IDEA, however, is far from perfect. Poor children who have less access to legal advocacy get less individualized treatment. Because, by definition, the individuals who are entitled to assistance under the statute are children, who also have disabilities that require special services, advocacy typically happens by the parents of a child. Parents with middle-class professional training find it easier to advocate within such a structure.[77] Moreover, the process of using an administrative structure is very time-consuming. Working class people or unemployed individuals with family responsibilities find it difficult to take off from work or family obligations to attend numerous administrative hearings and meetings.[78] In cases where parents have challenged the adequacy of the public school's placement for a child, often the parents pay for their child's private education while the inadequacy of the public education is being resolved legally.[79] That is not an option available to poor parents.

The IDEA model raises the question of whether an individu-alized treatment model is inherently class-based. This question is particularly troublesome in the context of the IDEA because the statute attempts to be sensitive to racial and ethnic biases that may be part of disability law through special rules.[80] Such rules may help states avoid using racial stereotypes in defining who has disabilities. Unfortunately, it does little for the child who has been correctly characterized as having a disability. Once the classification occurs, the statute requires no special sensitivity to that child's needs due to the race, ethnic, or class bias of our educational or legal system.

A further question is whether there would be less class bias in a system with more formal, categorical rules and less individualized treatment. In other contexts, some scholars have suggested that formality benefits disadvantaged individuals because less discretion exists on the part of decisionmakers.[81] Nonetheless, that critique does not offer us an obvious solution. By limiting ourselves to a formal system, because of our fear of the racial or class biases of discretionary systems of justice, we take a very pessimistic perspective that we cannot possibly rid our justice system of its discretionary biases. If we truly believe that children with disabilities fare best through individualized determinations, our obligation as a society is to try to make available the resources that allow those determinations to be made in a fair fashion. The IDEA does try to minimize the arbitrariness of such discretion by providing extensive procedural safeguards and administrative steps. Those safeguards are consistent with the argument that "Formality and adversarial procedures thus counteract bias among legal decisionmakers and disputants."[82] Nonetheless, such additional procedures are costly and therefore are not equally available to all children with disabilities. Free legal services for all children with disabilities who come from poor families could make those procedures more widely available. Unfortunately, the IDEA does not provide for such services, although many cities have public interest organizations that try to fill that need.[83] Finally, it is difficult even to formulate an effective way to use legal advocacy because, as many parents recognize, it is important to have a good long-term relationship with a school district if one has a child with disabilities. Contentious litigation could undermine a child's long-term interests, even if the litigation is successful.[84] Thus, it takes a very sophisticated parent and lawyer to advocate effectively on behalf of a child.

In sum, the disability model raises problems that we have seen before. Its bipolar framework operates clumsily in terms of maximizing our use of educational resources to assist children with disabilities. On the other hand, the disability model under the ADA and the IDEA can provide us with fresh ideas about how to incorporate more individualized consideration into race and gender anti-discrimination law. We do not need to make the mistake of replacing a group-based model entirely with an individualized model. The formal protections offered by a group-based model are important, but we should strive to find the resources to permit more individualized inquiries so that our scarce resources, especially in the affirmative action context, can be used most wisely.

Bipolar Injustice:
The Moral Code

·············

Dr. Jean Jew, an Asian-American woman, is a tenured professor at the University of Iowa College of Medicine.[1] In the 1980s, she was subjected to a relentless campaign of racial and sexual slurs because of her purported relationship with her supervisor, Dr. Terence Williams. Jew was referred to as a "slut," "bitch," "whore," and "chink," and "lesbian"[2] and denied promotion to full professor. Williams was forced to step down as Department Chair. Jew brought a Title VII[3] claim alleging sexual harassment and gender discrimination stemming from the denial of promotion. After a decade of litigation, she prevailed on the merits in a federal district court and obtained a favorable settlement from the University.[4]

J. Mario Carreno, a white man, was a licensed journeyman electrician.[5] He was subjected to derogatory comments such as "Mary" and "faggot,"[6] and was physically harassed by having his genitals and buttocks caressed as well as by having people simulate sexual intercourse or sodomy with him.[7] He brought suit in federal court under Title VII alleging sexual harassment and a gender-based constructive discharge. He lost.

After Sylvia DeAngelis, a white woman, became the first female sergeant on the El Paso Police Department, monthly columns in the association newsletter called her a dingbat and persistently stated that all women police officers were inherently incompetent.[8] These comments were then repeated by some of her male subordinates. She brought suit in federal court under Title VII alleging sexual harassment. She lost.

Allan Bakke, a white man, was not admitted at two dozen medical schools including the University of California at Davis.[9] Because of his race, Bakke was not eligible to compete for sixteen slots at Davis Medical School that were reserved for disadvantaged racial minorities and because of his socioeconomic status, he was not eligible to compete for five slots reserved for applicants from wealthy families.[10] Bakke had also been informed at Davis and elsewhere that his age (33) was a negative factor in his application. He brought suit in state court under Title VI of the Civil Rights act of 1964[11] and the equal protection clause of the United States Constitution[12] alleging race discrimination stemming from his failure to be admitted. He won.[13]

Melvin Hicks, an African-American shift commander, was suspended, reprimanded, and eventually discharged for rules infractions for which similarly situated whites were not even reprimanded.[14] These actions occurred after a report was authored recommending that blacks be demoted or discharged from supervisory positions to avoid racial tension within the prison system where he worked. He sued in federal court under Title VII alleging race discrimination stemming from his discharge. He lost.

These five cases reflect the moral code underlying federal anti-discrimination law. Women who are presumed to be heterosexual, such as Jean Jew, frequently prevail if they can show that they have been sexualized; merely showing gender-based conduct, such as in the case of Sylvia DeAngelis, is usually not sufficient. Men who are presumed to be homosexual,[15] such as Mario Carreno, rarely prevail upon a showing that they have been sexualized even if it is clear that the conduct is also gender-based. Whites who are presumed to be competent, such as Allan Bakke, frequently prevail upon a showing that race was a factor in an adverse decision. Blacks who are presumed to be incompetent, such as Melvin Hicks, rarely prevail upon a showing that race was a factor unless they can also present evidence of racial slurs or epithets. In other words, there is not one justice for all. Justice often depends upon plaintiff's race, gender, and sexual orientation.

The general outlines of Title VII's moral code are well known. Transsexuals,[16] cross-dressers,[17] and gay and lesbian people[18] are rarely successful in gender discrimination cases under Title VII. The role that sexual harassment doctrine plays in preserving this moral code, however, is usually not noticed, and the racial implications of this code are invisible.

I. Winner No. I: Presumptively Heterosexual Women

Barbara Stacks's employer had "closed parties" in which men were instructed not to bring their wives so that male representatives could bring their "dates" who were referred to as "road whores."[19] A party videotape showed two managers sitting in the front seat of an automobile with two female sales representatives in the back seat. After the men chanted, "Show us your tits," the women lifted their blouses and exposed their breasts.[20] The manager told another woman that she looked liked a "madam" and would not be promoted unless she had breast reduction surgery.[21] Ultimately, Stacks was fired for reasons that she alleged were pretextual.

The federal district court ruled against Stacks, concluding that she was not harassed because of her sex. The court believed that her supervisor was "unpleasant toward everybody."[22] As to her discharge claim, the trial court noted that Stacks was a "crackerjack salesperson" but nonetheless found for the defendant.[23] On appeal, the Eighth Circuit reversed.[24] Crediting Stacks's testimony that the harassment made her feel "less than human," the court found that the district court had erred and should enter judgment in favor of Stacks.[25] Being unpleasant toward everyone was not a proper defense when highly sexualized comments were made to a woman.

Other courts have agreed with the Eighth Circuit in *Stacks* that sexualized comments and behavior directed toward women constitute sexual harassment even if men are also exposed to sexual banter or insulting comments. For example, in *Faragher v. City of Boca Raton*,[26] the district court found for plaintiffs in a case involving harassment against female lifeguards. Male supervisors touched female lifeguards on their buttocks and breast without consent, used offensive language such as "cunts" and "bitches," mimicked cunnilingus in the presence of some of the women, and made repeated sexually suggestive comments.[27] Defendants unsuccessfully tried to excuse the behavior by noting the commonplace sexual banter and boisterousness at the pool. The court found that defense unavailing due to the "lack of respect" toward the female lifeguards evidenced by the men's conduct.[28] The highly sexualized nature of the comments allowed the women to prove gender discrimination even though the men were also the targets of sexual comments.

In other cases, defendants have tried to avoid liability by claiming that the supervisor was bisexual and therefore did not prey upon plaintiff *because of her sex.* In *Ryczek v. Guest Services, Inc.,*[29] Francine Ryczek alleged that defendant Catherine O'Brien sexually harassed her by telling plaintiff about her sexual preference for females, inquiring about plaintiff's sexual practices, dipping plaintiff's finger into a pot of sauce and licking the finger, looking at plaintiff suggestively and leaning against her, and removing her shirt when she was riding with plaintiff in an elevator. Defendant Guest Services defended the lawsuit by arguing that the actions were not gender-based, relying on precedent from the D.C. Circuit concerning bisexual supervisors, because O'Brien was a bisexual not a lesbian.[30] The court did not rule on this issue but noted the problems that argument raised in Title VII litigation:

This would be an anomalous result: a victim of sexual harassment in the District of Columbia would have a Title VII remedy in all situations except those in which the victim is harassed by a particularly unspeakable cad who harassed both men and women. In addition to this troubling possibility, the prospect of having litigants debate and juries determine the sexual orientation of Title VII defendants is a rather unpleasant one.[31]

Rather than engage in such an inquiry in the case before it, the court ruled against plaintiff on other grounds.[32]

The court did, however, pause to consider how to get around the bisexual supervisor defense problem. The court commented that it could simply "interpret the statute to cover sexual harassment by any individual, regardless of gender. This last interpretation would appear to require the court to interpret the word 'sex' as used in Title VII to mean something more than gender."[33]

In contending with the bisexual supervisor defense, the court did not really understand how that defense fits into Title VII doctrine generally. The word "sex" in Title VII already means something more than gender; it means *sexualized* harassment against heterosexual women. That is why women have been able to prevail in the "he's mean to everyone defense." If a woman is treated sexually, it does not seem to matter if men are also treated derogatorily. Thus, Jean Jew, an unmarried woman, prevailed in her case against the University of Iowa because she was repeatedly referred to as a "slut" for allegedly having an affair with her married supervisor. The court acknowledged that the sexual relationship rumors also implicated her male supervisor.[34] Under pressure to resign, Williams, in fact, stepped down as head of the department shortly before Jew's promotion case was considered.[35]

The court found that Jew had been subjected to unlawful gender-based sexual harassment because: "Were Dr. Jew not a woman, it would not likely have been rumored that Dr. Jew gained favor with the Department Head by a sexual relationship with him."[36] That response, however, does not respond to the argument that Jew (a woman) and Williams (a man) were both maligned by the rumors of a sexual relationship. It only tells us that Williams was considered to be a heterosexual and Jew was considered to be a heterosexual. Had their sexual orientations been different, such allegations would have been unlikely. Thus, there was no direct evidence that Jew's *gender* caused the rumors although the rumors did seem dependent on her and Williams's perceived sexual orientation.

Another factor which caused the court to be persuaded that Jew was a victim of gender-based harassment was that the two men in the department who were friends with Williams did not have their sexual habits or professional competency questioned.[37] One of them, in fact, was the subject of a graffiti incident which the court considered to be an isolated incident.[38] But, unlike Jew, the two male co-workers did not suffer adverse assessments of their professional competency due to their relationship with Williams. The two male co-workers, however, did not come up for promotion during this time period so that one could determine whether a man's association with Williams would have had the same detrimental effect. The court presumed that there would have been a difference in treatment without such evidence. The evidence that Jew was sexualized and the men were rarely sexualized was sufficient evidence for the court to support that presumption.

Because of the weight attached to sexualized evidence in harassment cases involving female plaintiffs, reaching bisexual supervisors who harass women would require no great modification to existing Title VII doctrine. A Wyoming district court has agreed that Title VII can reach an "equal opportunity harasser," finding liability when a supervisor verbally harassed members of both genders.[39] In a rather remarkable case under Title VII, two men and two women alleged that their supervisor subjected them to gender-based sexual harassment. Dale and Carla Chiapuzio alleged that they were sexually harassed by supervisor, Eddie Bell, whose incessant, sexually abusive remarks usually referred to the fact that Bell could do a better job of making love to Carla than Dale could.[40] Clint Bean alleged sexual harassment because Bell subjected him and his wife, who was not an employee, to sexually abusive remarks. On one occasion, Bell offered Bean's wife $100 if she would sit on his lap.[41] Christina Vironet alleged sexual harassment because Bell subjected her to an incessant series of sexual advances, particularly when she was pregnant.[42]

Despite the fact that Bell was an "equal-opportunity" harasser,[43] the court found in favor of the male and female plaintiffs. The court reached this conclusion because it concluded that each of the plaintiffs were harassed because of their gender.

Bell intended his remarks to demean the men as men by insulting their sexual prowess, and to demean the women as women by viewing them as sex objects. Through such logic, the court reached harassment of a man by another man. The court, however, drew the line at homosexual advances, observing "Bell never harassed male employees concerning sexual acts he desired to perform with them." [44]

The court's reasoning draws an illogical distinction between sexual orientation and gender. Bell's comments to the men and women did not solely relate to their gender; they also related to their sexual orientation. To the men, Bell was saying, "I am a better heterosexual than you are because I could give your wife more sexual pleasure." To the women, Bell was saying, "I am a better heterosexual than your husband because I could give you more sexual pleasure." The comments reflected Bell's sexual orientation and were intended as insults to the sexual prowess of the men. It is also true that sexual prowess insults are considered to be gender-based insults in our society. But it is wrong to say that Bell's comments were solely based on gender. The same analysis would apply if Bell had accused the men of being gay or had made sexual advances toward them. In both cases, his comments would have been based on his perception of their sexual orientation and might have insulted their integrity as men.

The court had no difficulty in concluding that Bell's comments toward the women was based on their gender rather than sexual orientation. But why should it be *gender* discrimination to make sexual advances toward women but not be gender discrimination to make sexual advances toward men? If sexual advances are gender-based because they are intended to demean and objectify the victim, then it should be irrelevant whether the source of the attraction is heterosexuality or homosexuality.

The *Chiapuzio* decision reflects one of the most awkward constructions of Title VII to preserve heterosexual chastity. Given Bell's character, it takes little imagination to speculate about the kinds of comments he would have made to an openly gay man or lesbian at the workplace. Undoubtedly, he would have found a way to insult their sexual practices with comments such as pussy and faggot to the men and comments about the lesbians just needing a "good lay." Such comments would have been demeaning and loaded with gender stereotypes, yet the *Chiapuzio* court would have been unwilling to reach them even within the scope of its "equal opportunity" harasser doctrine. In the future, supervisors who wish to demean the sexual practices of their employees should confine their hiring to gay men and lesbians!

Evidence of sexualized comments directed toward women, however, is no guarantee of quick or easy success under Title VII. Barbara Stacks's harassment had begun in 1986. She initially lost in the trial court and did not obtain a favorable judgment from the court of appeals until 1994. Similarly, Jean Jew endured a decade of harassment before obtaining a favorable judgment in the federal district court. Even so, her fate was uncertain until a massive public relations campaign was mounted to dissuade the University from pursuing its appeal of the decision.[45] Thus, on the hierarchy of successful lawsuits, cases involving presumptively heterosexual women who have faced highly sexualized comments may be the most promising but even those cases can be difficult to win.

The cases involving female and even male heterosexual plaintiffs, therefore, reveal that the word "sex" already means far more than gender under Title VII. Sex discrimination can be proven with evidence of sexualized harassment even when there is not strong evidence of gender-based discrimination. But, as we shall see further, this generalization does not usually apply to cases involving homosexual remarks and advances.

II. Loser No. 1: Presumptively Gay Men

Ernest Dillon was an employee of the U.S. Postal Service. He was routinely called a "fag" at work, and told that he "sucks dicks." [46] He was subjected to repeated graffiti with statements such as "Dillon gives head." [47] He was physically assaulted at work, and received numerous injuries. After three years of enduring this treatment, he resigned upon advice from his psychiatrist and sued in federal court under Title VII for sexual harassment.

Mario Carreno had "his genitals and buttocks caressed," was "grabbed or held from behind while simulated sexual intercourse or sodomy was performed on him by virtue of pelvic thrusts by other employees," and was exposed to "constant, explicit, vulgar and derogatory comments regarding sexual acts at his employment." [48] Carreno sued in federal court under Title VII for sexual harassment. Other men have filed similar claims of sexual harassment based on incidents involving sexual touching. [49]

These men did not prevail under sexual harassment doctrine because the courts concluded that their conduct was based on sexual orientation rather than gender. [50] (The courts presumed they were gay men although they do not appear to have made such concessions at trial.) In each case, they were targeted for sexualized comments and actions that were not directed at women at the workplace. No one seemed concerned if women "sucked dick" or were effeminate. As men, however, those traits were unacceptable. These were not cases like *Stacks* or *Faragher,* where the employer could offer the defense that they mistreated everyone. But, like *Stacks* and *Faragher*, they were cases where the comments clearly offended their dignity as persons.

The only defense in these cases was that the comments were homophobic rather than sexist. The line between homophobia and sexism, however, is invisible because homophobia frequently relies on sexual stereotyping about gender roles. Women who are perceived to be heterosexual frequently prevail under Title VII for what is called a "sexual stereotyping" theory even when the sexual stereotyping includes allusions about their sexual orientation. In the landmark 1989 Supreme Court case establishing this doctrine, Ann Hopkins prevailed by showing that she was sexually stereotyped as being too "macho," and for being told that she should "wear make-up and go to a charm school." [51] She did not fit the proper gender roles for women, including that of heterosexuality. As Professor Elvia Arriola has argued, mainstream society views " 'gayness' [as] about crossing the strict sexual boundaries between men and women." [52] Although Hopkins does not appear to have ever been explicitly accused of being a lesbian, other women who are considered to be heterosexual, such as Jean Jew, have faced such accusations. [53] It is rather peculiar for Title VII to protect women who are presumed to be heterosexual against sexual stereotyping when they are accused of being "macho" or "lesbian" but not to protect men, who are presumed to be homosexual, against sexual stereotyping when they are called epithets such as "Mary" and "fag." Dillon's and Carreno's perceived homosexuality was unacceptable, in part, because it did not fit the proper gender roles specified by society.

Courts have suggested that one would have to add the phrase "sexual orientation" to Title VII to reach cases like Dillon's and Carreno's. [54] In fact, it is the courts who have added the word "heterosexual" to Title VII already. The existing case law reads: A man can recover for being stereotyped as a "fag" and a woman can recover for being stereotyped as "macho" or "lesbian" *if* they are considered to be heterosexual. If Title VII would protect against gender discrimination for *all employees* then all employees, irrespective of their sexual orientation, would be able to complain against gender stereotyping epithets such as fag (for men) and macho (for women).

It would oversimplify the *Dillon* and *Carreno* cases, however, to conclude that men and women never can prevail under Title VII when there is harassment involving a perceived homosexual. When the *harasser* is a gay man or lesbian, and the person being harassed is considered to be heterosexual, the courts often find that Title VII covers such conduct.[55] For example, Robin McCoy, a female, prevailed under Title VII because her female supervisor allegedly rubbed McCoy's breasts, rubbed between McCoy's legs, and forced her tongue into McCoy's mouth while also calling McCoy "stupid poor white trash" and "stupid poor white bitch."[56] The sexual taunts and physical assaults to which McCoy was subjected were comparable to those faced by Dillon and Carreno. Unlike Dillon and Carreno, however, McCoy was considered to be heterosexual, so a ruling in her favor protected a plaintiff's heterosexual chastity while penalizing a purportedly lesbian supervisor.

The problem with this trend in this case law is that it requires a court to evaluate whether the plaintiff is a heterosexual or homosexual—a problem similar to the one noted by the *Ryczek* court in the context of the bisexual supervisor defense. This evaluation seems to particularly harm male plaintiffs who are often presumed to be homosexual when they are the subject of explicit sexual advances; women, by contrast, are often presumed to be heterosexual in such contexts. Thus, the courts have developed a distinction between sexual orientation and gender that they claim is based on Title VII's coverage of sexism but not homophobia. The application of this principle, however, reflects the courts' own prejudices and stereotypes about who is homosexual rather than any consistent principles.

III. Loser No. 2: Nonsexualized Women

Teresa Harris worked as a manager of Forklift Systems.[57] Charles Hardy was the President of the company and her supervisor. Her employment began in April 1985. The following kinds of comments were made until mid-August 1987:

> "You're a woman, what do you know?"
> "We need a man as the rental manager."
> She was a "dumb ass woman."
> He suggested in front of other employees that the two of them "go to the Holiday Inn to negotiate [her] raise."
> He asked Harris and other female employees to get coins from his front pants pocket.
> He threw objects on the ground in front of Harris and other women, and asked them to pick the objects up.
> He made sexual innuendos about Harris's and other women's clothing.[58]

In mid-August 1987, Harris complained to Hardy about his conduct. He said he was surprised that Harris was offended, claimed he was only joking, and apologized. Nonetheless, in early September, while Harris was arranging a deal with one of Forklift's customers, he said to Harris in front of other employees: "What did you do, promise the guy . . . some [sex] Saturday night?"[59] Harris soon quit, and filed a lawsuit for sexual harassment and constructive discharge.

After a hearing in the U.S. Supreme Court to clarify the

standards in a sexual harassment case,[60] the Magistrate found on remand that the "workplace did not become permeated with abusive conduct that rose to the level of a Title VII violation until the middle of August 1987, when the sexual comments became explicitly unwelcome."[61] The district court affirmed these findings[62] and no further appeal ensued. These findings are problematic because they rely entirely on the unwelcome *sexual* comments made to Harris, overlooking the derogatory gender-based comments that were also made. At least two of the comments related to the purported lack of intelligence of Harris as a woman. One comment suggested that all women are stupid; another comment suggested that Hardy, as a woman, was stupid. Such comments should have been per se gender-based (although nonsexualized) harassment.

Teresa Harris was not alone in having the courts ignore the nonsexualized aspects of her complaint. She ultimately prevailed for a portion of the harassment she faced,[63] because her complaint also contained sexualized elements. Women with purely gender-based cases (without a sexual element) have not been so fortunate. The most recent example of this trend is a 1995 Fifth Circuit decision, *DeAngelis v. El Paso Municipal Police Officers Association.*[64]

Sylvia DeAngelis was the first female promoted to sergeant on the police force. Within a few months of being promoted, she was subjected to repeated ridicule in the newsletter of the El Paso Municipal Police Officers Association.[65] The newsletter reached seven hundred police officer members each month. Most of the comments referred to women in general, dismissing them as incompetent with comments like "physically, the police broads just don't got it!", while a couple of the comments referred to plaintiff personally with statements that she was a "dingy woman."[66] The repeated theme of the comments was that women were not suited to be police officers, but none of the comments were sexual in nature. In a jury trial in federal district court, DeAngelis was awarded $10,000 in compensatory damages and $50,000 in punitive damages.[67]

On appeal, the Fifth Circuit reversed.[68] The three-judge panel unanimously concluded that the "column did not represent a boss's demeaning harangue, or a sexually charged invitation, or a campaign of vulgarity perpetrated by co-workers: the column attempted clumsy, earthy humor."[69] The Fifth Circuit's opinion was influenced by its desire to avoid First Amendment problems in concluding that an Association's newsletter could not invoke Title VII liability for sexual harassment. But, even there, the Court was dependent on a sexualized/nonsexualized dichotomy. In a footnote, the Court commented: "We do not mean that sexual propositions, quid pro quo overtures, discriminatory employment actions against women or 'fighting words' involve the First Amendment."[70] In other words, had the columnist called women "bitches" or "cunts" instead of incompetent, plaintiff could probably have prevailed without First Amendment problems.

To DeAngelis and Harris, however, being called incompetent may have been far more damaging than being called sexy or a whore. DeAngelis testified that the comments undermined her credibility at work. On two specific occasions following the publication of the first article (which maligned her personally), junior officers behaved insubordinately to her.[71] Further, these columns so undermined her self-confidence that she was reluctant to apply for a promotion to lieutenant. Being repeatedly labeled incompetent harmed her dignity in ways that are similar to the cases involving sexualized comments but the court of appeals discounted that testimony, in part, because "no physical or sexual advances were made on DeAngelis."[72] The word "sex" in Title VII was interpreted not to include nonsexualized, gender discrimination.

Fortunately, not every federal court has followed the trend typified by *DeAngelis* and *Harris*. In a 1987 decision by the Eighth Circuit, the court held that: "Intimidation and hostility toward women because they are women can obviously result from conduct other than explicit sexual advances."[73] Accordingly, it upheld the trial court judgment for the plaintiff in a case involving harassment both of a sexualized and nonsexualized nature.[74] Unfortunately, the Eighth Circuit's decision does not seem to reflect the more recent trends under Title VII where women in purely nonsexualized harassment cases have failed to prevail.[75] And, as we will see in Part VI, the Equal Employment Opportunity Commission has been unable to codify the Eighth Circuit holding.

IV. Loser No. 3: African-Americans

Melvin Hicks began working as a correctional officer at a half-way house, St. Mary's Honor Center, in August 1978.[76] In less than two years, he was promoted to shift commander although, unknown to Hicks at the time, a report was soon authored for the Department of Corrections recommending that blacks be demoted or discharged from supervisory positions to avoid racial tension within the prison system.[77] Until 1984, when Steve Long, a white man, became superintendent, and John Powell, a white man, became chief of custody, Hicks had a perfect work record with no suspensions or reprimands.[78] Shortly after Long and Powell took their positions, Hicks was targeted for reprimands and suspensions, and ultimately was discharged.

Hicks was treated harshly for minor rules infractions. During one incident, Hicks ordered a correctional officer to use a St. Mary's vehicle but failed to enter the vehicle's use into the log. Chief of Custody Powell recommended that Hicks be disciplined for failing to insure the vehicle was correctly logged-in; he was not recommended for discipline for authorizing the use of the vehicle. A four-person disciplinary board voted to demote Hicks as a result of that incident; Powell, who was a member of that board, voted to terminate Hicks for that infraction.[79]

When white shift commanders committed far more serious infractions of the rules, they received much more lenient treatment. For example, after Michael Doss, a white man, who was the acting shift commander, negligently allowed a prisoner to escape, he received only a letter of reprimand as discipline. Similarly, after Sharon Hefele, a white woman who was a shift commander, failed to lock certain doors to the main power room and annex building, she received no reprimand whatsoever.[80] Moreover, Powell, who had recommended Hicks's termination for the log-in error, *praised* a white transportation officer, Edward Ratliff, who had instructed an inmate in violation of prison rules to climb over a wall to obtain some keys from Superintendent Long's office.[81]

The second incident that demonstrated the disparate treatment of Hicks was the one that ultimately led to his termination. On April 19, 1984 (only three months after the personnel changes were made), Hicks was notified of his demotion at a meeting with Powell and Long, as well as Vincent Banks, the only remaining black supervisor. Hicks was upset by the news and requested the rest of the day off. Long granted the request. Nonetheless, Powell followed Hicks to his open locker to obtain his shift commander's manual. In the court's words:

Plaintiff refused, and the two exchanged heated words. Plaintiff indicated he would "step outside" with Powell, and Powell warned plaintiff that his words could be perceived as a threat. After several tense minutes, plaintiff left.[82]

Powell immediately sought disciplinary action against Hicks for these "threats." A disciplinary board met and voted to suspend Hicks for three days. Steve Long, however, disregarded their vote and recommended termination. One month later, Hicks was terminated.[83]

When a parallel incident regarding a white man occurred, Powell recommended that no disciplinary action be taken. Arthur Turney, a white man who was under Hicks's supervisory authority, "became indignant and cursed plaintiff with highly profane language"[84] after attending a meeting with Hicks to receive the results of his employment evaluation. In the court's words: "Powell concluded that Turney was merely venting justifiable frustration, and did not discipline Turney for the incident."[85] Thus, when a white man cursed a black male supervisor, no disciplinary action was taken. But, when a black man exchanged "heated words" with a white male supervisor, he was terminated despite an internal recommendation that he only be suspended.

The atmosphere at St. Mary's Honor Center was therefore charged with harassment against black male supervisors. Black male supervisors were demoted and fired, and replaced with whites. Hicks was subjected to demotion and discharge for misconduct that was less serious than conduct for which whites received no discipline or merely a reprimand. Hicks's authority was undermined in every way possible once Powell and Long became supervisors. His attempts to reprimand others and retain his authority were not validated by management. Instead, management seemed to try to build a file as quickly as possible that would lead to his termination. As early as the relatively minor log-in incident, Powell was recommending Hicks's discharge. The ultimate discharge occurred only because Long imposed a harsher penalty than was recommended by the disciplinary board.

To justify its conclusion that Hicks was not treated differently because of his race, the district court emphasized that two of the four persons on the disciplinary board consistently were black. One of those individuals was presumably Banks, the only remaining black supervisor after Hicks's discharge. Because there were no other black supervisors at St. Mary's, the other black member must have been a nonsupervisor. One of the two white members was apparently Powell; Long had the responsibility for making the final recommendation to the Department of Corrections.

The idea that the presence of two blacks, one of whom was a nonsupervisor, on the disciplinary board should insulate St. Mary's from a racial discrimination claim is contrary to core principles underlying Title VII and also distorts the facts underlying the case. It is clear that both Powell and Long, who were white men, treated Hicks more harshly than they treated whites. Long had the ultimate authority, which he exercised, to recommend to the Director of the Missouri Department of Corrections and Human Resources that Hicks be terminated. That decision did not result from the recommendation of the racially balanced board. Powell was always one-fourth of the votes on the disciplinary board, and consistently used that authority to seek the harshest possible penalty for Hicks. The two blacks on the board at the time of the log-in incident voted *inconsistently* with Powell, and thereby achieved the result that Hicks was demoted rather than terminated.[86] Blacks, of course, can help perpetuate racism especially in a situation like the one at St.

Mary's where they might be worried about losing their own jobs. But it is not fair to describe the trial court record as demonstrating that the black employees condoned the treatment of Hicks;[87] if anything, the record indicates that Powell and Long, white men, who had the cooperation of the Director of Corrections, engaged in a vendetta to systematically remove nearly all black supervisors.

Hicks's case was also strengthened by racially conscious documentary evidence. Unknown to Hicks at the time of his employment at St. Mary's, James Davis performed a study of the honor centers in St. Louis and Kansas City in 1980 and 1981 for the Missouri Department of Corrections. As the district court found, "In a section toward the end of the study Davis pointed out that too many blacks were in portions of power at St. Mary's, and that the potential for subversion of the superintendent's power, if the staff became racially polarized, was very real."[88]

Although the witnesses[89] at trial indicated that they were unaware of the Davis study in 1984,[90] dramatic personnel changes began occurring in 1984 that were consistent with the Davis study. The supervisory staff changed from being one white and five blacks to being four whites and two blacks. The black superintendent was demoted and transferred; his position was filled by a white. The black chief of custody was demoted and transferred; his position was filled by a white. The two black shift commanders other than Hicks were fired and replaced by whites. Hicks was formally retained, but was subjected to immediate and pervasive harassment. Although blacks were hired during this reorganization, none of them were hired for supervisory positions.[91] Until this time, Hicks had not been suspended, written up, or otherwise disciplined except for a mistaken reprimand for being absent when he, in fact, was on a

scheduled vacation.[92] His record was considered entirely satis-
factory.[93]

The court excused these dramatic race-based personnel
changes by noting that they were "not unusual" in light of the
problems at St. Mary's.[94] Implicitly, the court was ratifying the
Davis study's conclusion that one way to respond to racial
tension at the halfway house was to terminate black supervisors
and replace them with whites. Such reasoning, however, should
be unacceptable under Title VII's prohibition of race discrimination.

Ultimately, Hicks lost his case because the district court concluded that his discharge was the result of a personality dispute
rather than racism.[95] This holding was upheld by the Supreme
Court because it refined and tightened the burden of proof for
plaintiffs in race and gender discrimination cases. In the *Hicks*
case, the plaintiff had alleged that he was a black man who had
been fired for entirely pretextual reasons thereby raising a
strong inference of race discrimination. At trial, the defendants
had tried to explain their conduct by producing evidence that
Hicks was fired for merit-based reasons. That proof, however,
was unsuccessful, as Hicks was able to rebut the evidence with
the examples cited above concerning similarly situated whites
who were treated more favorably. One would therefore have
expected Hicks to prevail in his claim that a nonmerit-based
factor, such as racism, must explain his discharge. The trial
court and the Supreme Court, however, refused to presume that
racism motivated his discharge. Instead, the trial court came up
with an explanation for the discharge *that had not even been
offered by the defendants at trial*—that Hicks had been fired
due to a personality dispute rather than racism. Emphasizing
that a plaintiff in a race discrimination case always maintains
the burden of proving intentional discrimination, the court

found and the Supreme Court upheld that Hicks had failed to meet this burden even though he had proven that the explanations offered by the defendant were pretextual. In a dramatic shift in Title VII case law, the Supreme Court made clear that plaintiffs who allege discrimination face a virtually insurmountable assumption of incompetence. Even if they can demonstrate that the justifications offered by a defendant are pretextual, they may lose if the court chooses to substitute its own explanation such as a subjective feeling of a personality dispute.

The personality dispute defense has taken on added significance in cases after *Hicks* unless the plaintiff has evidence of explicit racial epithets. For example, Anita Bivens, a black woman, and Rodolfo Arzate, an Hispanic man, could not convince a judge to let them take their racial harassment cases to a jury. Bivens was not permitted to argue to the jury that pushing and shoving incidents along with loud altercations were due to her race in light of the fact that one employee did openly call her a "nigger."[96] Arzate was not allowed to argue that other employees "mocked" his speech, which had an Hispanic accent.[97] The court concluded that plaintiff and his co-workers did not talk to each other out of "choice" rather than because of plaintiff's race. "The fact that coworkers do not like the plaintiff, or that he does not like them, is not the basis of a cognizable Title VII racially hostile work environment claim."[98] The court refused to connect this "dislike" and noncommunication to stereotypes about plaintiff's Hispanic ancestry because of the absence of explicit racial epithets.[99]

Most African-American plaintiffs who win racial harassment or discrimination cases do provide evidence of racial epithets.[100] James Rodgers, a black man, prevailed in his racial harassment and discharge claims against Western-South Life Insurance.[101] He offered evidence that his supervisor, William Mann, repeatedly called him and another black employee "nigger," had referred to blacks as "too fucking dumb to be insurance agents," and had explicitly advised his superior not to hire any more blacks. As with the gender cases involving sexualized language, the defendants tried to argue that Mann insulted all of his employees. The evidence did support the conclusion that Mann regularly called his subordinates "knobheads," "knuckleheads," "dunderheads," and "goons" which contributed to much psychological anxiety. Despite the fact that everyone seemed to suffer abuse from Mann at that workplace, the court found and the circuit court affirmed that "Mann's racist comments and taunts, though perhaps not the sole factor, contributed significantly to the stress condition that compelled Rodgers to resign from Western-Southern." [102] What the court fails to tell us is whether white employees also frequently resigned because of the stress caused by Mann's abusive personality. The racialized nature of the comments caused the court not to make that comparison. Hicks, by contrast, could not prevail although he had strong comparative evidence of different treatment, because he did not have evidence of racialized comments. Without such evidence, his lawyer did not even characterize his case as harassment.

Evidence of repeated racial epithets, however, is not a guarantee that a plaintiff will prevail. James Bolden, a black man, was subjected to comments such as: "you better be careful because we know people in the Ku Klux Klan," "honky", and "nigger." [103] Bolden lost because the court found that although he was "tormented at work" and did report some events that "he did not alert his supervisor he felt he was being harassed because of his race." [104] In another case, the district court did not find credible the assertions of Vildred Davis, a black woman, which were supported by co-workers, that her supervisor "hurled racial epithets towards her, assigned her to difficult jobs without providing training, and otherwise verbally abused her in front of other employee." [105] Both decisions were affirmed on appeal. Evidence of racial epithets therefore strengthen a race discrimination case but are certainly not a guarantee of success.

V. Winner No. 2: Whites

Wendy Wygant, a white woman, was laid off from her job as a school teacher at a time of increasing racial tensions in the Jackson School District. [106] The Union, which represented both black and white teachers, achieved a compromise where the burden of being laid off would fall proportionately on white teachers and minority teachers as a group. Each group would experience a portion of that burden equal to its portion of the faculty. [107] Because black teachers, however, had disproportionately less seniority than white teachers, strict seniority rules had to be modified in order to achieve this racial balance. Wygant, along with some other white teachers, who were among the bottom of the seniority scale for white teachers, but who had more seniority than some of the black teachers who were retained, successfully challenged the compromise agreement. The Supreme Court rejected this compromise despite its purpose to alleviate racial tension, provide role models for minority students, and maintain racial balance. Wendy Wygant's competence and abilities were considered irrelevant to the Court's resolution of the case; not once did one member of the Court even mention plaintiff's full name in the hundreds of pages of opinions that were authored in the case. [108]

In *Hicks*, the racially conscious plan did not have the purpose of *maintaining* racial balance; instead, it had the purpose of overturning the gains at the supervisory level that had been made by blacks. In addition, the plan in *Hicks* had a disproportionate impact on "innocent" black third parties; blacks and whites were not equally affected. Finally, in *Hicks* the rationale of avoiding racial strife seemed much more attenuated than in *Wygant*. In *Wygant*, the school district wanted to develop and foster positive black role models; in *Hicks*, the Department of Corrections appeared to be perpetuating the negative stereotype that black supervisors would sympathize with minorities who might engage in racial strife in a prison context. Such negative stereotypes have no place in anti-discrimination doctrine.

Despite dramatic evidence of discrimination, Hicks lost his case because the district court concluded that Hicks had not proven that race was the true explanation for his discharge, although it agreed that Hicks had demonstrated that the reasons offered for his discharge were pretextual. As the court stated: "In essence, although plaintiff has proven the existence of a crusade to terminate him, he has not proven that the crusade was racially rather than personally motivated." [109] The court of appeals reversed,[110] but the Supreme Court reversed the court of appeals and remanded the case back to the district court.[111] For the second time, the district court ruled for the defendants, finding that Hicks had not offered sufficient evidence of race discrimination to prevail under Title VII.[112] Hicks never proved to the satisfaction of the court that race was the cause of his gross mistreatment at St. Mary's.

A comparison between *Hicks* and reverse discrimination cases reveals that courts are exceedingly strict with determinations of causation in cases involving race discrimination claims brought by minority claimants but quite generous with determinations of causation in cases involving reverse race discrimination claims brought by white claimants. For example, in the leading affirmative action case, *Bakke v. Board of Regents,*[113] the courts barely paused to consider whether Allan Bakke's race was the source of his failure to be admitted by Davis Medical School. Bakke had applied to twelve medical schools over two years, and had been turned down by all of them.[114] When he inquired as to why he was rejected, two medical schools indicated that the explanation was his age. The newest and least prestigious of these two dozen schools was the University of California at Davis.[115] Nonetheless, Bakke was aware that his age might be a negative factor at Davis; he therefore wrote to Davis in 1971 asking how his age (33) would affect his application. The associate dean responded "that when an applicant is over thirty, his age is a serious factor which must be considered."[116] Despite the concerns raised by this letter, Bakke applied for admission late in 1972 and received an interview in March after most of the places in the class had been filled.[117] He was rejected for admission; his request to be waitlisted was also rejected.

Bakke sued under Title VI of the Civil Rights Act, as well as the U.S. Constitution in state court. He argued that he was not admitted because his race precluded him from competing for sixteen positions that were set aside for racial minorities. The trial court held that the special admissions program was unlawful, but refused to order Bakke's admission, holding that he had failed to carry his burden of proving that he would have been admitted but for the existence of the special program.[118] Bakke appealed from the portion of the trial court judgment denying him admission and the University appealed from the decision that its special admissions program was unlawful. On appeal, the California Supreme Court ruled in favor of Bakke, because the University conceded that it could not demonstrate that Bakke would not have been admitted in the absence of the special admissions program. Accepting this admission, the California Supreme Court ordered the trial court to order Bakke admitted to Medical School.[119] The U.S. Supreme Court affirmed the judgment of the California Supreme Court.

The role that Bakke's qualifications played in this litigation was very peculiar. Several *amici* suggested that the University "fabricated" Bakke's qualifications in order to permit him to have standing in the case.[120] The courts accepted the assumption that Bakke was qualified for admission despite the strong evidence that his age had been an adverse factor. For this white plaintiff, qualification and causation were presumed; for black plaintiff Hicks, incompetence and lack of causation were presumed even after he showed that the defendants' explanations were pretextual.

The Supreme Court rejected the suggestion by *amici* that Bakke did not have standing to sue due to his fabricated qualifications.[121] Nonetheless, six years later, when a group of parents of black school children brought suit alleging that the Internal Revenue Service helped perpetuate segregated schools, thereby depriving their children of an integrated education, by permitting segregated private schools to maintain their tax-exempt status, the Supreme Court was much more rigorous in its assessment of causation.[122] The Supreme Court found that plaintiffs could not adequately demonstrate that the injury of attending segregated schools was "fairly traceable" to the challenged actions of the IRS. Although the Davis special admissions program supposedly caused Bakke's harm of being excluded from fair consideration to medical school, the Court rejected the argument that the federal subsidy of segregated schools contributed to the harm of black children who are denied an integrated education. As Justice Brennan stated in dissent, "More than one commentator has noted that the causation component of the Court's standing inquiry is no more than a poor disguise for the Court's view of the merits of the underlying claim. The Court today does nothing to avoid that criticism."[123] Thus, it may be true that the University of California made it easier for the Supreme Court to rule in Bakke's favor by not contesting Bakke's qualifications. On the other hand, the Supreme Court would probably have seen through that attempt if Bakke had been a black schoolchild trying to gain access to a white school. Moreover, the University of California probably would not have conceded Bakke's qualifications during litigation if he were not white and male. Although Jean Jew, for example, had a strong record of sexual harassment, the University of Iowa was unwilling to concede her qualifications for promotion during litigation. As an Asian-American woman, Jean Jew did not garner the presumption of competence accorded to white men such as Bakke.

Similarly, in the recent *Duquesne Light* case[124] which was decided in favor of a white plaintiff for $400,000 punitive damages (in a case where the compensatory damages were only $25,000), the courts never seriously considered whether Claus's race was the source of his failure to be promoted. Frederick Claus had worked for Duquesne Light since 1964 and had been made director of engineering in 1985. In 1987, he was denied promotion to manager of construction and engineering and, in 1989, was rejected for promotion to manager of construction coordination and underground for the western division. In 1987, he was passed over in favor of a black man; in 1989, he was passed over in favor of a white man. The district court concluded that the black man who received the first promotion was qualified for it, but that Duquesne Light violated its own affirmative action plan when it promoted him.[125] Four other white individuals had also applied for and been rejected for that promotion. No one asked whether Claus was more qualified than the other whites who were also rejected for the position.[126]

As for the failure to obtain the second promotion, the EEOC concluded that Claus was passed over in retaliation for having filed a complaint regarding the first promotion.[127] Claus, like Bakke, was presumed to be qualified; no consideration was given to whether some of the other white candidates might be more qualified. Moreover, no one questioned why an engineer with more than twenty years of experience had not been promoted previously to a manager position. Reverse discrimination could not possibly explain the other times that Claus was not promoted, since only two of eighty-two middle and upper-middle management positions at Duquesne were held by minorities. Quite possibly, Claus was denied a promotion over the years because of some work-related problems with his performance, not his race. Or possibly, his age (55) had become an (illegal) adverse factor in the employment process. Nonetheless, in reverse discrimination cases plaintiffs are not required to prove causation with the same rigor that they are required to prove causation in cases brought by women and minorities. Once they establish that race was a factor in the selection process, the courts presume that they were more qualified than the minority who was selected.[128] Melvin Hicks, by contrast, was not able to benefit from that presumption. White male plaintiffs are presumed to be competent and victims of discrimination when they are not selected; minority and female plaintiffs are presumed to be incompetent and victims of a meritocracy when they are not selected.

There are occasional counterexamples to this trend, nonetheless. A federal district court in *Hopwood v. State of Texas*,[129] for example, recently applied the *Hicks* doctrine to the liability stage of a reverse discrimination case. At stage one, plaintiffs had established that the University of Texas violated Title VI and the U.S. Constitution by using a race-based quota system for law school admissions.[130] At stage two (the liability phase), however, the court cited *Hicks* for the proposition that the " 'ultimate burden of persuasion' remains at all times with the plaintiff."[131] Then, citing *Bakke,* the court concluded that the plaintiffs should not prevail if the defendants could "establish legitimate grounds for the decision not to admit these plaintiffs, notwithstanding the procedure followed."[132] Applying these two doctrines, the court accepted the university's argument that the plaintiffs would not have been admitted even in the absence of the race-based admissions program. This decision was not appealed to the Fifth Circuit.

Although the district court cited *Hicks* in its opinion, it was not really following the *Hicks* doctrine. In *Hicks,* the Supreme Court concluded that a plaintiff in a race case *never* establishes a presumption of race discrimination even after he or she disproves the justifications offered by the defendant. In *Hopwood,* by contrast, the district court concluded that the evidence that race was a factor in the admissions process *shifted the burden of proof to the defendant.* The plaintiffs would presumptively prevail unless the defendant could demonstrate that the plaintiffs were unqualified. Because the defendants met this burden of proof, plaintiffs failed to prevail at the liability stage for an order of admission. Had the defendants not met this burden of proof, then the presumption in favor of the plaintiffs would have prevailed and plaintiffs would have won. Had the *Hicks* court employed such a framework, Hicks would have won after defendants failed to establish that plaintiff was unqualified. Thus, even when whites fail to obtain relief in reverse discrimination cases, they have played under an easier set of rules than have blacks.

The case that brings together the different presumptions that apply to cases being brought by white and minority plaintiffs and the role that racialized evidence can play in such cases is Jean Jew's case. Jew's case contained two separate allegations: that she was a victim of sexual harassment and that she was not promoted because of her gender. (She did not raise a race claim although some of the sexual epithets were racially charged.) Her failure-to-be-promoted allegation was a difficult claim under existing law, because cases challenging tenure and promotion in the educational context are usually unsuccessful.[133] The presumption of incompetence that is usually accorded to plaintiffs in race and gender discrimination cases is particularly strong in that context. Nonetheless, Jew was able to prevail on both her harassment and promotion claims because of the strength of the evidence of sexualized comments.

The comments that formed the basis of Jew's sexual harassment case, however, centered on her sexuality not her intelligence or abilities as a research scientist. She was called a "whore," not a "dumb broad." If the issue is whether harassment taints a promotion process, one would think that comments like "dumb broad" would be more powerful than comments like "whore" because they speak directly to an individual's ability to be a research scientist. Yet, the remand decision in *Harris,* the Fifth Circuit's decision in *DeAngelis,* and the Supreme Court's decision in *Hicks* all suggest that nonsexualized and nonracialized comments are not particularly problematic at the workplace. Only sexualized and racialized comments reflect lack of respect for an individual's ability to perform his or her work. It is time to remember that the words "sex" and "race" are unmodified in Title VII. One should be able to prevail on a claim of sex or race discrimination without evidence of sexual or racial epithets.

Ironically, when sexual harassment doctrine was first being developed, the lower courts ruled against the female plaintiffs under the misconception that sexual harassment does not constitute gender discrimination.[134] Those courts were wrong, because, as Catharine MacKinnon has powerfully argued, "the sexual harassment of working women presents a closed system of social predation in which powerlessness builds on powerlessness."[135] Jean Jew was the victim of this social predation as her sexualization ultimately infected the promotion process in which men who had openly insulted her voted against her promotion. In their minds, she was a "slut" rather than a competent professional. It is therefore a positive development in Title VII jurisprudence for such women as Jean Jew to prevail. The development of sexual harassment doctrine, however, should not make us forget that sexual harassment is only one form of discrimination that women and men may face at the workplace. Gender and race discrimination can and do happen in the absence of sexualized or racialized insults.

VI. Beyond the Moral Code

As we have seen, the courts have overemphasized the sexual nature of harassment as a component of gender-based harassment for claims brought by heterosexual women. Similarly, it increasingly requires evidence of racial epithets for blacks to prevail in claims of racial discrimination. This overemphasis originated with the first harassment guidelines issues by the Equal Employment Opportunity Commission nearly fifteen years ago.[136] Although the purpose of these guidelines was to clarify that sexual harassment constituted gender-based discrimination, contrary to the holdings of many lower courts, the guidelines failed to state clearly that harassment could be proven without evidence of sexual comments or actions. As the EEOC has recently recognized, the focus on harassment that is sexual in nature has led some people not to realize that harassment based on race, color, religion, gender, age, and disability "is egregious" and prohibited by the various civil rights acts.[137] Accordingly, the EEOC recently decided to "put in guideline form the rule that sex harassment is not limited to harassment that is sexual in nature, but also includes harassment due to gender-based animus."[138] Because the original EEOC guidelines focused on harassment that was sexual in nature which needed to be distinguished from appropriate sexual interactions, the Guidelines included an inquiry as to whether the sexual conduct was "welcome." The special problem of deciding whether conduct is "welcome," however, does not exist for nonsexualized harassment and therefore is not part of the EEOC's recently proposed guidelines for conduct that is not sexual in nature.[139]

Unfortunately, the EEOC's attempt to highlight nonsexualized harassment has not been successful. The proposed guidelines have been withdrawn after being subjected for much criticism that they violate employers' First Amendment rights. Moreover, the proposed guidelines offer little guidance to courts on how to interpret statements and conduct to determine if they constitute "sex harassment" when they are not sexual in nature.[140] In many cases, like that of Teresa Harris, gender-based comments are combined with sexualized comments. The proposed guidelines give no special instruction as to how to evaluate such comments to determine if they are sufficiently severe and pervasive to constitute unlawful harassment.

The New Jersey Supreme Court, by contrast, has recognized that both gender-based and sexually-based harassment should violate Title VII. In *Lehmann v. Toys 'Я' Us*,[141] the Court stated that comments and actions of a nonsexualized nature that serve to degrade women's value at the workplace constitute gender-based harassment and provided the following framework for evaluating such comments:

> When the harassing conduct is sexual or sexist in nature, the but-for element will automatically be satisfied. . . . However, not all sexual harassment is sex-based on its face. . . . When the form of the harassment is not obviously based on the victim's sex, the victim must make a prima facie showing that the harassment occurred because of her sex. . . . In such non-facially sex-based harassment cases a plaintiff might show that such harassment was accompanied by harassment that was obviously sex-based. Alternatively, she might show that only women suffered the non-facially sex-based harassment. All that is required is a showing that it is more likely than not that the harassment occurred because of the plaintiff's sex. For a female plaintiff, that will be sufficient to invoke the rebuttable presumption that the harassment did in fact occur because of the plaintiff's sex.[142]

The New Jersey doctrine represents an enormous advance over existing Title VII doctrine for two reasons. First, it recognizes that harassing conduct can be gender-based even if it is not "sex-based on its face." The doctrine therefore allows plaintiffs to use circumstantial evidence to infer the gender-based aspect of harassing conduct. Under existing Title VII doctrine, cases involving such circumstantial evidence usually are required to utilize the more rigorous *Burdine-Hicks* doctrine.[143] Second, it recognizes that the gender-based aspect of harassing conduct can be inferred from evidence that other harassment or conduct was sex-based. This insight helps clarify that harassing conduct often occurs in a situation where it is not exclusively and explicitly gender-based. The New Jersey doctrine allows a plaintiff to combine nongender-based harassment with gender-based harassment to meet the threshold of "offensive and pervasive" that is required under Title VII.[144] If applied to *Harris,* this framework would expand the scope of Harris's recovery. The derogatory comments to Teresa Harris about her intelligence, because accompanied by overt sexualized comments, would easily constitute sex-based harassment.

A problem with the New Jersey standard is that it does not discuss how courts should apply the "unwelcomeness" standard to cases of mixed sexual and nonsexual gender-based conduct. Courts need to clarify that the "unwelcomeness" inquiry is only relevant to sexual conduct. As applied to Harris's situation, for example, comments about her purported stupidity should have been considered per se unwelcome; Harris should have had a successful claim based on those comments before her discussion with Hardy about the unwelcomeness of the sexualized comments. Moreover, under the New Jersey guidelines, those comments about her stupidity could be used to infer that the sexual comments were intended to harm her at the time they were uttered; they were not reflective of "joking" behavior. In other words, an individual who is making entirely unacceptable comments about stupidity that must have been intended to cause harm could be understood to be making contemporaneous comments about sexuality that also must have been intended to cause harm. There is no policy reason to tolerate any derogatory and gender-based comments about one's intelligence. Sex harassment doctrine should clarify this policy.

Not addressed by the proposed EEOC guidelines or the New Jersey Supreme Court rule is how to address claims brought by individuals who are perceived to be gay men or lesbians. These individuals have not been able to take advantage of the long-standing sexualized harassment doctrine. We should retain the principle that sexualized comments are prohibited by Title VII but extend that protection to individuals who are perceived as being gay and lesbian.

Moreover, the focus of the EEOC and the New Jersey Supreme Court has been to reinvigorate gender-based, nonsexualized cases. The fact that race cases brought by racial minorities are also suffering the same problem has been largely unaddressed. The stereotype that all blacks are incompetent and deserve to be discharged remains. The EEOC has done nothing to level the playing field between white and black plaintiffs in race discrimination lawsuits. Thus, the modest steps being taken by the EEOC and New Jersey Supreme Court are unlikely to unravel the emerging moral code under Title VII.

Sexual harassment is an important problem at the workplace that Title VII should continue to redress. Title VII should reach "equal opportunity harassers" who demean both men and women at the workplace with sexualized comments, because those comments are intended to cause gender-based injury to them. To the individual woman who is called a "slut" or "whore" at the workplace, the injury is not lessened because men are also called sexually derogatory names. Since Title VII promises protection against discrimination to the "individual," an individual should be able to recover who can demonstrate that comments reflect gender stereotyping or gender-based animus.

Nonetheless, our recognition that harassment that includes conduct that is sexual in nature is egregious should not blind us to the fact that harassment that is not sexual in nature also occurs at the workplace, and is equally egregious. It is as pernicious to call a woman "stupid" as it is to call her "sexy." Both comments should be illegal when based on gender stereotypes.

Race discrimination against minorities, irrespective of whether it includes the use of racial epithets, is also pernicious and should be redressed by Title VII. Given the direction in

which Title VII case law has gone in the last decade, it is easy
to forget that harassment doctrine originated with a recognition
of the pernicious nature of racial harassment, and that Congress' primary motivation in passing Title VII was to rid the
workplace of racism against blacks. *Hicks* reflects a growing
presumption that blacks do not face harassment and are discharged at work due to incompetence.[145] By contrast, the "reverse discrimination" cases reflect a presumption that whites
who are discharged are victims of race-based affirmative action
plans that cheat them out of their entitlement to employment
and advancement.

Three modifications to Title VII are greatly needed to solve
the problems discussed above. First, the EEOC guidelines emphasizing the importance of race and sex harassment that is not
overtly racial or sexual in nature must be implemented and
followed by the courts. Second, Congress must overturn *Hicks*
in order to level the playing field between white male plaintiffs
and female and minority plaintiffs. Racial minorities and
women deserve the presumption of competence that is routinely
accorded to white men. If a woman or racial minority establishes a prima facie case of discrimination and a defendant can
offer no credible nondiscriminatory and legitimate explanations
for its conduct then a plaintiff should prevail as a matter of law.
Third, the courts must develop more skepticism toward the
claims of reverse discrimination brought by white men. As they
do in cases of intentional discrimination brought by women and
minorities, courts should consider legitimate and nondiscriminatory explanations that are offered for their failure to promote, employ, or even discharge white men. There are many
explanations other than reverse discrimination which can explain why white men do not attain certain jobs; courts must be
cognizant of that reality when they consider reverse discrimina-

tion cases. They might want to consider hypothetically how they would evaluate the facts if alleged by a black man.

Some people snidely speculate that a conservative Congress may try to repeal Title VII. As I interpret the case law, however, there is no need for conservatives to call for the repeal of Title VII. By further developing existing doctrine, they can simply transform Title VII into a civil rights statute for women who are victims of sexualized harassment and white men who are purported victims of reverse discrimination. We can only hope that Title VII may one day again become a statute to protect women and minorities from all forms of discrimination at the workplace.

EIGHT

Invisible Hybrids
under the U.S. Census

. . . .

The point of this book is not that we should abandon categories. A legal system without categories is impossible, and a society without a legal system invites anarchy. If one thing is clear about American society, it is that it always will be dependent upon a legal system that relies heavily on categories.

The point of this book is not that categories are inherently harmful and destructive. Categories can be very important to self-identity as well as to political coalition-building. In addition, the formal use of categories within the legal system can provide a foundation of fairness and justice by insuring that decisions are not made in an entirely subjective and biased manner.

The point of this book is that the legal system is overly reliant on *bipolar* categories. By focusing our intention on hybrids, we can see the awkwardness, unfairness, and injustice caused by such a bipolar legal system. We can break down this needless bipolarity by adding more individualized decisionmaking to the legal system while not entirely displacing the use of categories. Sometimes, breaking down this bipolarity will cause us to add *new* categories such as bisexual, transsexual, or multiracial. At other times, it will help us to focus our attention on whom we want to devote our attention or resources within such a category as African-American or female. Yet at other times, it will cause us to see the stark differences in justice that are accorded to people who lie on one end of the bipolar spectrum (e.g., whites, men, or heterosexuals) and to people who lie on the other end (e.g., blacks, women, or homosexuals). A focus on the bipolarity of our legal system can therefore broaden our vision enormously.

A current political issue that can illuminate the central themes of this book is the controversy concerning the inaccuracy and even disrespectful nature of the U.S. census data collection on race. A census has been with us since the founding of our country. Article I, Section 2 of the Constitution requires an enumeration of all "free Persons, including those bound to Service for a Term of Years, and excluding Indians not taxed, three fifths of all other Persons." The U.S. decision to require a census followed a well-established European tradition of gathering statistics about its people. *Statistics* and *state* come from the same root, because statistics were historically a means of "ascertaining the political strength of a country."[1] The power to collect statistics can include the power to dominate a citizenry; thus, the story of a census is important to understanding the power of the state.

The first enumeration in the United States took place in 1780, and every ten years thereafter. It inquired whether individuals were free white males over sixteen, free white males under sixteen, free white females, all other free persons, or slaves.[2] The questions concerned status rather than race. Enumeration occurred on a family basis; individuals were enumerated as they related to the head of the household.[3] Beginning in 1850, the Census began enumerating individuals rather than families.

Slowly, all persons began to be counted without regard to status. In 1870, pursuant to the ratification of the Fourteenth Amendment, there was no longer any special designation for "slaves." "Indians not taxed" were enumerated for the first time as persons in the census of 1890.[4]

Beginning in 1870, the Census tried to gather information about "the new free man of color" by adding racial categories for the first time—"black" (for those of more than three-fourths African descent), "mulatto" (three-eighths to one-half African descent), "quadroon" (one-quarter to three-eighths African descent), and "octoroon" (one-eighth or less of any African descent).[5] These determinations were made solely on the basis of personal observation; no questions were asked to the respondents concerning their race.[6] The 1890 Census inquired for the first time whether people were "Chinese" or "Japanese."[7] The mixed-race categories were dropped in 1900; mulatto was reintroduced for the 1910 and 1920 enumerations. Census enumerators were instructed to designate, by visual observation, whether people were white, black, mulatto, Indian, Chinese, or Japanese.[8]

The census of 1910 began asking questions about nationality, country of origin, mother tongue, and language spoken at home in response to the large influx of immigrants around the turn of the century.[9] But these questions created more confusion than precise data:

The Austro-Hungarian Empire was then called a "prison-house of nations." What nationality then was a Serbian who had come from there, or a Finn or Pole who came from Czarist Russia? If a family left Poland and stopped in England for a while, as many did, before continuing to the United States, what was its "country of origin"? What was learned about a Jewish family whose "language spoken at home" was Yiddish?[10]

In 1930, four new categories were added: Mexican, Filipino, Hindu, and Korean.[11] The designation of "Mexican" as a race, however, had a very brief history. Beginning in 1940, "Mexican" was eliminated as a separate race. In 1950, Hindu and Korean were omitted and the "Indian" category was modified to read "American Indian." The move to a smaller list was short-lived; in 1960, eleven racial classifications were used. The categories Hawaiian, Part Hawaiian, Aleut, and Eskimo were added. Census takers also were instructed that people of Latin descent were to be considered white unless they were "definitely Negro, Indian, or some other race."[12] Although the Hindu category had been formally eliminated, enumerators were instructed to write in "Hindu" for the race of Asian Indians. The 1970 Census modified the categories again, deleting the categories of Part Hawaiian, Aleut, and Eskimo. Most importantly, for the first time, the instructions were that the respondent should complete the Census form, although enumerators were still given permission to write in the race based on personal observation if this was possible.[13]

In the 1970s, racial questions on the Census also began to reflect broader race-based record-keeping in society. "Directive No. 15" was issued in 1977; it provides for the racial categories used on *all* government recordkeeping. Instead of racial designation being an event that occurred once a decade, racial designation became a routine part of filling out applications for employment and enrollment in school. The move toward this widespread and uniform racial recordkeeping was to monitor enforcement of the recently enacted Civil Rights laws. Ironically, racial categories grew to have a more sweeping impact on American life. Americans soon became used to being racially categorized as part of many life activities.

Directive No. 15 also ended enumerator designation of race.

In 1980, even in cases where enumerators had to do follow-up interviews, they were instructed to designate race solely on the basis of respondents' statements. Fifteen options were used for the racial question in 1980 and 1990: white, black or Negro, Indian (American), Eskimo, Aleut, Asian-Pacific Islander—Chinese, Filipino, Hawaiian, Korean, Vietnamese, Japanese, Asian Indian, Samoan, and Guamanian. Alternatively, individuals could check the category "other." [14] If an individual wrote in "brown" or "Mexicano," they were not reassigned to another category, such as white. Instead, they were counted as "other."

The term "other" has been on the Census form since 1910 but really has never been a separate category. When a respondent checks "other," the census enumerator is instructed to write down the person's race based on observation, ask the respondent to choose which one of the listed race he or she identifies with, or to write in specifically what he or she considers to be his or her race. When an individual writes in a racial category, the response is reassigned to one of the listed racial classifications so that the person is still classified as monoracial. Before 1980, a mixed-race person was assigned the father's race but, since 1980, a mixed-race person is assigned the mother's race. [15]

Various rules govern how people who identify as multiracial are currently classified. People who designate they are biracial or multiracial are left in the "other" racial classification. People who respond "black-white" are designated as "black" and people who respond "white-black" are designated as white. Finally, data collected elsewhere on the form, or from similarly situated households, also sometimes is used to impute race for individuals who check "other" race. [16]

In sum, the Census has not always employed racial categories. But we have used five categories without interruption for the last one hundred years—white, black or Negro, American Indian, Chinese, and Japanese. We have moved from recognizing multiracial blacks to only recognizing monoracial categories. We have also moved from enumerator observation to self-identification. We have added an "other" category but never used its results to permit multiracial designation.

Although the current debate about whether a "multiracial" category should be added to the racial categories in Directive No. 15 focuses on whether such an addition would be a more respectful way to categorize people, a historical analysis of racial designations shows no correlation between respecting a group and designating it separately. In the first several census enumerations, we counted the number of slaves in order to determine the representation of the white community in Congress. These slaves, of course, were not even counted as whole persons for that purpose. The move toward multiracial categories in the late nineteenth century with the highly ambiguous categories of mulattos, quadroons, and octoroons was described as an "heroic attempt" to "prevent racially mixed individuals from crossing the racial line into the White population."[17] This enumeration reflected an attempt to keep tabs on the degree of racial mixing as part of an anti-miscegenation political effort.[18] (This data was also collected from visual identification, not self-identification.) Similarly, the separate enumeration for Chinese and Japanese populations must "be interpreted within the context of prevailing anti-Chinese and anti-Japanese sentiments and restrictive immigration and other policies directed at these groups."[19] The increase in the number of Asian racial classifications since 1980 also reflects "political and social reactions to the growing Asian presence in U.S. society."[20] There has been no similar move to have white Americans designate their country of origin in the Census race question.

Given the peculiar history of our Census race questions, it is not surprising that the question of whether our current classification scheme is appropriate is contentious. For some reason, however, the current controversy has been a rather confined one. No one seems to be questioning whether we should collect race data on a national level at all. (Canada, as we will see, does not inquire about "race" on its census; it only inquires about the ethnic or cultural identities of one's ancestors.) Racial questions on the census were historically really "status" questions—whether one was free or black. The initial movement toward "race" questions was motivated by attempts to keep people out of our society or to deter interracial marriage. The impetus behind Directive No. 15 in the 1970s, however, was arguably ameliorative. The Secretary of Health, Education, and Welfare, Caspar Weinberger, had deplored the lack of useful data on racial and ethnic groups in 1973 to assess how the federal government could improve educational opportunities for Chicanos, Puerto Ricans, and American Indians.[21] The coordinated development of common definitions for racial and ethnic groups soon emerged as a recommendation. An Ad Hoc Committee on Racial and Ethnic Definitions was created in 1974 to fulfill that recommendation; three years later, Directive No. 15 emerged as the solution.

The impetus behind Directive No. 15 was twofold: to find a consistent definition for minority groups other than blacks and to have definitions that would be used uniformly throughout society. The definition of "black" has not undergone change as a result of this evaluation whereas other minority groups have been added or deleted from the categories. The issue today of whether a "multiracial" category should be added again primarily reflects the experiences of minority groups without a significant African-American heritage, because the most common group to intermarry with whites is Asian-Americans. Thus, in recent years, modification of the categories has not reflected dissatisfaction with the way "blacks" are counted. Nonetheless, as we will see, adding the category multiracial might affect the way "blacks" are counted.

The changes in the census since 1974 also have assumed that uniform racial and ethnic data best could answer the kinds of questions that were being asked by Secretary Weinberger. Weinberger's highly centralized approach, however, may have been flawed. We assume that we *should* have one model for asking race-based questions in all walks of life rather than fine-tuning the questions as appropriate. For example, if we wanted to know how many children in a school district might need special English classes if English is not the language spoken in their home, then it might make sense to ask people in that school district with children of school age what language they speak at home. But is it really helpful to know how many of those children (or their parents) identify as Hispanic? Are we asking race or ethnicity questions in some situations instead of the real questions that we want answered? Until we address the issue of what is the purpose of all of these racial and ethnic questions, it will be difficult to assess whether the given categories are useful.

Finally, few people acknowledge the gross inaccuracy of census data. The census has been collecting information about "whites" and "slaves" since the first census, yet the enumeration of the African-American population has always been considered extremely inaccurate. "The error in counting the black population of the country has often exceeded that of the white by as much as ten times! In the *details* of the census—for example, Negro men from 25 to 34 years of age—the differences in the size of the error between black and white become even more extreme."[22] If we want answers to the kinds of questions posed by Secretary Weinberger, sophisticated sampling of targeted populations might make much more sense. The census notoriously undercounts poor people because census collection requires an individual to have a street address. If a major purpose of the census is to provide us with information about the most disadvantaged members of our society, then a census would seem to be a particularly inappropriate form of data collection.

Although one might expect that basic questions about why we have a census and collect racial data at all would be a basic part of the current debate about modifying Directive No. 15, they are not. Instead, everyone assumes that Directive No. 15 will continue to exist indefinitely and that the real challenge is to figure out how to improve Directive No. 15. Reluctantly accepting that assumption, we therefore should consider how Directive No. 15 could be improved.

The current proposal to improve Directive No. 15 is to add a separate category of "multiracial." The addition of a multiracial category is quite controversial within some black civil rights organizations. Because nearly all blacks who have been in the United States for several generations have some white ancestry, a multiracial category could virtually wipe out the monolithic category of "black." They argue that it makes little sense to reclassify these people from "black" to "multiracial" since the one drop of blood rule predominates American life. Reclassification will not eliminate racism although it might permit government data collectors to hide or distort its existence.

Their argument has a strong historical foundation because

the modification in data collection for African-Americans has never been for the purpose of serving their interests. White slave owners and proponents of anti-miscegenation have dominated the racial classification system in the past. With the recent onslaught against affirmative action, they have every reason to be skeptical that this multiracial data would be in their interest.

Deborah Ramirez summarizes the implications of moving from monoracial classification to multiracial classification:

Creating a multiracial category would dilute the statistical strength of established minority groups. As the number of people claiming multiracial identity increases, membership in existing minority groups would necessarily decrease. This statistical change would have an enormous impact on matters immensely important to minority communities: electoral representation, the allocation of government benefits, affirmative action, and federal contracting rules. Certain districts created under the Voting Rights Act of 1965 to encourage minority representation might have to be redrawn as minority group numbers decrease. This statistical shift would also affect local school boards and civil rights agencies that utilize traditional minority categories. The federal government relies on monoracial categories to monitor a wide array of programs and entitlements, including: minority access to home mortgage loans under the Home Mortgage Disclosure Act, enforcement of the Equal Credit Opportunity Act, public school desegregation plans, minority business development programs, and enforcement of the Fair Housing Act. Creation of a multiracial category also has the potential to disrupt equal employment opportunity recordkeeping and affirmative action planning on the part of employers who are required to collect ethnic data under Title VII of the Civil Rights Act of 1964.[23]

Ramirez's exhaustive list of the implications of changing our definitional scheme is daunting. The list, alone, should cause us not to be surprised that abandoning a monoracial classification system is contentious. Interestingly, the consequences flow because everyone assumes that it will be people who are currently labeled as minorities who will become multiracial rather than people who are currently classified as whites. That assumption flows from the pervasive "one drop of blood rule."

Other civil rights organizations that represent parents in multiracial marriages, however, favor the multiracial category. In their case, a multiracial lineage is not a distant past plagued by the knowledge of slave masters and rape of young black women. Their multiracial lineage is the result of a consensual, contemporary marriage. The multiracial community is composed of many households with a mixture of Asian-Americans and Caucasians who may not feel tainted by the one drop of blood rule in the same way that the children of African-American and Caucasian parents are tainted. They may feel that they can help construct their children's identities by calling them multiracial. More fundamentally, they feel that their children's basic rights are invaded by forcing them to favor one parent over the other in choosing a monoracial designation.[24]

The search for a solution that can satisfy all of these different communities is difficult, especially if we think that a monolithic solution is required. Although Ramirez examines many areas of life in which interracial conflict is occurring over definitional questions, such as who should qualify for affirmative action, she offers no solution to the thorny census issue. I suggest that we could revamp the race questions entirely to satisfy the interests of the diverse communities with multiracial backgrounds. In order to do so, we need to ask some basic questions.

First, we have to ask: why do we need this information at all? It is odd to try to improve Directive No. 15 without a clear answer to that question. On a general level, it seems that we want racial designation information for three separate purposes: (1) to determine how people *self-identify*, (2) to determine how the *community* classifies people, and (3) to determine people's backgrounds.

Historically, we have asked each of these questions at different times. When census enumerators determined race, we asked the second question. Since 1980, we have asked the first question through self-enumeration. And for those people who have checked "other" since 1910, we have classified them based on the third question. Our historical census data on race is therefore virtually meaningless because we have conflated each of those three questions. Census data is infamous for its inaccuracy on racial questions;[25] the shifting perspectives embodied in prior census data perpetuates such inaccuracy.

It is therefore time to ask why we have this confusing color and ethnic topography that will not permit recognition of multiple or hybrid categories, and that does not separate self-identity from social identity from country of origin. In Canada, for example, the topography is not structured around race. Instead, the Canadian Census form indicates that an individual should check *all the categories that apply*. Moreover, the categories are based on country of origin, not race. All Africans are not alike under the Canadian scheme, nor are all Europeans alike. People have an identifiable country of origin rather than meaningless "race." There is no separate category for "multiracial." It is presumed that a large portion of the population is "multi-ethnic"; the forms therefore reflect that presumption. In the United States, by contrast, we have constructed our forms around the false presumption of monoracial backgrounds.

The Canadian model, however, does not appear to respond to the purported purposes of the U.S. census. Secretary Weinberger proposed that we collect more consistent race and ethnic data to help us track the status and needs of minority communities in the United States. An inquiry limited to country of origin would not provide us with that information. For example, an individual who indicated that her ancestors were from South Africa might be white or black.

The Canadian model also does not adequately respond to the conflicting concerns raised by multiracial and black civil rights organizations. Multiracial organizations want an opportunity to indicate their self-identity irrespective of how society might categorize them visually. Black civil rights organizations want to make sure that their numbers are not diluted so that we can continue to recognize that people who are "pure" black as well as multiracial "black" face racism in our society. They are concerned with the community definition of their race rather than self-definition. The Canadian model might induce some people to report that their racial background includes European and African ancestors without an opportunity to indicate that the community nonetheless regards them as black. In other words, the Canadian approach is not designed to collect useful data in a society that has been dominated by the legacy of slavery.

To overcome these problems, we could modify the Census forms by asking three different types of questions:

1. What is your self-identity?

2. If your self-identity is different than your community identity, what is your community identity?

3. What are the countries of origin of your parents, to the extent that you are aware of them?

For each of these questions, we could allow individuals to list as many categories as apply (including the category "multiracial" for people who prefer to think of themselves in that way). Asking the questions in this way would allow us to separate out people who are aware of a multiracial background, people who visibly look multiracial, and people who identify as multiracial. Then, we could use the data in ways that conform to people's actual lives. If the question is whether there is a large percentage of people in an area who are treated as if they are "black," then we would have that answer. But if the question is whether a particular area consists of people with varied, multiracial backgrounds, we would also have that information. In other words, we would recognize the social construction of race in the ways that we asked the questions. We would not assume that race is a static category.

The problem with this solution is that it requires a degree of trust in our government and society that may not be appropriate. Why should an individual who self-identifies as an African-American but who knows that he or she has a white ancestor trust our government by acknowledging his or her multiracial background? The consequences of moving away from monoracial categories may be wide-ranging as catalogued by Ramirez. Our historical experience suggests that that information will be misused. Our contemporary politics provides no reason for positive reassurance. But, of course, changing the census questions will not force anyone to admit to having ancestors from different racial groups. It will simply provide them with the opportunity to do so. By making that opportunity available, many parents of multiracial children will feel as if their ethnic heritage has obtained more respect.

When I read the testimony of parents in interracial marriages, I deeply understand their desire to transform the society in which their children will grow up. They want their children to share in the culture and heritage of both parents, and not to be judged by the "one drop of blood rule." I hope that adding new categories to the census will help in the achievement of that objective. But I also know that history tells us that these parents face an insurmountable challenge. No matter how frequently they tell their children that they are multiracial, their children will be identified and classified on one end of the bipolar spectrum in many aspects of their lives. But if we do not begin to embark on the journey of honoring the values of these parents, we will never take any steps toward erasing the "one drop of blood" rule. Thus, we should embrace the attempt to move toward a multicultural society while recognizing that it will be a slow and difficult process.

By examining one series of questions on the census concerning race and ethnic identity, I have tried to show how we could separate out questions of self-identity, community identity, and ancestry. These distinctions might allow us to recognize people's multiracial backgrounds while respecting people's self-identity and understanding the history of oppression in our society. The same insights might benefit our categorization system for gender, sexual orientation, and disability on the census. In each of these areas, we also use highly bipolar categories that fail to reflect hybrids and the distinction between self-identity, community identity, and background. A post-operative transsexual is given a monolithic gender category which hides the fluidity of gender categories in that person's life. Why ask about gender on the census if the gender of some people is not counted?

In this book, I have tried to render hybrids visible although the official census may still render them invisible. I hope that we will have such individuals in mind in the future as we create ameliorative programs to redress a history of group-based subordination in our society. I hope that we will do a better job in the future of considering how the life histories of individuals make them deserving of ameliorative treatment. We need to be less stereotypical and bipolar in our thinking about how race, sexual orientation, gender, and disability matter in people's lives.

Aside from these legal discussions, I also hope this book has helped each of us learn more about the hybrids within us. As I was finishing this book, I was playing with my three year old daughter. She said to me, "Mommy, today I am going to be a boy. Tomorrow, I am going to be a girl." She then smiled mischievously and said, "No, today I am going to be a girl. Tomorrow I am going to be a boy. You're always going to be a girl because you're a mommy." I wonder when society will socialize her into believing that she can only conform to female gender roles. I hope, instead, that she can grow up to see the hybrids within each of us, including herself.

Notes

....

Notes to Preface

1. *See* MARTIN S. WEINBERG, COLIN J. WILLIAMS, AND DOUGLAS W. PRYOR, DUAL ATTRACTION: UNDERSTANDING BISEXUALITY 7 (1994).

2. *See, e.g.,* James Bovard, *The Disability Act's Parade of Absurdities,* WALL ST. J., June 22, 1995, A16; Max Boot, *A Rye Look at ADA,* WALL ST. J., June 22, 1995, A16.

3. *See* WEBSTER'S NEW COLLEGIATE DICTIONARY (1979) (defining hybrid as "an offspring of two animals or plants of different races, breeds, varieties, species or genera").

4. MARJORIE GARBER, VICE VERSA: BISEXUALITY AND THE EROTICISM OF EVERYDAY LIFE (1995).

5. GREGORY HOWARD WILLIAMS, LIFE ON THE COLOR LINE: THE TRUE STORY OF A WHITE BOY WHO DISCOVERED HE WAS BLACK (1995).

6. John Leleand et al., *Bisexuality: Not Gay. Not Straight. A New Sexual Identity Emerges,* NEWSWEEK, July 17, 1995, at 44 (cover story).

7. Tom Morganthau et al., *What Color Is Black?,* NEWSWEEK, February 13, 1995, at 44 (cover story).

8. Amy Bloom, *The Body Lies,* NEW YORKER, July 18, 1994, at 38.

9. Judy Scales-Trent, *Commonalities: On Being Black and White, Different, and the Same,* 2 YALE J. OF LAW & FEMINISM 305 (1990).

Notes to Chapter One

1. SANDRA LIPSITZ BEM, THE LENSES OF GENDER: TRANSFORMING THE DEBATE ON SEXUAL INEQUALITY vii (1993).

2. Judy Scales-Trent, *Commonalities: On Being Black and White Different, and the Same*, 2 YALE J. OF LAW & FEMINISM 305, 32₄ (1990) [hereinafter *Commonalities*]. *See also* JUDY SCALES-TRENT NOTES OF A WHITE BLACK WOMAN: RACE, COLOR, COMMUNITY (1995)

3. *Commonalities, supra* note 2, at 305.

4. Linda Alcoff, *Mestizo Identity* in AMERICAN MIXED RACE: EX PLORING "MICRODIVERSITY" (ed. Naomi Zack, 1995). Although Al coff describes herself in this chapter as both white and Latina, she has told me that she recently discovered that she also has African ances tors. Thus, I make that observation although it is not contained in her chapter.

5. *Id.* at 278.

6. *Id.*

7. Rohan Preston, *Battle to Keep Black Professor Leaves Bruised Egos and Reputations*, N.Y. TIMES, Mar. 8, 1995, at B8.

8. Equality Foundation of Greater Cincinnati, Inc. v. City of Cincinnati, 54 F.3d 261 (6th Cir. 1995).

9. 163 U.S. 537 (1896).

10. Neil Gotanda, *A Critique of "Our Constitution is Color-Blind,"* 44 STAN. L. REV. 1 (1991).

11. *See infra* chapter 8.

12. *See* Jeffrey S. Byrne, *Affirmative Action for Lesbians and Gay Men: A Proposal for True Equality of Opportunity and Workforce Diversity*, 11 YALE L. & POL'Y REV. 47 (1993).

13. *See, e.g., Obesity Bias Lawsuit: Woman Sues Movie Theater Over Access*, NEWSDAY, Feb. 25, 1994, Business Section, Nassau & Suffolk Edition, at 53 (woman who went with her niece to see *Jurassic Park* not allowed to use her own chair in the wheelchair section).

14. Our tort system, by contrast, gives people an incentive to be labeled as "white" rather than "black" when race-based tables are used to determine lost compensation. *See generally* Martha Chamallas, *Questioning the Use of Race-Specific and Gender-Specific Economic Data in Tort Litigation: A Constitutional Argument*, 63 FORDHAM L. REV. 73 (1994).

Notes to Chapter Two

1. *See* Trip Gabriel, *A New Generation Seems Ready to Give Bisexuality a Place in the Spectrum*, N.Y. TIMES, June 12, 1995, at C10.

2. A bisexual perspective has emerged within feminist theory through the publication of two anthologies, BI ANY OTHER NAME: BISEXUAL PEOPLE SPEAK OUT (ed. Loraine Hutchins and Lani Kannhumanu, 1991) and CLOSER TO HOME: BISEXUALITY & FEMINISM (ed. Elizabeth Reba Weise, 1992).

3. Marjorie Garber's six hundred page discussion of bisexuality makes only two references to multiracial categories and then only in quotation. She does not discuss other hybrid categories. See MARJORIE GARBER, VICE VERSA: BISEXUALITY AND THE EROTICISM OF EVERYDAY LIFE 48, 88 (1995).

4. MARTIN S. WEINBERG, COLIN J. WILLIAMS, AND DOUGLAS W. PRYER, DUAL ATTRACTION: UNDERSTANDING BISEXUALITY 27–29 (1994).

5. *Id.* at 6.

6. GARBER, *supra* note 3, at 49.

7. *See* Dvora Zipkin, *Why Bi?* in CLOSER TO HOME, *supra* note 2, at 55–73 (describing an experience where women were asked to join one of four groups—bisexual, heterosexual, or choose not to label; twice, she picked "choose not to label").

8. Ruth Gibian, *Refusing Certainty: Toward a Bisexuality of Wholeness*, in CLOSER TO HOME, *supra* note 2, at 5.

9. ALFRED C. KINSEY ET AL., SEXUAL BEHAVIOR IN THE HUMAN MALE (1948).

10. John L. Peterson, *Black Men and Their Same-Sex Desires and Behaviors*, in GAY CULTURE IN AMERICA: ESSAYS FROM THE FIELD 147, 148 (ed. Gilbert Hendt, 1992).

11. *See id.* at 148 (reporting that black men in a prison population were more likely than white males to engage in anal intercourse with another man).

12. *Id.* at 150. This failure to identify as homosexual or bisexual despite the experience of same-sex sexual relationships may be reflective of the racism within the white gay movement. *Id.* at 152. Thus, bisexuality within the African-American male community might be-

come more evident if the larger society in which we live were not so racist. Sexual identity and racism therefore may be deeply connected.

13. I have not seen any discussion of sexual behavior within the female African-American community. Discussions of "women" do not distinguish between African-American and white women.

14. As Brenda Marie Blasingame has noted: "I once talked with a Latino male doing AIDS education in the Latino community about his approach to educating the community about safe sex. He said there was no word for bisexual per se, but that bisexuality existed in the community and that this had to be addressed in order to teach safe sex. It was very much like the black community. When they talk about safe sex they have to refer to it as 'when you have sex with another man.'" Brenda Marie Blasingame, *The Roots of Biphobia: Racism and Internalized Heterosexism,* in CLOSER TO HOME, *supra* note 2, at 51–52.

15. *Id.* at 51–52.

16. Gibian, *supra* note 8, at 13–14.

17. I carefully use the word "some" because nearly all individuals who identify as black have a multiracial heritage. The majority of those individuals comfortably identify as black. A subgroup of those individuals identify as multiracial along with individuals who consist of other multiracial backgrounds. In this book, I focus on individuals who are black/white multiracial, but the category of multiracial, of course, involves endless combinations of ethnic and racial backgrounds.

18. GARBER, *supra* note 3, at 37.

19. Stacey Young, *Breaking Silence About the "B-Word": Bisexual Identity and Lesbian-Feminist Discourse,* in CLOSER TO HOME, *supra* note 2, at 77.

20. Nina Silver, *Coming out as a Heterosexual,* in CLOSER TO HOME, *supra* note 2, at 45.

21. *Id.* at 84 (quoting Micki Siegel, *Bisexual Invisibility,* GAY COMMUNITY NEWS, Mar. 11–17, 1990).

22. WEINBERG, *supra* note 4, at 19–20.

23. Further experiences perpetuated that pattern. A lesbian activist reportedly said that it was unfortunate that I was involved with a man because I was such a good role model for lesbian law students. As a

bisexual, I apparently could no longer be a good role model. Problems with role model theory will be discussed in chapter 4.

24. For further discussion, see Stacey Young, in CLOSER TO HOME, *supra* note 2, at 75–87.

25. *See* BI ANY OTHER NAME, *supra* note 2 and CLOSER TO HOME, *supra* note 2.

26. Irene Sege, *Not Black Enough?* BOSTON GLOBE, Feb. 9, 1995, Living Section, at 63.

27. *Id.*

28. Rohan Preston, *Battle to Keep Black Professor Leaves Bruised Ego and Reputations,* N.Y. TIMES, Mar. 8, 1995, at B8.

29. GREGORY HOWARD WILLIAMS, LIFE ON THE COLOR LINE: THE TRUE STORY OF A WHITE BOY WHO DISCOVERED HE WAS BLACK 272 (1995).

30. *See* WEINBERG, *supra* note 4, at 402–3 (reporting incidence of celibacy, monogamy, and multiple relationships among bisexuals, heterosexuals, and homosexuals).

31. GARBER, *supra* note 3, at 66.

32. BETTY FAIRCHILD AND NANCY HAYWARD, NOW THAT YOU KNOW: WHAT EVERY PARENT SHOULD KNOW ABOUT HOMOSEXUALITY 75 (1989).

33. *Id.* at 76.

34. Interestingly, homosexuality also is often invisible. Polls consistently report that few adults in the United States believe that they know any gay or lesbian people. Sylvia Law, *Homosexuality and the Social Meaning of Gender,* WIS. L. REV. 187 (1988). I know of no poll, however, that has even asked people if they know anyone who is bisexual. Poll data also show that people who report that they know gay or lesbian people tend to be more tolerant of them. *Id.* at 194. The invisibility of bisexuality therefore probably contributes to stereotypical attitudes but, again, it is hard to prove this assertion since researchers do not even ask questions about bisexuals.

35. A major contributor to that myth was Freud. Although he believed that all humans have a bisexual capacity and that even people who are heterosexual retain homosexual tendencies, he did not challenge the dichotomous categories of heterosexual and homosexual. For further discussion, see Law, *supra* note 34, at 204.

36. JOHN J. MCNEILL, S.J., THE CHURCH AND THE HOMOSEXUAL 148 (1976).

37. WEINBERG, *supra* note 4, at 319.

38. *Id.,* at 288 (emphasis in original).

39. Heather MacDonald, *SSI Fosters Disabling Dependency,* WALL ST. J., Jan. 20, 1995, at A12.

40. For example, in Pennsylvania, children with disabilities can receive services through the Early and Periodic Screening, Diagnosis and Treatment program ("EPSDT"). Money for this program goes directly to the health care provider, not to the parent or guardian. *See generally* PA. STAT. ANN. t.t. 62 5001.701 (1992).

41. 493 U.S. 521 (1990).

42. *Id.* at 534 n. 13.

43. *Id.* at 536 n. 17.

44. Michael Winerip, *A Disabilities Program that "Got out of Hand,"* N.Y. TIMES, Apr. 8, 1994, at A1.

45. Angela Harris, *Race and Essentialism in Feminist Legal Theory,* 42 STAN. L. REV. 581 (1990).

Notes to Chapter Three

1. Jacobson v. Jacobson, 314 N.W.2d 78 (S.D. 1981).

2. Watkins v. United States Army, 837 F.2d 1428, 1446 (9th Cir. 1988), *opinion withdrawn,* 825 F.2d 659 (9th Cir. 1989).

3. The first ballot initiative against homosexuals surfaced in 1979 in Dade County, Florida, when Anita Bryant successfully mounted a campaign to overturn Dade County's ordinance prohibiting sexual orientation discrimination. More recent attempts include a ballot initiative in 1992 in Oregon which attempted to restrict the rights of gay men, lesbians, and bisexuals. In 1994, ballot initiatives were attempted in ten states. *See generally* William E. Adams, Jr., *Pre-Election Anti-Gay Ballot Initiative Challenges: Issues of Electoral Fairness, Majoritarian Tyranny, and Direct Democracy,* 55 OHIO ST. L.J. 583 (1994).

4. Ordinance No. 490–1992.

5. This is the language of the proposed Charter amendment: "NO SPECIAL CLASS STATUS MAY BE GRANTED BASED UPON SEXUAL ORIENTATION, CONDUCT OR RELATIONSHIPS. The City of Cincinnati . . . may not enact, adopt, enforce or administer any

ordinance, regulation, rule or policy which provides that homosexual, lesbian, or bisexual orientation, status, conduct, or relationship constitutes, entitles, or otherwise provides a person with the basis to have any claim of minority or protected status, quota preference or other preferential treatment." *See* Equality Foundation of Greater Cincinnati, Inc. v. City of Cincinnati, 54 F.3d 261, 264 (6th Cir. 1995) (quoting proposed Article XII to City Charter).

6. 54 F.3d at 266 (describing trial court's opinion).

7. 478 U.S. 186 (1986).

8. 54 F.3d at 268.

9. JUDY SCALES-TRENT, NOTES OF A WHITE BLACK WOMAN: RACE, COLOR, COMMUNITY (1995).

10. N.H. HB 70, as quoted in *In re* Opinion of the Justices, 530 A.2d 21, 22 (N.H. 1987).

11. 530 A.2d at 24.

12. *Id.* at 24.

13. N.H. REV. STAT. ANN. 170-B:2 (XV) (1992).

14. The ambiguity problem did not end with this case. Foster parents unsuccessfully challenged the new rules on grounds of ambiguity. *See* Stuart v. State Division of Children and Youth Services, 597 A.2d 1076 (N.H. 1991). The foster parents unsuccessfully argued that they could not certify that there were no homosexuals in their household because the definition of homosexuality in the statute was so vague.

15. The FBI and CIA also have had their share of problems in trying to restrict gay and lesbian people from employment. *See, e.g.,* Padula v. Webster, 822 F.2d 97 (D.C. Cir. 1987). The current official policy of the FBI and CIA, however, is not to exclude individuals from employment based on sexual orientation.

16. 632 F.2d 788 (9th Cir. 1980).

17. *Id.* at 794.

18. *Id.* at 794.

19. *Id.* at 794.

20. *Id.* at 802 n. 9.

21. *Id.* at 802.

22. *Id.* at 802 n. 9 (quoting SECNAV Instruction 1900.9C).

23. 741 F.2d 1388 (D.D.C. 1984).

24. *Id.* at 1389.

25. *Id.* at 1398.

26. *Id.* at 1398.

27. 489 F. Supp. 964 (E.D. Wis. 1980).

28. *Id.* at 969.

29. *Id.* at 969.

30. *Id.* at 974.

31. *Id.*

32. These regulations are codified at 10 U.S.C. 654 (1993).

33. *See generally* Robinson v. California, 370 U.S. 660 (1962).

34. 871 F.2d 1068 (Fed. Cir. 1989).

35. 875 F.2d 699 (9th Cir. 1989), *cert. denied,* 498 U.S. 957 (1990).

36. 703 F. Supp. 1372 (E.D. Wis. 1989), *reversed,* 881 F.2d 454, *cert. denied,* 110 S. Ct. 1296 (1989).

37. 871 F.2d at 1974 n. 6.

38. benShalom v. Marsh, 703 F. Supp. 1372, 1373 (E.D. Wis. 1989).

39. Watkins v. United States Army, 847 F.2d 1329 (9th Cir. 1988).

40. 871 F.2d at 1069.

41. *Id.* at 1070.

42. *Id.* at 1070.

43. 837 F.2d at 1430.

44. Watkins v. United States Army, 837 F.2d 1428 (9th Cir. 1988), *opinion withdrawn on rehearing by* 875 F.2d 659 (9th Cir. 1989), *cert. denied,* 498 U.S. 957 (1990).

45. 837 F.2d at 1446.

46. *Id.* at 1446.

47. 875 F.2d at 707.

48. *Id.* at 711.

49. *Id.* at 710.

50. 690 F. Supp. 774 (E.D. Wis. 1988).

51. 881 F.2d at 456.

52. *Id.* at 457.

53. 703 F. Supp. 1372 (E.D. Wis. 1989).

54. 881 F.2d at 460.

55. *Id.* at 460.

56. Elaborating further on that issue, the Court of Appeals said: "Plaintiff's lesbian acknowledgment, if not an admission of its practice, at least can rationally and reasonably be viewed as reliable evidence of a desire and propensity to engage in homosexual conduct. Such an assumption cannot be said to be without individual exceptions, but it is compelling evidence that plaintiff has in the past and is likely to again engage in such conduct. To this extent, therefore, the regulation does not classify plaintiff based merely upon her status as a lesbian, but upon reasonable inferences about her probable conduct in the past and in the future." *Id.* at 464.

57. 10 U.S.C. 654(b) (1993).

58. 847 F. Supp. 1038 (E.D.N.Y. 1994).

59. 880 F. Supp. 968 (E.D.N.Y. 1995).

60. 847 F. Supp. at 1042.

61. Arthur A. Murphy and John P. Ellington, *Homosexuality and the Law: Tolerance and Containment II,* 97 DICK. L. REV. 693 (1993).

62. *Id.* app. A at 709.

63. *Id.* app. A at 709–10

64. *Id.* at 698 (footnotes omitted).

65. Murphy and Ellington are not alone in proposing new initiatives to penalize gay, lesbian, and bisexual people. Recent initiatives in Oregon, Colorado, and elsewhere have tried to repeal the minimal nondiscrimination advances made by gay, lesbian, and bisexual people in the last twenty-five years. See *id.* apps. B-C at 710–11 (Oregon and Colorado initiatives).

66. Unsuccessful legal efforts are reflected in the following cases: Baker v. Nelson, 191 N.W.2d 185 (Minn. 1971); Jones v. Hallahan, 501 S.W.2d 588 (Ky. Ct. App. 1973); DeSanto v. Barnsley, 476 A.2d 952 (Pa. Super. Ct. 1984); Singer v. Hara, 522 P.2d 1187 (Wash. Ct. App. 1974). Litigation, however, may prove to be successful in Hawaii. The Hawaii Supreme Court recently remanded a case to the lower court to see if a gender-specific marriage law could be sustained under heightened scrutiny. Baehr v. Lewin, 852 P.2d 44 (Haw. 1993).

67. For example, by 1991, 44 couples had registered as domestic partners in San Francisco, and 125 had registered as domestic partners in Berkeley. Ken Hoover, *Same-Sex Marriage Bill Stalls,* UPI, Apr. 24, 1991.

68. MARTHA ALBERTSON FINEMAN, THE NEUTERED MOTHER, THE SEXUAL FAMILY, AND OTHER TWENTIETH CENTURY TRAGEDIES 229 (1995).

69. *See generally* Peter Rusk, *Same-Sex Spousal Benefits and the Evolving Conception of Family,* 52 U. OF T. FACULTY OF L. REV. 170 (1993).

70. *Id.*

71. *See* Egan v. Canada, File No. 23636 (Supreme Court of Canada, decided May 25, 1995). The Attorney General of Canada conceded the argument that sexual orientation is a suspect class, entitled to protection under Canada's equality provision.

72. *Id.* The Supreme Court of Canada ruled that federal pension benefits did not need to be available to same-sex couples, despite the fact that sexual orientation is a suspect class. The Court's reasoning focused on the "fact" that heterosexual partnerships "uniquely [have] the capacity to procreate children and generally care[] for their upbringing." *Id.* at 25.

73. *Id.,* at 25.

74. These examples appear in MATTHEW A. COLES, SEXUAL ORIENTATION AND THE LAW (Boalt Hall Law School, Spring 1993).

75. Jody Freeman, *Defining Family in Mossop v. DSS: The Challenge of Anti-Essentialism and Interactive Discrimination for Human Rights Litigation,* 44 U. TORONTO L.J. 41, 72 (1994).

76. *Id.* at 71–72.

77. Bill 167, An Act to amend Ontario Statutes to Provide for the Equal Treatment of Persons in Spousal Relationships, 3d Session, 35th Legislature, Ontario (1st Reading, May 19, 1994).

78. The term "spouse" was defined as: "(a) a person to whom the person is married, or (b) a person of either sex with whom the person is living in a conjugal relationship outside marriage, if the two persons, (i) have cohabited for at least one year, (ii) are together the parents of a child, or (iii) have together entered into an agreement under section 53 of the Family Law Act."

79. FINEMAN, *supra* note 68.

80. *Id.* at 230.

81. 618 N.Y.S.2d 356 (1994).

82. *See generally* MARGARET MAHONEY, STEPFAMILIES AND THE

LAW 130 (1994) (reporting that one-third of all states confer visitation rights to stepparents).

83. *See* Jeffrey S. Byrne and Bruce R. Deming, *On the Prudence of Discussing Affirmative Action for Lesbians and Gay Men: Community, Strategy, and Equality,* 5 STAN. L. & POL'Y REV. 177, 179 (1993). Proposed federal legislation to create nondiscrimination protection on the basis of sexual orientation explicitly prohibits affirmative action. See *A Bill to Prohibit Employment Discrimination on the Basis of Sexual Orientation* Sec. 6 ("A covered entity shall not give preferential treatment to an individual on the basis of sexual orientation") (103d Cong. 2d Sess.) (available from author). If this bill became law, the institutions that have publicly announced use of affirmative action for lesbians and gay men arguably would be violating the statute.

84. Byrne and Deming, *supra* note 83. Northeastern University has also recently announced an affirmative action program for lesbians and gay men. *See* Glen Johnson, *University Starts Recruiting Gay Faculty,* THE RECORD A06 (June 27, 1994); Alice Dembner, *Northeastern Takes Steps to Hire More Gays,* BOSTON GLOBE, June 28, 1994, Metro/Region Section, at 20. Nonetheless, some institutions have tried to distance themselves from suggestions that they engage in affirmative action on the basis of sexual orientation. *See, e.g.,* Anthony Flint and Kay Longcope, *Kennedy School Shows Caution on Gay Initiative,* BOSTON GLOBE, Feb. 28, 1991, Metro/Region Section, at 25 (school spokesman released a statement saying that institution does not recruit or admit students, staff, or faculty on the basis of sexual orientation despite a report recommendation that the institution engage in affirmative gay and lesbian recruitment).

85. Byrne and Deming, *supra* note 83, at 186.

86. *See* Jeffrey S. Byrne, *Affirmative Action for Lesbians and Gay Men: A Proposal for True Equality of Opportunity and Workforce Diversity,* 11 YALE L. & POL'Y REV. 47, 69–70, 77–78 (1993).

87. *See id.* at 92.

88. *Id.* at 93.

89. *See, generally,* Ruth Colker, *A Bisexual Jurisprudence,* 3 LAW & SEXUALITY: REV. OF LESBIAN AND GAY LEGAL ISSUES 127 (1994).

90. Someone could make up stories of disadvantage but those

stories will often be verifiable. Even if fraud problems existed with my proposal, I still believe that it is the fairest approach.

91. *See, e.g.,* Adrienne Rich, *Compulsory Heterosexuality and Lesbian Existence,* 5 SIGNS 631 (1980).

Notes to Chapter Four

1. Bottoms v. Bottoms, 457 S.E. 2d 102 (Va. 1995).

2. Bowers v. Hardwick, 478 U.S. 186 (1986).

3. Doe v. The Boeing Company, 846 P.2d 531 (Wash. 1993).

4. Phillips v. Michigan Department of Corrections, 731 F. Supp. 792 (W.D. Mich. 1990).

5. *Id.* at 794.

6. *See id.* at 795 n. 5 (distinguishing between a transsexual, homosexual, and transvestite). Gay and lesbian groups recently seem to have become concerned with transgender issues. The 1993 March on Washington for lesbian and gay civil rights, for example, included transgender concerns in its list of concerns. *See* Dan Levy and David Tuller, *Transgender People Coming Out,* S.F. CHRON., May 28, 1993, at A1. Nonetheless, transgendered individuals report that they have faced many obstacles from mainstream homosexuals who say that the presence of cross-dressers at gay marches and parades offends straight people and undermines overall support for the gay rights movement. *Id.*

7. *See, e.g.,* Phillips v. Michigan Department of Corrections, 731 F. Supp. 792, 795 n. 5 (W.D. Mich. 1990).

8. *See* ANNIE WOODHOUSE, FANTASTIC WOMEN: SEX, GENDER, AND TRANSVESTISM 19 (1989).

9. *Id.* at 19–20.

10. *Id.* at 46–47.

11. *Id.* at 47.

12. Hermaphrodites constitute three sub-groups: (1) they possess one testes and one ovary, (2) they possess testes and some aspects of female genitalia but not ovaries, or (3) they have ovaries and some aspects of male genitalia but lack testes. Anne Fausto-Sterling, *How Many Sexes Are There?*, N.Y. TIMES, Mar. 12, 1993, at A29.

13. *See supra* chapter 5.

14. *See infra* Part IIC.

15. Tina Gaudoin, *Prisoner of Gender: Androgyny,* HARPER'S BA-ZAAR, June 1993, at 114.

16. *Id.*

17. MARTIN S. WEINBERG, COLIN J. WILLIAMS, AND DOUGLAS W. PRYOR, DUAL ATTRACTION: UNDERSTANDING BISEXUALITY 60 (1994).

18. *Id.* at 60 (transsexual bisexual challenges the assumption that "gender identity and sexual preference fit together in some necessary way").

19. 457 S.E. 2d 102 (Va. 1995).

20. Elizabeth Kastor, *The Battle for the Boy in the Middle: Little Tyler's Mom Is a Lesbian, So Grandma Got to Take Him Away,* WASH. POST, Oct. 1, 1993, at C1.

21. *Id.*

22. 348 S.E.2d 18 (Va. Ct. App. 1986).

23. *Id.* at 20.

24. *Id.* at 20.

25. *Id.*

26. B. v. B., 585 N.Y.S.2d 65 (App. Div. 1992).

27. *Id.* at 66.

28. *See, e.g.,* Stanley v. Stanley, 592 So. 2d 862 (La. Ct. App. 1991) (male role model for son); Seeley v. Jaramillo, 727 P.2d 91 (N.M. Ct. App. 1986) (reversing modification of custody agreement that had relied on importance of female role model for daughter).

29. As recently as 1991, the Tennessee Court of Appeals in Jones v. Leisure, 1991 WL 10971 (Tenn. Ct. App., Feb. 5, 1991), noted that the "tender years" doctrine is a positive factor for consideration in a mother's lawsuit for custody of her young daughter.

30. *See, e.g., In re* Diehl, No. 2–90–1217, 1991 Ill. App. LEXIS 1972, *22 (Ill. Ct. App., Nov. 22, 1991) (denying custody to an alleged lesbian and stating that because of the child's "tender years . . . it is in her best interest not to be exposed to a lesbian relationship").

31. Constant A. v. Paul C.A., 496 A.2d 1, 3 (Pa. Super. Ct. 1985).

32. 457 S.E. 2d 102 (Va. 1995).

33. *See generally* Stephen B. Pershing, *"Entreat Me Not to Leave Thee": Bottoms v. Bottoms and the Custody Rights of Gay and Lesbian Parents,* 3 WM. & MARY BILL RTS. J. 289 (1994).

34. Leisge v. Leisge, 292 S.E. 2d 352 (Va. 1982).

35. *Id.* at 7.

36. *Lesbian Loses Custody of Her Son*, NAT'L L.J., May 8, 1995, at A10.

37. *See, e.g., In re* Marriage of Patricia O'Brien and Mark Thomas O'Brien, 491 N.W.2d 202 (Iowa Ct. App. 1992) (awarding custody of three boys to father despite admission of physical abuse of spouse).

38. *See* Mason v. Moon, 385 S.E.2d 242 (Va. Ct. App. 1989).

39. *See, e.g.,* Ferris v. Underwood, 348 S.E.2d 18 (Va. Ct. App. 1986); Walker v. Brooks, 124 S.E.2d 195 (Va. 1962).

40. *Id.*

41. *See* Testimony of Mary Beth Harrison, Defense Advisory Committee on Women in the Services, 1988 Spring Conference (Apr. 16–20, 1988).

42. *See* William B. Rubenstein, *Challenging the Military's Antilesbian and Antigay Policy,* 1 LAW & SEXUALITY: REV. OF LESBIAN AND GAY LEGAL ISSUES 239 (1991).

43. *See* Michelle M. Benecke and Kirstin S. Dodge, *Military Women in Nontraditional Job Fields: Casualties of the Armed Forces' War on Homosexuals,* 13 HARV. WOMEN'S L.J. 215 (1990).

44. GA. CODE ANN. 16–6-2 (1984).

45. Sodomy statutes sometimes also are used to prosecute female prostitutes who engage in oral sex with their clients. They are never used to prosecute more traditional heterosexual relationships.

46. 478 U.S. 186 (1986).

47. KATE BORNSTEIN, GENDER OUTLAW: ON MEN, WOMEN AND THE REST OF US 36 (1994).

48. *See, e.g.,* DeSantis v. Pacific Telephone & Telegraph Co., Inc., 608 F.2d 327 (9th Cir. 1979) (sexual orientation discrimination not recognized as gender-based under Title VII).

49. I believe that it would be more coherent for the courts to acknowledge that the discrimination is gender-based and then decide whether that discrimination can be justified. At present, the courts allow their conclusion that the discrimination can be justified to color their conclusion as to whether the discrimination is gender-based. They seem to be afraid to let cases proceed to the stage of justification.

50. 852 P.2d 44 (Haw. 1993).

51. *Id.* at 52 n. 11.

52. *Id.* at 52 n. 12.

53. BORNSTEIN, *supra* note 47.

54. *Id.* at 24.

55. *Id.* at 27.

56. Doe v. Boeing Company, 846 P.2d 531 (Wash. 1993).

57. *Id.* at 533.

58. *Id.* at 534.

59. *Id.* at 537.

60. Ulane v. Eastern Airlines, 742 F.2d 1081 (7th Cir. 1984).

61. 667 F.2d 748 (8th Cir. 1982).

62. *See* Sommers v. Iowa Civil Rights Commission, 337 N.W.2d 470 (Iowa 1983).

63. *Id.*

64. Kirkpatrick v. Seligman & Latz, 636 F.2d 1047 (5th Cir. 1981).

65. Holloway v. Arthur Andersen and Company, 566 F.2d 659 (9th Cir. 1977).

66. *See, e.g.,* Phillips v. Martin Marietta Corp., 400 U.S. 542 (1971) (employer's refusal to hire women with preschool children violated Title VII).

67. *See generally* HERMA HILL KAY, SEX-BASED DISCRIMINATION 484–535 (1981) (explaining sex-plus theory).

68. 388 U.S. 1 (1967).

69. *See, e.g.,* Fagan v. National Cash Register Co., 481 F.2d 1115, 1124–25 (D.C. Cir. 1973).

70. SANDRA L. BEM, THE LENSES OF GENDER: TRANSFORMING THE DEBATE OF SEXUAL INEQUALITY 149 (1993).

71. *See, e.g.,* Doe v. Boeing Co., 846 P.2d 531 (Wash. 1993) (male-to-female transsexual fired because she wore a strand of pink pearls to the workplace).

72. Katharine T. Bartlett, *Only Girls Wear Barrettes: Dress and Appearance Standards, Community Norms, and Workplace Equality,* 92 MICH. L. REV. 2541, 2559 (1994).

73. *See* Rappaport v. Katz, 380 F. Supp. 808 (S.D.N.Y. 1974).

74. Mary Whisner, *Gender-Specific Clothing Regulation: A Study in Patriarchy,* 5 HARV. WOMEN'S L.J. 73, 102 (1982).

75. 507 F. Supp. 599 (S.D.N.Y. 1981).

76. Fountain v. Safeway Stores, Inc., 555 F.2d 753 (9th Cir. 1977).

77. Fagan v. National Cash Register Co., 481 F.2d 1115 (D.C. Cir. 1973).

78. *See, e.g.,* Carroll v. Talman Federal Savings and Loan Association, 604 F.2d 1028 (7th Cir. 1979) (demeaning for women to be required to wear uniforms and men only required to wear customary business attire); O'Donnell v. Burlington Coat Factory Warehouse, 656 F. Supp. 263 (S.D. Ohio 1987) (demeaning for female sales clerks to be required to wear a "smock" and for male sales clerks to be required to wear business attire consisting of slacks, shirt, and a necktie).

79. Patricia Williams, *The Obliging Shell: An Informal Essay on Formal Equal Opportunity,* 87 MICH. L. REV. 2128, 2144–46 (1989).

80. *Id.* at 2146.

81. Barbara A. Brown et al., *The Equal Rights Amendment: A Constitutional Basis for Equal Rights for Women,* 80 YALE L.J. 871, 902 (1971).

82. See *Woman Is Acquitted in Trial for Using the Men's Room,* N.Y. TIMES, Nov. 3, 1990, Section 1, at 8.

83. *See, e.g.,* In the Matter of Anonymous, 293 N.Y.S.2d 834 (Civ. Ct. 1968), In the Matter of Anonymous, 314 N.Y.S.2d 668 (Civ. Ct. 1970).

84. *See, e.g.,* Hartin v. Director of the Bureau of Records and Statistics, 347 N.Y.S.2d 515 (1973) (Department did not act capriciously in issuing a new certificate changing only the first name of petitioner and omitting any designation of sex); Anonymous v. Weiner, 270 N.Y.S.2d 319 (1966) (judicial intervention not appropriate to reverse Department's refusal to change birth certificate designation); Anonymous v. Mellon, 398 N.Y.S.2d 99 (N.Y. 1977) (judicial intervention not appropriate). *But see* K. v. Health Division, 552 P.2d 840 (Oregon Ct. App. 1976) (court had authority to order change of name and sex designation on birth certificate).

85. M.T. v. J.T., 355 A.2d 204 (N.J. Super. Ct. 1976). For another case involving positive treatment of a transsexual, see Christian v. Randall, 516 P.2d 132 (Colo. Ct. App. 1973) (denying custody petition by father who objected to children staying with wife who was undergoing female to male transsexual procedure). *But see* Frances B.

v. Mark B., 355 N.Y.S.2d 712 (1974) (post-operative female to male transsexual could not succeed on divorce claim as no valid marriage had been entered into, since he had no male sex organs); Daly v. Daly, 715 P.2d 56 (Nev. 1986) (parental rights of post-operative female to male transsexual terminated).

86. 355 A.2d at 210.

87. *Id.* at 207.

88. See, e.g., *In re* Declaratory Relief for Ladrach, 513 N.E.2d 828 (Ohio Probate Ct. 1987) (denying marriage license to post-operative male to female transsexual to marry male).

89. *See, e.g.,* Pinneke v. Preisser, 623 F.2d 546 (8th Cir. 1980) (Iowa's policy of denying medicaid benefits for sex reassignment surgery found not to be consistent with the objectives of the medicaid statute); Doe v. Lackner, 145 Cal. Rptr. 570 (Ct. App. 1978) (Medi-Cal benefits found to cover radical sex conversion surgery for treatment of transsexualism); G.B. v. Lackner, 145 Cal. Rptr. 555 (Ct. App. 1978) (Medi-Cal claimant entitled to benefits for surgery to treat transsexualism); Doe v. State Department of Public Welfare, 257 N.W.2d 816 (Minn. 1977) (decision to deny medical assistance benefits to adult male transsexual found to be arbitrary and unreasonable); Denise R. v. Lavine, 364 N.Y.S.2d 557 (1975) (denial of benefits for sex conversion operation found to be arbitrary and capricious). Prison inmates, however, have not been successful in obtaining estrogen therapy as a treatment for transsexualism. *See* Farmer v. Carlson, 685 F. Supp. 1335 (M.D. Pa. 1988); Meriwether v. Faulkner, 821 F.2d 408 (7th Cir. 1987); Supre v. Ricketts, 792 F.2d 958 (10th Cir. 1986); Bowring v. Godwin, 551 F.2d 44 (4th Cir. 1977); Lamb v. Maschner, 633 F. Supp. 351 (D. Kan. 1986).

90. *See* Richard Green, *Spelling "Relief" for Transsexuals: Employment Discrimination and the Criteria of Sex,* 4 YALE L. & POL'Y REV. 125 (1985). Nonetheless, the American Psychiatric Association, at its 1993 annual conference proposed that well-adjusted transsexuals not automatically be considered to have a mental disorder. Levy and Tuller, *supra* note 6, at A1.

91. *See, e.g.,* Farmer v. Carlson, 685 F. Supp. 1335 (M.D. Pa. 1988) (transsexual inmate found to be denied proper medical care by being denied conjugated estrogens); Phillips v. Michigan Dept of

Corrections, 731 F. Supp. 792 (W.D. Mich. 1990) (transsexual inmate entitled to preliminary injunction ordering correctional officials to provide her with estrogen therapy); White v. Farrier, 849 F.2d 322 (8th Cir. 1988) (summary judgment not appropriate on issue of whether transsexual inmate subjected to deliberate indifference through failure to be given estrogen therapy); Meriwether v. Faulkner, 821 F.2d 408 (7th Cir. 1987) (transsexual inmate stated claim under Eighth Amendment for failure to provide estrogen therapy); Lamb v. Maschner, 633 F. Supp. 351 (D. Kansas 1986) (inmate not found to have constitutional right to pre-operative hormone treatment and sex change operation).

92. *See supra* note 90.

93. In order for plaintiffs to prevail in the prison context, they typically have to attempt to commit suicide or remove some of their own sexual organs. For example, in Supre v. Ricketts, 596 F. Supp. 1532, 1533 (D. Colo. 1984), plaintiff attempted to remove his testicles six times, attempted to kill himself by hanging, and incised and removed a portion of his scrotum. Before successful judicial intervention occurred, the prison took the position that treatment for gender dysphoria could not occur in a penal setting. In concluding that medical treatment was appropriate, the judge ruled that "plaintiff's life was in jeopardy." *Id.* at 1535. It is appalling that an individual has to attempt mutilations, castrations, and suicide before a court can find that he or she is entitled to medical treatment for gender dysphoria.

94. *See* Fausto-Sterling, *supra* note 12.

95. *Id.*

96. There are life-threatening conditions that can occur as a result of being a hermaphrodite: hernias, gonadal tumors, and adrenal malfunction. *Id.*

Notes to Chapter Five

1. 388 U.S. 1 (1967).

2. The term "race" is itself a socially constructed term. As James Lindgren has noted: "According to most population geneticists, what we call 'races' arise when members of species become separated over a long enough period of time to develop different distributions of

characteristics. When those differences are substantial enough, races are said to have developed. The point to keep in mind, however, is that 'the level of differences used as a threshold is entirely arbitrary.' Ultimately, if differentiation increases, interfertility decreases between the various races of a species. Human race differentiation has not proceeded to the point where interfertility has decreased, and, given current interaction between races, a decrease in interfertility between human races is unlikely to develop. Race is therefore principally a social construct that gives meaning to certain characteristics of groups within a species." James Lindgren, *Seeing Colors,* 81 CAL. L. REV. 1059, 1084–85 (1993) (footnotes omitted). *See also* Lawrence Wright, *One Drop of Blood,* NEW YORKER, July 25, 1994, at 46, 50 (noting that scientific research indicates that the genetic variation among individuals from accepted racial groups was only slightly greater than the variation within the groups).

3. Gabrielle Sandor, *The "Other" Americans,* AMERICAN DEMOGRAPHICS 36 (June 1994).

4. *Id.*

5. *Id.*

6. Wright, *supra* note 2, at 46, 49.

7. *See, e.g.,* Wheeler Tarpeh-Doe v. United States, 771 F. Supp. 427, 455–56 (D.D.C. 1991) (court considering whether mixed-race child should be considered black or white for determination of lost wages).

8. Neil Gotanda, *A Critique of "Our Constitution is Color-Blind,"* 44 STAN. L. REV. 1, 25 (1991).

9. *See supra* chapter 1.

10. *See* GREGORY HOWARD WILLIAMS, LIFE ON THE COLOR LINE: THE TRUE STORY OF A WHITE BOY WHO DISCOVERED HE WAS BLACK (1995).

11. SHIRLEE TAYLOR HAIZLIP, THE SWEETER THE JUICE (1994).

12. *See* Martha Minow, *The Supreme Court—Foreword,* 101 HARV. L. REV. 10, 70 (1987).

13. *See* Anita L. Allen, *Racial Counting: Government Data Collection and the Census* (available from Anita Allen, Georgetown University Law Center).

14. 163 U.S. 537 (1896).

15. JACK GREENBERG, CASES AND MATERIALS ON JUDICIAL PROCESS AND SOCIAL CHANGE: CONSTITUTIONAL LITIGATION 585 (1977).

16. Brief of Plaintiff in Error, *Plessy v. Ferguson* 3 (reprinted in LANDMARK BRIEFS AND ARGUMENTS OF THE SUPREME COURT OF THE UNITED STATES: CONSTITUTIONAL LAW 30 (ed. Philip B. Kurland and Gerhard Casper, 1975) [hereinafter PLESSY BRIEF].

17. *Id.* at 10.

18. GREENBERG, *supra* note 15, at 585.

19. 52 So. 500 (La. 1910).

20. The court does not specify Treadway's first name; he is referred to as the "defendant" throughout the case.

21. 52 So. at 508.

22. Ridgway v. Cockburn, 296 N.Y.S. 936 (Sup. Ct. 1937).

23. 278 So. 2d 915 (La. Ct. App. 1973).

24. *Id.* at 917.

25. State v. Louisiana State Board of Health, 296 So. 2d 809 (La. 1974).

26. *Id.* at 812–13 (Barham, J., dissenting).

27. *Id.* at 812.

28. For example, in Messina v. Ciaccio, 290 So. 2d 339 (La. Ct. App. 1974), the court of appeals upheld a lower court order requiring the birth certificate be issued designating an adopted child to be white. It found that the Bureau could not meet its burden of proving that the child was more than 1/32 Negro, as required by Louisiana law, because of the imprecise categories that were used to determine racial heritage.

29. 479 So. 2d at 372.

30. *See* LA. REV. STAT. ANN. 40:34 (West 1992) (repealed 1988) ("race or races of parents as reported by the parents").

31. Although I call these individuals "light-skinned blacks" during this discussion, they could more accurately be considered to be mixed-race individuals. I use the term "light-skinned" because we never had discussions with these individuals about their racial heritage. My discussion of "light-skinned" blacks could also apply to other characteristics that blacks may have which may make them more acceptable to whites. For example, a colleague of mine has told me that his

African-American wife was told at a job interview with a bank that they would consider hiring her if she would "relax" her hair. Similarly, African-American men are often requested to shave their beards in order to be hired or retained at a job. In both cases, blacks are being asked to conform their physical appearance to a "white" standard. Light skin color is therefore not the only trait that might make some blacks more acceptable to white society.

32. To the best of my knowledge, this case was never litigated on the merits. I was not involved with the case when it finally was resolved.

33. Cheryl Harris, *Whiteness as Property,* 106 HARV. L. REV. 1709, 1710–1713 (1993).

34. *Id.* at 1710.

35. I also wonder if the grandmother truly "passed" in the way that Harris describes. Did any of her co-workers suspect her black racial background? Had they been taught that it was alright to ignore such background when a person was light-skinned? In the gay rights context, it has often been my experience that people who think they are "passing" as heterosexual are not really passing. Many people may know of their homosexuality but have been taught to tolerate it so long as the person does not "flaunt" it. The grandmother certainly tried to hide her black heritage but we cannot fully tell from Harris's account whether she truly "passed." Finally, I want to emphasize that by discussing the spectrum on which race may be experienced that I am not trying to discount that Harris's grandmother suffered disadvantage because of her race. My point is simply that her skin color allowed her to mitigate some of those disadvantages while she still faced other disadvantages. Harris's grandmother, for example, probably attended racially segregated, black schools and lived in racially segregated, black neighborhoods.

36. *See infra* Part IB.

37. *See, e.g.,* STEPHEN L. CARTER, REFLECTIONS OF AN AFFIRMATIVE ACTION BABY (1991).

38. *See infra* note 105.

39. Michael Rezendes, *Debate Intensifies on Adoptions across Racial Lines,* BOSTON GLOBE, Mar. 13, 1994, Metro Section at 1 (reporting that Randall Kennedy says that "race should never be consid-

ered in adoptions, even if there comes a day when enough black families can be found to adopt all the black children waiting for families to call their own."). *See also* Randall Kennedy, *Racial Critiques of Legal Academic,* 102 HARV. L. REV. 1745, 1819 n. 305 (1989) (describing a race conscious placement as "scandalous").

40. 59 Fed. Reg. 29,831–01 (1994) (quoting 1977 Directive).

41. The classification problem also frequently occurs for the label "Hispanic." *See generally* Alex M. Saragoza et al., *Concepcion,* 5 LA RAZA L.J. 1 (1992) (discussing question of whether Spaniards should be included in the Hispanic category for the purposes of affirmative action). *See also* Ian F. Haney Lopez, *The Social Construction of Race: Some Observations on Illusion, Fabrication, and Choice,* 29 HARV. C.R.-C.L. L. REV. 1 (1994) (describing how he and his other brother, both of whom had a fourth-generation Irish father and Salvadoran immigrant mother chose different racial identities).

42. Elizabeth Kulbert, *White Officers Seek Minority Status* N.Y. TIMES, Dec. 6, 1985, Metropolitan Desk, at B16.

43. Steven Marantz and Peggy Hernandez, *Defining Race Sensitive, Elusive Task, Bostons Hiring Probe Brings System Under Fire,* BOSTON GLOBE, Oct. 23, 1988, Metro/Region Section at 33.

44. *See* Wright, *supra* note 2, at 47 (quoting the mother of multiracial children who said that multiracial individuals know "to check the right box to get the goodies"). Even for groups that are recognized as "minorities," which minority classification they are put in can make a big difference in terms of social or economic entitlements. For example, some Native Hawaiians have sought to be labeled as Native Americans rather than as Asian or Pacific Islanders, which would entitle them to enjoy privileges concerning gambling concessions that they would not otherwise enjoy. *Id.*

45. 59 Fed. Reg. 29,831–01 (June 9, 1994).

46. *Id.*

47. *Id.*

48. *Id.*

49. *Id.*

50. *Id.*

51. The Columbia Law School application contains the following

categories: American Indian/Alaskan; Black/African-American; White/
Caucasian; Chicano/Mexican-American; Asian/Pacific Islander;
Puerto Rican; Other Hispanic; East Indian; Other; Unknown. The
accompanying instructions state: "If you wish to have our Admissions
Committee consider your racial or ethnic background in its evaluation
of your candidacy for admission, please indicate your status by check-
ing one or more of the following categories. Also, please attach a
separate statement describing your ethnic, cultural and linguistic heritage, and how this identification may have found expression in your
academic, extracurricular or community undertakings."

Columbia Law School, Application for Admission (1994).

52. Lindgren, *supra* note 2, at 1084.

53. NAOMI ZACK, RACE AND MIXED RACE (1993).

54. *Id.* at xii.

55. *Id.* at xiii.

56. *Id.* at xii.

57. 438 U.S. 265 (1978).

58. *Id.* at 312.

59. *Id.* at 316–17.

60. *Id.* at 317.

61. *See* Kennedy, *supra* note 39. *See also* CARTER, *supra* note 37,
at 27 (arguing that blacks should insist on an affirmative action "that
rewrites the standards for excellence, rather than one that trains us to
meet them").

62. 480 U.S. 616 (1987).

63. Id. at 624 n. 5.

64. JOEL DREYFUSS AND CHARLES LAWRENCE III, THE BAKKE CASE:
THE POLITICS OF INEQUALITY 5 (1979).

65. *See generally* ANDREW HACKER, TWO NATIONS: BLACK AND
WHITE, SEPARATE, HOSTILE, AND UNEQUAL (1995).

66. Anita L. Allen, *The Role Model Argument and Faculty Diversity,* 24 PHILOSOPHICAL FORUM 267, 276 (1992–93).

67. *Id.* at 270.

68. *Id.* at 267.

69. *Id.* at 268.

70. *Id.* at 269.

71. 476 U.S. 267 (1986).

72. Wygant v. Jackson Board of Education, 746 F.2d 1152, 1156 (6th Cir. 1984).

73. Randall Kennedy, *Persuasion and Distrust: A Comment on the Affirmative Action Debate,* 99 HARV. L. REV. 1327, 1329 (1986).

74. 476 U.S. at 275.

75. Allen, *supra* note 66, at 272.

76. 476 U.S. at 279.

77. *Id.* at 279.

78. *Id.* at 276.

79. 438 U.S. at 369.

80. *Id.* at 371.

81. *Id.* at 377.

82. *Id.* at 310.

83. *Id.* at 365–66.

84. 115 S.Ct. 2097 (1995).

85. 438 U.S. at 377.

86. *See* Laura Brown, *Small-Business Group Slammed as Ineffective,* BOSTON HERALD, June 14, 1995, News Section at 6 (reporting that one-third of the businesses assisted through a Massachusetts program that targets disadvantaged businesses were non-minority, male-owned firms); Richard Whitt, *Minority Deals Raise Grady Price,* ATLANTA CONSTITUTION, May 21, 1991, at D1 (reporting that William Coleman, owner of a white-owned company qualified as a disadvantaged business enterprise).

87. Limited evidence existed that some minorities were periodically found not to be disadvantaged. *See, e.g.,* Autek Systems Corp. v. United States, 835 F. Supp. 13 (D.D.C. 1993) (upholding determination that Native American was not "disadvantaged" under Small Business Administration regulations). *See generally* Brief Amicus Curiae of the Latin American Management Association in Support of Respondents, *Adarand v. Pena* No. 93–1841 (filed Dec. 5, 1994) (providing examples of small businesses owned by minorities and found not to be disadvantaged). The *Autek* case is cited in the *Adarand* briefs as reflecting a case where a Native American was disqualified for not being disadvantaged. Others, however, have described the case as not involving an "authentic" Native American. Hacker reports, for

example, that in "one egregious case, a white contractor won an award because he claimed he had a Native American great-grandmother." HACKER, *supra* note 65, at 128. Thus, some of the "disadvantage" cases may actually be "mixed-race" cases where the Small Business Administration is also questioning the validity of the racial presumption.

88. 115 S.Ct. at 2130 (Stevens and Ginsburg, J.J., dissenting).

89. HACKER, *supra* note 65.

90. Robert E. Suggs, *Rethinking Minority Business Development Strategies,* 25 HARV. C.R.-C.L. L. REV. 101, 108 (1990).

91. *Id.* at 109–10.

92. 438 U.S. at 376.

93. *Id.* at 377.

94. Telephone conversation with Robert Suggs (June 26, 1995).

95. *See generally* ROBERT E. SUGGS, MINORITIES AND PRIVATIZATION: ECONOMIC MOBILITY AT RISK (1989).

96. NATIONAL RESEARCH COUNCIL, A COMMON DESTINY: BLACKS AND AMERICAN SOCIETY 140 (ed. Gerald David Jaynes and Robin N. Williams, Jr., 1989).

97. Richard B. Freeman, *Decline of Labor Market Discrimination and Economic Analysis,* 63 AM. ECONOMIC REV. 280 (1973).

98. Finis Welch, *Black-White Differences in Returns to Schooling,* 63 AM. ECONOMIC REV. 893 (1973).

99. Jeremiah Cotton, *Opening the Gap: The Decline in Black Economic Indicators in the 1980s,* 70 SOCIAL SCIENCE QUARTERLY 803, 817 (1989).

100. *See, e.g,* Autek Systems Corp. v. United States, 835 F. Supp. 13 (D.D.C. 1993).

101. CARTER, *supra* note 37, at 252.

102. Brief of Petitioner at 13, Regents of the University of California v. Bakke, 438 U.S. 912 (1978).

103. 476 U.S. at 315 (Steven, J., dissenting).

104. Jody Armour, *Stereotypes and Prejudice: Helping Legal Decisionmakers Break the Prejudice Habit,* CAL. L. REV. (1995) (in press) (citing Birt L. Duncan, *Differential Social Perception and Attribution of Intergroup Violence: Testing the Lower Limits of Stereotyping of Blacks,* 34 J. OF PERSONALITY AND SOCIAL PSYCHOLOGY 590 (1976)).

105. National Assn. of Black Social Workers, Position Paper (Summer 1973) (as cited in Forde-Mazrui, *infra* note 107, at 926).

106. *Id.*

107. *See, e.g.,* Kim Forde-Mazrui, *Black Identity and Child Placement: The Best Interests of Black and Biracial Children,* 92 MICH. L. REV. 925 (1994); Zanita E. Fenton, *In a World Not Their Own: The Adoption of Black Children,* 10 HARV. BLACKLETTER J. 39 (1993); Timothy P. Glynn, *The Role of Race in Adoption Proceedings: A Constitutional Critique of the Minnesota Preference Statute,* 77 MINN. L. REV. 925 (1993); Jo Beth Eubanks, *Transracial Adoption in Texas: Should the Best Interests Standard Be Color-Blind,* 24 ST. MARY'S L.J. 1225 (1993); Joan Mahoney, *The Black Baby Doll: Transracial Adoption and Cultural Preservation,* 59 U.M.K.C. L. REV. 487 (1991); Twila L. Perry, *Race and Child Placement: The Best Interests Test and the Cost of Discretion,* 29 J. FAM. L. 51 (1990/1991).

108. Although I have not seen figures on the number of mixed-race children available for adoption, it appears that the number of such children is increasing. The number of black-white interracial marriages has increased from 65,000 in 1970 to 218,000 in 1988. Perry, supra note 107, at 52 n. 4. In 1984, there were approximately one million mixed-race children in the United States. Kathi Overmier, *Biracial Adolescents: Areas of Conflict in Identity Formation,* 14 J. APPLIED SOC. SCI. 157 (1990).

109. By "mixed-race" children, I will be referring to children who are part "black" and part "white," because that is the most common example of "mixed-race" discussed by the courts. Interestingly, I have found no cases involving, for example, a child with an Hispanic parent and African-American parent, although that combination probably is not unusual. It seems that racial classification issues most frequently arise when the child is white and black, which probably reflects our culture's preoccupation with the purity of the white race.

110. *See, e.g.,* Ward v. Ward, 216 P.2d 755 (Wash. 1950); Farmer v. Farmer, 439 N.Y.S.2d 584 (Sup. Ct. 1981); *In re* Davis, 465 A.2d 614 (Pa. 1983).

111. Thorwald Esbeusen, *Children Need Homes, Not Ethnic Politics,* CRISIS, 22 (Nov.-Dec. 1992).

112. *See, e.g.,* Drummond v. Fulton County Department of Family

and Children's Services, 547 F.2d 835 (5th Cir. 1977); Reisman v. State of Tennessee Department of Human Services, 843 F. Supp. 356 (W.D. Tenn. 1993).

113. The literature on the construction of race typically argues that white society unilaterally has defined the category "black." *See, e.g.,* Gotanda, *supra* note 8. The labeling of mixed-race children in the adoption context, nonetheless, has not occurred exclusively by white society. Some members of the black community have insisted on considering mixed-race children to be black for adoption purposes. *See, e.g.,* Fenton, *supra* note 107.

114. *See, e.g.,* Reisman v. State of Tennessee Department of Human Services, 843 F. Supp. 356 (W.D. Tenn. 1993). In *Drummond,* the social service agency appears to have eventually sought a mixed-race placement for the mixed-race child. *See* Larry I. Palmer, *Adoption: A Plea for Realistic Constitutional Decisionmaking,* 11 COLUM. HUM. RTS. L. REV. 1, 7 (1979).

115. In Drummond v. Fulton County Department of Family and Children's Services, 547 F.2d 835 (5th Cir. 1977), the agency belatedly acknowledged the adoptive child's mixed-race heritage when, after removing him from the white family where he had lived happily for two years, they attempted at least two placements with mixed-race couples before he reached the age of five, one of which was apparently unsuccessful. Larry I. Palmer, *Adoption: A Plea for Realistic Constitutional Decisionmaking,* 11 COLUM. HUM. RTS. L. REV. 1, 7 (1979). The agency's belated recognition of the child's mixed-race heritage accentuated "foster care drift" but did little for the well-being of child. Randall Kennedy has called race-conscious placements like in the *Drummond* case "scandalous." Kennedy, *supra* note 39, at 1819 n. 305.

116. Moreover, it is not unusual in our society for a child to be raised by one parent. A mixed-race child who is raised by one parent will therefore often be raised by a white parent or a black parent, not a mixed-race couple. Accordingly, a mixed-race couple adoption rule often does not replicate the family structure that that child would have had in the absence of adoption.

117. As Professor Harris notes: "It is not at all clear that even the slaves imported from abroad represented 'pure Negro race'. . . . many

of the tribes imported from Africa had intermingled with peoples of the Mediterranean, among them Portuguese slave traders. Other slaves brought to the United States came via the West Indies, where some Africans had been brought directly, but still others had been brought via Spain and Portugal, countries in which extensive interracial sexual relations had occurred. By the mid-nineteenth century it was, therefore, a virtual fiction to speak of 'pure blood' as it relates to racial identification in the United States." Harris, *supra* note 33, at 1791 n. 141.

118. *See, e.g.,* Fenton, *supra* note 107.

119. Gotanda, *supra* note 8, at 24.

120. Since my argument is premised on the need to engage in more individualized understandings of our racial heritage, I do not have sufficient information to know how important it may be to some or many black children to have black adoptive parents. In talking to my friends who have engaged in what is commonly described as a "transracial" adoption, I have been struck by how many of them indicate that the biological mother was white and the biological father was black. In one case, a friend, who is an adoptive mother, told me that the white biological mother of her adoptive daughter had two children by the same black man to whom she was not married. One of the children was dark and the other was light. The mother relinquished only the darker child for adoption. My friend, however, who was considered to have engaged in a transracial adoption, shared many physical characteristics with the biological mother who would have otherwise raised the child as a single parent. I believe that the term "transracial adoption" is a misnomer in that context, because the child was transferred from one white mother to another white mother. Although it is important for the white mother in this context to fully respect the child's racial heritage, there is no reason for her to face a higher burden to qualify for adoption because of the purportedly "transracial" nature of the adoption.

121. Zack has therefore argued, "it is now clear that the form of black family history is inherently problematic in comparison with the form of white family history. Not only does black family history contain self-undermining recollections of being oppressed, but its racial diversity may lead a descendant to an irreconcilable slave and

slave-owning genealogy. If one would liberate oneself through identification by means of family history, one may also have to liberate one's ancestors." Zack, *supra* note 53, at 65.

Notes to Chapter Six

1. 42 U.S.C. 12211(b)(1). *See also* 29 C.F.R. 1630.3(d) (1991).
2. *See* 134 CONG. REC. 2400 (daily ed. Mar. 17, 1988).
3. Adrienne L. Hiegel, *Sexual Exclusions: The Americans with Disabilities Act as a Moral Code,* 94 COLUM. L. REV. 1451, 1452 (1994).
4. Peter M. Panken, *The Disabled and Work,* ALI-ABA COURSE OF STUDY, Apr. 27, 1995.
5. *Id.*
6. *Id.*
7. "Overweight" refers to individuals who exceed their "ideal weight" as defined by insurance tables. "Medically significant obesity" includes those who are at least twenty percent above their "ideal weight" as defined above. "Morbidly obese" refers to an individual who weights more than twice his or her optimal weight, or more than 100 pounds over optimal weight. *See* Scott Petersen, *Discrimination against Overweight People: Can Society Still Get Away with It?,* 30 GONZ. L. REV. 105 (1994/1995); Steven M. Ziolkowski, *Case Comment,* 74 B.U. L. REV. 667 (1994).
8. PITTSBURGH POST-GAZETTE, July 30, 1995, at E-3 (Rob Rogers cartoon).
9. Commentary, *Fat, Female, and Poor,* LANCET (Dec. 24/31, 1994).
10. Richard F. Gillum, *Overweight and Obesity in Black Women: A Review of Published Data from the National Center for Health Statistics,* 79 J.A.M.A. 865 (1987).
11. *Review & Outlook: Disabling Mandate,* WALL ST. J., Jan. 6, 1995, at A12 (editorial).
12. Betsy Hart, *What Are the Rights of the Obese?* ROCKY MOUNTAIN NEWS, Mar. 10, 1994, at 49A (editorial).
13. *Id.*
14. *See, e.g.,* Scott Petersen, *Discrimination against Overweight People: Can Society Still Get Away with It?,* 30 GONZ. L. REV. 105

(1994/1995); Karen M. Kramer and Arlene B. Magerson, *Obesity, Discrimination in the Workplace: Protection through a Perceived Disability Claim under the Rehabilitation Act and the Americans with Disability Act,* 31 CAL. W. L. REV. 41 (1994); William C. Taussig, *Weighing in against Obesity Discrimination,* 35 CAL. L. REV. 927 (1994); Patricia Hartnett, *Nature or Nurturing Lifestyle or Fate: Employment Discrimination against Obese Workers,* 24 RUTGERS L.J. 807 (1993).

15. New York State Department of Human Rights v. New York-Pennsylvania Professional Baseball League, 320 N.Y.S.2d 788 (App. Div. 1971).

16. State Division of Human Rights v. New York City Department of Parks and Recreation, 38 A.D.2d 24 (App. Div. 1971).

17. Hardy v. Stumpf, 37 Cal. App. 3d 958 (1974).

18. Smith v. Troyan, 520 F.2d 492 (6th Cir. 1975).

19. *Id.* at 496.

20. *Id.* at 496.

21. 433 U.S. 321 (1977).

22. *Id.*

23. Linda A. Jackson and Kelly S. Ervin, *Height Stereotypes of Women and Men: The Liabilities of Shortness for Both Sexes,* 132(4) THE J. OF SOC. PSYCHOL. 433–45.

24. SANDRA BEM, THE LENSES OF GENDER 188 (1993).

25. *Id.* at 189.

26. *Proverbs* 23:21.

27. Mary Voboril, *Battling Fat Bias in the Workplace,* NEWSDAY, Dec. 5, 1993, at 95.

28. *See* Stephen A. Richardson et al., *Cultural Uniformity in Reaction to Physical Disabilities,* 26 AM. SOC. REV. 241 (1961).

29. Janet Cawley, *Last Target of Legal Bigotry: Obesity,* CHIC. TRIB., May 12, 1993, News Section, Zone N, at 1.

30. Dolores Tropiano, *Fat and Doing Fine Says "Enough" to Size Discrimination,* ARIZ. REPUBLIC, July 2, 1990, at C1.

31. Gillum, *supra* note 10, at 866.

32. James D. Sargent and David Blanchflower, *Obesity and Stature in Adolescence and Earnings in Young Adulthood,* 148 J. ARCHIVES, PEDIATRICS, AND ADOLESCENT MED. 681, 682–85 (1994).

33. *See* EEOC v. USAIR, 6:92CV00272, 1994 U.S. Dist. LEXIS 12135 (M.D. N.C. June 27, 1994).

34. *See, e.g.,* Gerdom v. Continental Airlines, Inc., 692 F.2d 602 (9th Cir. 1982).

35. *Id.*

36. 856 P.2d 1143 (Cal. 1993).

37. *Id.* at 1153.

38. Cook v. State of Rhode Island, 10 F.3d 17 (1st Cir. 1993).

39. *Id.* at 23 n. 7.

40. *Id.* at 23.

41. *See generally* Sheryl McCarthy, *No Apologies for Being Fat,* NEWSDAY, Feb. 29, 1994, News Section, at 8.

42. *See* Tudyman v. United Airlines, 608 F. Supp. 739 (D.C. Cal. 1984).

43. *See,* Dianne Neumark-Sztainer, *Excessive Weight Preoccupation: Normative But Not Harmless,* NUTRITION TODAY, April 1995, at 68.

44. *See, e.g.,* Chandler v. City of Dallas, 2 F.3d 1385 (5th Cir. 1993).

45. *See, e.g.,* Bryne v. Board of Education, 979 F.2d 560 (7th Cir. 1992).

46. *See, e.g.,* Jasany v. United States Postal Service, 755 F.2d 1244 (6th Cir. 1985); Roth v. Lutheran General Hospital, 5 A.D.D. 458 (N.D. Ill. 1994).

47. Taylor v. United States Postal Service, No. 93–3502, 1995 U.S. App. LEXIS 2833 (6th Cir. Feb. 10, 1995).

48. *See, e.g.,* Clark v. Virginia Board of Bar Examiners, 3 A.D. Cases 1066 (E.D. Va. 1994).

49. 20 U.S.C. 1401 *et seq.* (1988).

50. ROGER E. VOGLER AND WAYNE R. BARTZ, THE BETTER WAY TO DRINK: MODERATION & CONTROL OF PROBLEM DRINKING 25 (1982).

51. *Id.* at 11.

52. Ellenwood v. Exxon Shipping Co., 984 F.2d 1270, 1272 (1st Cir. 1992).

53. *Id.* at 1272.

54. 43 Op. Att'y Gen. 12 (1977).

55. 29 U.S.C. 706(7)(B)(1982).

56. VOGLER AND BARTZ, *supra* note 50, at 15.

57. Traynor v. Turnage, 485 U.S. 535 (1988).

58. 951 F.2d 511 (2d Cir. 1991).

59. *Id.* at 517.

60. Teahan v. Metro-North Commuter Railroad Company, 3 A.D. Cases 1694 (S.D.N.Y. 1994).

61. 42 U.S.C. 12114(c)(4) (1990). *See also* 29 C.F.R. 1630.16(b)(4) (1991).

62. VOGLER AND BARTZ, *supra* note 50.

63. *Id.* at 141–42.

64. This stigma is quite complicated in the disability context. We tend to think of individuals with disabilities in the educational context as "retarded" or "stupid." Children with physical disabilities that do not affect their mental capacity therefore often find it difficult to find an appropriate educational setting, since the special programs are usually for "retarded" children. In such a case, our shortsightedness in defining "disability" leaves a child with physical disabilities few acceptable educational choices. *See generally* Engel, *infra* note 77, at 185 (describing difficulties in finding placement for an intelligent handicapped child, because school districts often assume that "the physically handicapped person is automatically retarded").

65. This example comes from my own experience in a ninth-grade biology class as well as my experience teaching in a classroom with some blind students.

66. Board of Education v. Rowley, 458 U.S. 176, 197 n. 21 (1982).

67. *Id.* at 201.

68. *Id.* at 198.

69. Federal nondiscrimination law does just the opposite. An individual, for example, is not "disabled" in some circumstances under section 504 of the Rehabilitation Act or the Americans with Disabilities Act unless the impairment substantially limits an individual's employment potential. Thus, an individual with strabismus who is discharged because he cannot perform one discrete function at a job is not sufficiently impaired to come under the statutory definition of disability. *See* Jasany v. United States Postal Service, 755 F.2d 1244 (6th Cir. 1985). I am arguing, by contrast, that we examine the concrete situation to see if a disability poses a disadvantage rather than

worry about whether the individual experiences disability in other facets of his or her life. To the unemployed postal worker in *Jasany,* it is no solace to realize that his disability does not impair his ability to perform other employment.

70. Title I of the ADA prohibits discrimination against a qualified individual with a disability who, with or without reasonable accommodation, can perform the essential functions of the employment position such individual holds or desires. A reasonable accommodation is required unless the covered entity can demonstrate that the accommodation would impose an undue hardship on the operation of the business of such covered entity. The term "qualification standards" may include a requirement that an individual shall not pose a direct threat to the health or safety of other individuals in the workplace. *See* 42 U.S.C. 12111 (1991) (definitions); 12113 (1990) (defenses).

71. *Compare* Bradley v. University of Texas, 3 F.3d 922 (5th Cir. 1993) (HIV-positive surgical technician was not otherwise qualified to continue in his employment) *with* Roe v. District of Columbia, 842 F. Supp. 563 (D.D.C. 1993) (HBV-positive firefighter permitted to perform job without any accommodation).

72. Hindman v. GTE Data Services, 3 A.D. Cases 641 (M.D. Fla. 1994).

73. Hindman v. GTE Data Services, 4 A.D. Cases 182 (M.D. Fla. 1995).

74. Under the IDEA: "The term 'children with disabilities' means children (A) with mental retardation, hearing impairments including deafness, speech or language impairments, visual impairments including blindness, serious emotional disturbance, orthopedic impairments, autism, traumatic brain injury, other health impairments, or specific learning disabilities; and (B) who, by reason thereof need special education and related services." 20 U.S.C. 1401(a)(1) (1988).

75. Under the IDEA: "The term 'individualized education program' means a written statement for each child with a disability developed in any meeting by a representative of the local educational agency or an intermediate education unit who shall be qualified to provide, or supervise who shall be qualified to provide, or supervise the provision of, specially designed instruction to meet the unique needs of children with disabilities, the teacher, the parents or guardian

of such child, and, whenever appropriate, such child, which statement shall include [six criteria]." 20 U.S.C. 1401(a)(20) (1988).

76. Nonetheless, there is a policy decision contained within the statute that education in an integrated setting (both able-bodied and disabled children being educated together) is preferable, if possible. *See* 28 U.S.C. 1412(5) (safeguarding that "to the maximum extent appropriate, children with disabilities, including children in public or private institutions or other care facilities, are educated with children who are not disabled, and that special classes, separate schooling, or other removal of children with disabilities from the regular educational environment occurs only when the nature or severity of the disability is such that education in regular classes with the use of supplementary aids and services cannot be achieved satisfactorily").

77. David Engel studied parent participation in individualized educational plans and found that "effective parental participation in the IEP conference, however, proved to be the exception rather than the rule." David M. Engel, *Law, Culture, and Children with Disabilities: Educational Rights and the Construction of Difference,* 1991 DUKE L.J. 166, 178 (1991).

78. Engel found that most parents stopped attending their individual hearing after the first few years. See Engel, *supra* note 77, at 188.

79. *See, e.g.,* Tribble v. Montgomery County Board of Education, 798 F. Supp. 668 (M.D. Ala. 1992); W.G. v. Board of Trustees of Target Range School Dist. No. 23, 960 F.2d 1479 (9th Cir. 1992); Dreher v. Amphitheater Unified School District, 797 F. Supp. 753 (D. Ariz. 1992).

80. For example, the section on eligibility requirements states that each state must have procedures "to assure that testing and evaluation materials and procedures utilized for the purposes of evaluation and placement of children with disabilities will be selected and administered so as not to be racially or culturally discriminatory." 28 U.S.C. 1412(5) (1988).

81. *See* Delgado et al., *Fairness and Formality: Minimizing the Risk of Prejudice in Alternative Dispute Resolution,* 1985 WIS. L. REV. 1359, 1389 (arguing that racial prejudice is more likely to occur in informal, discretionary settings than in formal, adjudicatory settings because the "human propensity to prejudge and make irrational cate-

gorizations is . . . checked by procedural safeguards found in an adversarial system").

82. *Id.* at 1389 (footnote omitted).

83. In Pittsburgh, for example, we have the Education Law Center which tries to provide those services for free to children with disabilities. Nonetheless, it takes a sophisticated parent or guardian to find such services and use them aggressively.

84. *See* Engel, *supra* note 77, at 194–203.

Notes to Chapter Seven

1. Jew v. University of Iowa, 749 F. Supp. 946 (S.D. Iowa 1990).

2. Plaintiff's Memorandum in Opposition to Defendants' Motion for Summary Judgment at 20, Jew v. University of Iowa, 749 F. Supp. 946 (S.D. Iowa 1990) ("Jean Jew is a lesbian" appearing on department men's room wall).

3. 42 Title VII of the Civil Rights Act of 1964 makes it "an unlawful employment practice for an employer . . . to discriminate against any individual with respect to his compensation, terms, conditions, or privileges of employment, because of such individual's race, color, religion, sex, or national origin." 42 U.S.C. 2000e-2(a)(1).

4. Martha Chamallas, *Jean Jew's Case: Resisting Sexual Harassment in the Academy,* 6 YALE J. L. & FEMINISM 71, 82 (1994) (Jew was retroactively promoted to full professor, given back pay, compensated for a related state defamation judgment, and awarded $895,000 in attorney's fees).

5. Carreno v. Local Union No. 226, 54 Fair Empl. Prac. Cas. (BNA) 81 (D. Kan. 1990).

6. *Id.* at 81.

7. Samuel A. Marcosson, *Harassment on the Basis of Sexual Orientation: A Claim of Sex Discrimination Under Title VII,* 81 GEO. L.J. 1, 1 (1992) (quoting Plaintiff's Response to Defendant Local Union No. 226's Motion for Summary Judgement at 13).

8. DeAngelis v. El Paso Municipal Police Officers, 51 F.3d 591 (5th Cir. 1995).

9. *See* Regents of the University of California v. Bakke, 438 U.S. 265 (1978). *See generally* JOEL DREYFUSS AND CHARLES LAWRENCE III, THE BAKKE CASE: THE POLITICS OF INEQUALITY 5 (1979).

10. *See* DREYFUSS AND LAWRENCE *supra* note 9, at 24.

11. 42 U.S.C. 2000(d) *et seq.*

12. U.S. CONST. amend. XIV.

13. The Supreme Court granted Bakke the injunction enforcing his admission and invalidated the Medical School's special admissions program. *Bakke,* 438 U.S. at 320.

14. St. Mary's Honor Center v. Hicks, 113 S. Ct. 2742 (1993).

15. Although this trend might apply to women who are perceived to be lesbians, the cases reflect the pattern that courts assume that women are heterosexual even when accused of being lesbians. *See, e.g.,* McCoy v. Johnson Controls World Services, 878 F. Supp. 229 (S.D. Ga. 1995); Jew v. University of Iowa, 749 F. Supp. 946 (S.D. Iowa 1990).

16. *See, e.g.,* Holloway v. Arthur Andersen & Co., 566 F.2d 659 (9th Cir. 1977); Sommers v. Budget Marketing Inc., 667 F.2d 748 (8th Cir. 1982); Powell v. Read's Inc., 436 F. Supp. 369 (D. Md. 1977).

17. *See, e.g.,* Ulane v. Eastern Airlines, Inc., 742 F.2d 1081 (7th Cir. 1984).

18. *See, e.g.,* DeSantis v. Pacific Telephone & Telegraph Co., Inc., 608 F.2d 327 (9th Cir. 1979).

19. Stacks v. Southwestern Bell Yellow Pages, 27 F.3d 1316, 1320 (8th Cir. 1994).

20. *Id.* at 1320.

21. *Id.* at 1321.

22. *Id.* at 1322.

23. *Id.*

24. *Id.* at 1327.

25. *Id.*

26. 864 F. Supp. 1552 (S.D. Fla. 1994).

27. *Id.* at 1557.

28. *Id.* at 1562.

29. 877 F. Supp. 754 (D. D.C. 1995).

30. Bundy v. Jackson, 641 F.2d 934, 942 n.7 (D.C. Cir. 1981); Barnes v. Costle, 561 F.2d 983, 990 (D.C. Cir. 1977).

31. *Ryczek,* 877 F. Supp. at 762.

32. "[T]he company's response to the alleged harassment was sufficiently prompt and adequate to negate any liability." *Id.* at 759.

33. *Id.* at 762 n. 9.

34. *Jew,* 749 F. Supp. at 958.

35. *Id.* at 952.

36. *Id.* at 958.

37. *Id.* at 958.

38. *Id.* at 958.

39. Chiapuzio v. BLT Operating Corp., 826 F. Supp. 1334 (D. Wyo. 1993). *But see* Hopkins v. Baltimore Gas & Elec. Co., 871 F. Supp. 822 (D. Md. 1994) (no liability against bisexual supervisor).

40. *Id.* at 1335.

41. *Id.*

42. *Id.*

43. *Id.* at 1337.

44. *Id.* at 1338.

45. *See generally* Chamallas, *supra* note 4.

46. Dillon v. Frank, 952 F.2d 403 (6th Cir. 1992) (table case) (not published but available on LEXIS, No. 90–2290, 1992 U.S. App. LEXIS 766, at *2 (6th Cir. Jan. 15, 1992)).

47. *Id.* at *3.

48. Carreno v. IBEW Local No. 226, 54 FEP Cases 81 (D. Kan. 1990). For a statement of the facts, see Samuel A. Marcosson, *Harassment on the Basis of Sexual Orientation: A Claim of Sex Discrimination under Title VII,* 81 GEO. L.J. 1, 1 (1992).

49. *See, e.g.,* Garcia v. Elf Atochem North America, 28 F.3d 446 (5th Cir. 1994) (Freddy Garcia was approached from behind by Rayford Locke, a plant supervisor, who grabbed "Garcia's crotch area and made sexual motions from behind Garcia"); Benekritis v. Johnson, 882 F.Supp 521 (D.S.C. 1995) (David Benekritis was approached by fellow teacher R. Earl Johnson at two school basketball games where Johnson placed "his genitals against Plaintiff's backside" and placed "his hand on Plaintiff's genitals").

50. *Dillon,* 1992 U.S. App. LEXIS 766 at *22 ("Thus, Dillon cannot escape our holding, and those of the other circuits, that homosexuality is not an impermissible criteria on which to discriminate with regards to terms and conditions of employment"). *Carreno,* 54 Fair Empl. Prac. Cas. (BNA) at 82 ("The issue before the court is

whether a homosexual male may recover under Title VII of the Civil Rights Act of 1964").

51. Price Waterhouse v. Hopkins, 490 U.S. 228, 235 (1989).

52. Elvia R. Arriola, *Gendered Inequality: Lesbians, Gays, and Feminist Legal Theory*, 9 BERKELEY WOMEN'S L.J. 103, 122 (1994).

53. For example, Jean Jew was called a "lesbian" as part of the sexual harassment she faced at the University of Iowa. She ultimately prevailed. *Jew*, 749 F. Supp. 946. For a compelling account of the *Jean Jew* case, see Chamallas, *supra* note 4.

54. *Dillon*, 1992 U.S. App. LEXIS 766 (by implication) and *Carreno*, 54 Fair Empl. Prac. Cas. (BNA) 81 (by implication).

55. *See, e.g.*, McCoy v. Johnson Controls World Services, 878 F. Supp. 229 (S.D. Ga. 1995).

56. *Id.* at 229, 231.

57. Harris v. Forklift Systems, Inc., 114 S. Ct. 367 (1993).

58. *Id.* at 369.

59. *Id.*

60. "When the workplace is permeated with 'discriminatory intimidation, ridicule, and insult,' that is 'sufficiently severe or pervasive to alter the conditions of the victims employment and create an abusive working envirconoment,' Title VII is violated" (internal citations omitted). *Id.* at 370.

61. Harris v. Forklift Systems, Inc., No. 3:89–0557, 1994 U.S. Dist. LEXIS 19928, at *1 (M.D. Tenn. Nov. 9, 1994).

62. *Id.* at *2.

63. *Id.* at *1 (Harris was awarded $151,435).

64. 51 F.3d 591 (5th Cir. 1995).

65. *Id.* at 592.

66. *Id.* at 595.

67. *Id.* at 593.

68. *Id.* at 597.

69. *Id.* at 595.

70. *Id.* at 597 n. 6.

71. *Id.* at 596.

72. *Id.* at 596.

73. Hall v. Gus Construction Company, 842 F.2d 1010 (8th Cir. 1988).

74. The purportedly nonsexualized episodes included calling one of the women "herpes," male crew members urinating in one of the plaintiff's gas tank, and failing to fix the pilot truck that gave off fumes. *Id.* at 1013–14. Of course, the first two of those episodes could have been characterized as sexual. Therefore, the court's ruling had limited application to this fact pattern.

75. Although about a dozen courts have cited *Gus Construction* for the proposition that women can prevail for sexual harassment solely on the basis of gendered comments, few of these women have, in fact, prevailed. *See, e.g.,* Trotta v. Mobil Oil Corp., 788 F. Supp. 1336, 1347 (S.D.N.Y. 1992) (concluding that plaintiff would have resigned whether or not the events that allegedly created a sexually hostile work environment occurred); Ott v. Perk Development Corporation, 846 F. Supp. 266, 274 (W.D.N.Y. 1994) (concluding that examples of purportedly nonsexualized harassment were, in fact, examples of legitimate, nondiscriminatory actions); EEOC v. A. Sam & Sons Produce Company, Inc., 872 F. Supp. 29 (W.D.N.Y. 1994) (concluding that female employee who was called a "whore" could recover for sexual harassment but that second female employee who was not directly called a "whore" could not recover); Cram v. Lamson Sessions Co., 49 F.3d 466, 474 (8th Cir. 1995) (concluding that defendant's "interactions with [plaintiff] . . . were brief, sporadic, nonsexual, nonthreatening, and polite" thereby not meeting the required showing of "sustained, severe harassment required to make a claim of hostile working environment"). *But see* Cronin v. United Service Stations, Inc., 809 F. Supp. 922, 929 (M.D. Ala. 1992) (finding liability where comments and behavior were derogatory and insulting to women generally, and overtly demeaning to the plaintiff personally but where comments were not overtly sexual); Laughinghouse v. Risser, 754 F. Supp. 836 (D. Kansas 1990) (denying summary judgment for defendant where most of the comments were not sexual in nature).

76. *Hicks,* 113 S. Ct. 2742.

77. Hicks v. St. Mary's Honor Ctr., 970 F.2d 487, 490 (8th Cir. 1992).

78. *Id.* at 489 ("Plaintiff's supervisors had consistently rated his performance as competent. He had not been suspended, written up, or otherwise disciplined").

79. *Hicks,* 756 F. Supp. 1244, 1247 n. 7 (E.D. Mo. 1991).
80. *Id.* at 1248.
81. *Id.* at 1248 n. 10.
82. *Id.* at 1247.
83. *Id.* at 1248.
84. *Id.*
85. *Id.*
86. *Id.* at 1247 n. 7.
87. By failing to differentiate between the actions of Powell and Long, which were instituted by white men who had considerable power at St. Mary's, and the actions of the black members of the discipline board, who appeared to have little authority at St. Mary's, the court confused participation with power. The fact that blacks *participate* in a process does not mean that they have a powerful role in that process.
88. *Hicks,* 756 F. Supp. at 1249.
89. The trial court record does not specifically indicate whether the Director of the Missouri Department of Corrections and Human Resources had read the Davis study. It only states that none of the witnesses at the trial had read the Davis study before 1984; it is not clear whether the Director testified at the trial.
90. Although no witnesses at trial admitted to having seen the Davis study at the time of the 1984 personnel changes, *someone* at the Department of Corrections's central office must have seen the report. More importantly, that report must have been written to reflect information that the writer collected from some supervisory personnel at St. Mary's; recommendations rarely arise out of "thin air."
91. 756 F. Supp. at 1246.
92. *Id.* at 1246.
93. *Id.*
94. The court offered the following explanation: "The fact that most of the supervisory staff was terminated or transferred is not alarming given the widespread problems that St. Mary's experienced under their control. . . . It is not unusual that several black supervisors were replaced by whites because blacks held nearly all the supervisory positions before January, 1984." *Id.* at 1252.
95. *Id.* at 1252 (calling the comments "personally motivated").

96. Bivens v. Jeffers Vet Supply, 873 F. Supp. 1500 (M.D. Ala. 1994).

97. Arzate v. City of Topeka, Case No. 93–4128-SAC, 1995 U.S. Dist. LEXIS 6545 (D. Kan. Feb. 27, 1995).

98. *Id.* at *24.

99. *Id.* at *18.

100. *See, e.g.,* Daniels v. Essex Group, 937 F.2d 1264 (7th Cir. 1991) (black plaintiff called "Buckwheat," criticized for conversing with white women at work, and confronted with a human-sized black dummy hanging from a doorway); Daniels v. Pipefitters' Association Local Union No. 597, 945 F.2d 906 (7th Cir. 1991) (blacks at workplace called "nigger," "porch monkeys," "baboons," "ghetto assholes," "super nigger" and other epithets in Italian). In *Daniels,* however, the court also explicitly considered a physical threat that was not specifically racial in nature as part of the claim for a hostile work environment. *Id.* at 1273.

101. Rodgers v. Western-Southern Life Ins. Co., 12 F.3d 668 (7th Cir. 1993).

102. *Id.* at 677.

103. Bolden v. PRC Inc., 43 F.3d 545 (10th Cir. 1994).

104. *Id.* at 549.

105. Davis v. Northrop Corporation, 24 F.3d 245 (9th Cir. 1994) (not published but available on LEXIS and WESTLAW).

106. Wygant v. Jackson Board of Education, 476 U.S. 299 (1986).

107. *Id.* at 299 (Marshall, J., dissenting).

108. Arguably, the courts did not consider her qualifications because this was only phase one of the trial. Her merits would be considered at the relief stage. But, as we will see with the *Bakke* case, courts fail to consider the merits of the white plaintiff even in cases involving individual acts of discrimination rather than class actions.

109. *Hicks,* 756 F. Supp. at 1252.

110. Hicks v. St. Mary's Honor Center, 970 F.2d 487 (8th Cir. 1992).

111. *Hicks,* 113 S. Ct. 2742.

112. Hicks v. St. Mary's Honor Center, 2 F.3d 265 (8th Cir. 1993).

113. 438 U.S. 265 (1978).

114. JOEL DREYFUSS AND CHARLES LAWRENCE III, THE BAKKE CASE: THE POLITICS OF INEQUALITY 5 (1979).

115. *Id.* at 13.

116. *Id.*

117. *Id.*

118. 438 U.S. at 279 (describing trial court decision).

119. *Id.* at 281.

120. *Id.* at 280 n. 14.

121. *Id.* at 280–81 n. 14.

122. Allen v. Wright, 468 U.S. 737 (1984).

123. *Id.* at 782 (Brennan, J., dissenting).

124. Claus v. Duquesne Light Co., 46 F.3d 1115 (3rd Cir. 1994), *cert. denied,* 115 S. Ct. 1700 (1995).

125. Mike Bucsko, *Worker Wins Suit against Utility,* PITTSBURGH POST-GAZETTE, Dec. 17, 1993, at A11.

126. *Id.*

127. *Id.*

128. Another case that follows this pattern is Johnson v. Transportation Agency, 480 U.S. 616 (1987). Although the white male plaintiff, Paul Johnson, lost his reverse discrimination case, the Court never questioned whether he was, in fact, less qualified on nongendered grounds. Diane Joyce, who was selected for the position, had more experience than Johnson, and appears not to have been selected initially because of overt gender bias. Two of the three members of the interview panel (which was the only factor on which she scored lower than the male plaintiff), had treated Joyce in overtly negative ways because of her gender. For example, one of them had described her as a "rebel-rousing, skirt-wearing person." *Id.* at 624 n. 5. Joyce had had to seek guidance from the affirmative action officer to be treated in a *nondiscriminatory* manner so that she could attain a promotion that was rightfully hers. Rather than recognize the blatant discrimination that had precluded Joyce from initially being selected for the position, the Supreme Court characterized the case as one of lawful affirmative action, suggesting that Joyce only became more qualified than Johnson by giving her a "plus" for her gender. The fact that Johnson's case was even treated as a "reverse discrimination" case reflects the presumption of qualification that is accorded to white male plaintiffs.

129. 861 F. Supp. 551 (W.D. Texas 1994).

130. *Id.*

131. *Id.* at 580.

132. *Id.* at 580.

133. *See, e.g.,* Fields v. Clark University, 966 F.2d 49 (1st Cir. 1992), *cert. denied,* 113 S. Ct. 976 (1993); Brousard-Norcross v. Augustana College Association, 935 F.2d 974 (8th Cir. 1991); Namenwirth v. Board of Regents of University of Wisconsin System (7th Cir. 1985), *cert. denied,* 474 U.S. 1061 (1986); Zahorik v. Cornell University, 729 F.2d 85 (2d Cir. 1984); Smith v. University of North Carolina, 632 F.2d 316 (4th Cir. 1980).

134. CATHARINE MACKINNON, THE SEXUAL HARASSMENT OF WORKING WOMEN 59 (1979) (citing lower court decisions in Corne and DeVane v. Bausch & Lomb, 390 F. Supp. 161 (D. Ariz. 1975); Miller v. Bank of America, 418 F. Supp. 233 (N.D. Cal. 1976); and Tomkins v. Public Service Electric & Gas Co., 422 F. Supp. 552 (D.N.J. 1976)).

135. *Id.* at 55.

136. 45 Fed. Reg. 74,677 (1980)(codified at 29 C.F.R. 1604.11).

137. 58 Fed. Reg. 51,266 (1993).

138. *Id.*

139. *See Id.* (Guidelines withdrawn, however).

140. The proposed guidelines stated that "harassing conduct" includes, but is not limited to: "(I) epithets, slurs, negative stereotyping, or threatening, intimidating, or hostile acts that relate to race, color, religion, gender, national origin, age, or disability; and (ii) Written or graphic material that denigrates or shows hostility or aversion toward an individual or group because of race, color, religion, gender, national origin, age, or disability and that is placed on walls, bulletin boards, or elsewhere on the employer's premise, or circulated in the workplace." *Id.* at 51,268.

141. 626 A.2d 445 (N.J. 1993).

142. *Id.* at 454.

143. Under the *Burdine-Hicks* framework, a plaintiff must first allege a prima facie case of discrimination. The burden of proof stays with the plaintiff, but the burden of coming forward with evidence then shifts to the defendant. The defendant must then articulate a legitimate, nondiscriminatory explanation for the employment action.

Plaintiff is then given an opportunity to rebut the explanations offered by defendant. Even if plaintiff successfully rebuts each of defendant's explanations, the court is not required to rule for plaintiff. Despite disproving each of defendant's explanations, plaintiff still has burden of establishing that unlawful factor (i.e., race or gender) was the true explanation for the adverse employment action. In a sense, the prima facie case disappears from the case once the defendant comes forward with evidence, even if that evidence is found not to be credible. *Hicks,* 113 S. Ct. 2742; Texas Dept. of Community Affairs v. Burdine, 450 U.S. 248 (1981).

144. The doctrinal importance of this framework is that a plaintiff is not subject to the burden shifting regime of *Burdine-Hicks.* In a sexual harassment case, a plaintiff will prevail if she can demonstrate that: the conduct was gender-based, it was severe and pervasive, it was unwelcome, and management had legal liability for the conduct. In contrast to *Hicks,* a court cannot find for the defendant on the theory that the conduct just reflected a "personality dispute." *Hicks,* 756 F. Supp. at 1252.

145. This presumption is particularly problematic in light of a recent governmental study indicating that black federal employees are more than twice as likely to be dismissed as their white, Hispanic, or Asian counterparts. *See* Karen De Witt, *Blacks Prone to Dismissal by the U.S.,* N.Y. TIMES, Apr. 20, 1995, at A19.

Notes to Chapter Eight

1. IAN HACKING, THE TAMING OF CHANCE 16 (1990).

2. HYMAN ALTERMAN, COUNTING PEOPLE: THE CENSUS IN HISTORY 195 (1969).

3. *Id.* at 221.

4. *Id.* at 228.

5. *Id.* at 276.

6. *Id.* at 276.

7. Sharon M. Lee, *Racial Classifications in the U.S. Census: 1890–1990,* 16 ETHNIC AND RACIAL STUDIES 75, 77 (1993).

8. *Id.* at 77.

9. ALTERMAN, *supra* note 2, at 233.

10. *Id.* at 233.

11. Lee, *supra* note 7, at 79.

12. *Id.* at 79.

13. *Id.* at 79.

14. *Id.* at 80.

15. *Id.* at 83.

16. *Id.* at 83–84.

17. *Id.*

18. *Id.* at 82.

19. *Id.* at 82.

20. *Id.* at 83.

21. 59 FR 29831.

22. HACKING, *supra* note 1, at 263.

23. Deborah Ramirez, *Race and Remedy in a Multicultural Society: Multicultural Employment: It's Not Just Black and White Anymore,* 47 STAN. L. REV. 957, 968 (1995).

24. Carlos Fernández, President, Association of MultiEthnic Americans, *Congressional Hearings* 127 (June 30, 1993).

25. *See generally* PETER S. LI, RACE AND ETHNIC RELATIONS IN CANADA (1990).

Index

·············

Able v. United States of America, 65–
66
Adarand Constructors, Inc. v. Pena,
145–47
Adoption, of multiracial children, 130,
156–62, 269–70 n. 39, 274 n. 108,
275 n. 115–16, 276 n. 120
Affirmative Action, for bisexuals, 80;
and color, 154–55; diversity of ideas
rationale, 136–40; employing positive use of categories, 6–7, 32–33;
and fraud, 259–60 n. 90; for multiracials, 4; need for group-based categories, 7–8; overcoming disadvantage
rationale, 81–83, 144–53, 272 n.
86–87; overcoming stereotypes rationale, 153–54; redefining merit,
271 n. 61; role model rationale, 82–
85, 140–44
African-Americans, invisibility of, 18;
sexual practices of, 17
AIDS crisis, ramifications of bisexual invisibility, 17–18
Alcoff, Linda, 2, 3, 250 n. 4
Alcoholism, 179–84
Allen, Anita, 140–41, 142–43
Ameliorative treatment, and color,
128–29
Androcentrism, defined, 6

Androgyne, 90
Armour, Jody, 151–52

Baehr v. Lewin, 102–3
Bakke v. Board of Regents, 196, 220–
22, 224, 284 n. 13
Ballot initiatives, as used against homosexuals, 257 n. 65. See also Cincinnati voter initiative
Barham, Justice, 126–27
Bartlett, Katharine, 109
Bathrooms, and gender differentiation,
112–15
Bell, Derrick, 141
Beller v. Midendorf, 50–52, 57
Bem, Sandra Lipsitz, 1, 2, 3, 6, 7, 19,
104, 109, 170
benShalom v. Secretary of Army, 55,
56, 57, 58, 62–63, 64, 257 n. 56
Bi Perspective, critical aspects of, 36–
38; defined, 15; differing implications for sexual orientation, race, gender, and disability, 33–36
Bipolar injustice, epidemic proportions
of, 16
Birdwell, Deborah, 176
Bisexuals, and affirmative action, 80–
85; categorization within racial minority communities, 18; as category

295